# THE POWER OF
# PEER LEARNING

From 1995 to 2005, Jean-H. Guilmette was the Director of IDRC's Division for Central and Eastern Europe Initiatives. He is former Executive Director of the African Development Bank, Director of the OECD's Sahel Club, and Director General of the Strategic Planning Unit in the Africa and Middle-East branch of the Canadian International Development Agency. In 2001, the Norman Paterson School of International Affairs (NPSIA) of the Carleton University, appointed Mr. Guilmette Adjunct Research Professor. Now semi-retired, Jean-H is a practising sculptor, based in Gatineau, Canada.

# THE POWER OF PEER LEARNING

## Networks and Development Cooperation

**JEAN-H. GUILMETTE**

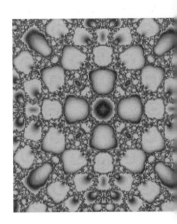

ACADEMIC FOUNDATION
NEW DELHI

————— *in association with* —————

**International Development Research Centre**
Ottawa • Cairo • Dakar • Montevideo • Nairobi • New Delhi • Singapore

Published in 2007
*by*
ACADEMIC FOUNDATION
4772-73 / 23 Bharat Ram Road, (23 Ansari Road),
Darya Ganj, New Delhi - 110 002 (India).
Tel : 23245001 / 02 / 03 / 04.
Fax : +91-11-23245005.
E-mail : academic@vsnl.com
www.academicfoundation.com

*in association with*

INTERNATIONAL DEVELOPMENT RESEARCH CENTRE (IDRC)
PO Box 8500, Ottawa, ON, K1G 3H9
Canada
info@idrc.ca / www.idrc.ca

*The Power of Peer Learning:*
*Networks and Development Cooperation*

by
Jean-H. Guilmette

ISBN-13: 978-81-7188-622-7
ISBN-10: 81-7188-622-1

Printed and bound in India.

# CONTENTS

Section 1: Alliances and Cooperation: Emergence of a New Post-War Paradigm

1.1 Fifteen Hundred Years of War
1.2 Five Characteristics of the New Paradigm
1.3 Overall Impact of the New Paradigm
1.4 Role of Human Rights and Democratic Governance
    in Functioning of OECD Methodologies

Section 2: From Paradigm Shift to Institutional Activities

2.1 Multilateral Organizations with Universal Membership
2.2 International and Regional Organizations with Limited Membership
2.3 The North Atlantic Treaty Organization (NATO)
2.4 International Policy Regimes and Coordinating Institutions

Section 3: International Development Cooperation

3.1 The Marshall Plan
3.2 The Colombo Plan
3.3 Official Development Assistance (ODA)
3.4 Aid and the International Projection of Ideas
3.5 Aid Volumes and Impact

Section 4: The Cooperation Paradigm and the Former Eastern Bloc

4.1 The 'Magic' of the Market
4.2 Reform: A Complex, Multifaceted Process
4.3 Need for New and Relevant Aid Instruments

Section 5: Relevance of the IDRC and OECD Experience to Eastern European Countries

# List of Tables and Boxes

## TABLES

## BOXES

# Foreword

Canada's International Development Research Centre (IDRC) has recognized the power of peer learning and knowledge sharing—the subject of this book—since its foundation in 1970. Working with partners in both South and North and establishing and participating in North-South and South-South exchanges are important aspects of the Centre's work. Our experience has proven that this is an efficient way to transmit knowledge across a wide range of groups or regions. Peer learning, based on jointly generated evidence, is also an effective means to build capacity and foster scientific excellence. The body of knowledge it generates is a powerful tool for the development of evidence-based policy.

IDRC is not alone in its belief in the value of this cooperative approach: it is also the hallmark of the Organisation for Economic Co-operation and Development (OECD). This book was born of the conviction that the OECD could provide a useful model for regional cooperation in nations of the former Soviet Union, and was originally conceived as a tool to assist these countries to understand the principles and inner workings of the OECD, a model of transparent, cooperative decision making. In doing so, IDRC sought to allay Soviet skepticism about how information sharing can foster growth, the possibility of adopting a joint approach without compromising sovereignty, and the potential of a rigorous negotiating process for resolving policy problems between nations.

How this works in practice was well demonstrated in work supported by IDRC in Eastern Europe from 1994 to 2001. The Environmental Management Development in Ukraine program, a massive clean-up effort of the Dnipro River, was managed by IDRC's Office for Central and Eastern Europe Initiatives (OCEEI), directed by author Jean-H. Guilmette. The program provided more than the nuts and bolts of pollution control and water conservation: it also addressed the mechanics of institutional reform. By bringing together Ukrainian experts who used to work independently, it promoted collaboration and the sharing of information and emphasized working in multidisciplinary teams, networking, and policy development—all novel approaches in the region at that time.

The program was instrumental in enabling local decision-makers to manage the Dnipro more effectively and resulted in improved environmental policy. The success of this program led to a larger transboundary project to draft a strategic action plan to rehabilitate the entire Dnipro basin, which required collaboration between Ukraine, Russia, and Belarus.

In describing the approach of both the OECD and IDRC, Jean-H. Guilmette demonstrates how peer learning, based on sharing knowledge and evidence, now underpins technological and economic growth. He also shows that managing this type of network is fundamentally different from managing companies, organizations, or other bodies that fall under a single authority.

Although Guilmette's active research for the book ended in December 2003, the principles describing and highlighting the organizational behaviour of both the OECD and IDRC—and their commitment to being inclusive agents of knowledge transmission—remain as described in the following pages. I commend the author for his devotion to this work and truly hope that you will find it useful and informative.

Maureen O'Neil

*President—International Development Research Centre*

# Preface

*Why, how, and when was this research undertaken*

This book had its genesis when solutions were being sought in the mid-1990s to problems and questions raised in the management of the water resources of the Dnieper River Basin. A project, managed by the International Development Research Centre (IDRC), provided research grants and assistance to Ukraine to help it design a relevant program for the river basin rehabilitation: it began in 1994 and ended in 2001. Because the Dnieper River flows through Belarus, Russia, and Ukraine, its management requires international cooperation between those three sovereign nations. In 1998, it became obvious that it was necessary to draft a Strategic Action Plan for the entire River Basin, which would involve Belarus and Russia in addition to Ukraine. The resources of the Global Environmental Fund (GEF) were sought for that purpose by UNDP. Nations, however, are unlikely to delegate the drafting of national policy and parts of its sovereignty to any international or even regional organization. As well, existing technical assistance management models often fail to bring about the changes in mentality essential to the task. This challenge prompted the IDRC team involved in assisting Ukraine to draft and propose an alternative management model as a means to better manage and develop policies for the rehabilitation of this most important European body of water.

Aid to developing countries and emerging economies is often confronted with two sources of resistance. On the one hand, donors are met with suspicion of foreign ideas and of the motivation of foreigners, with the result that money is welcomed by recipients but the ideas that come with it may not be. Those ideas are often rejected or politely shelved, and donors wonder why their ideas are not accepted. On the other hand, there often exists a deep conviction that the country's problems come from outside, and are manufactured by foreigners. Implicitly, those who believe this also believe that the solution must come from outside the country. Populations and governments often wait out the good donor who has the solution to the country's problems, with the result that ideas embedded in project activities often wait for appropriation to take place.

In this respect, IDRC's approach is almost unique among donors, because it rests entirely on the capacity of the beneficiary to design and undertake its own development. It is essentially based on self-help. This method seems more likely to produce long-term results, because the proposed policy comes from research carried out in the country by local experts and institutions, and is therefore more likely to be quickly adopted.

This leads us to ask whether we can expect cooperation between nations, especially countries such as Belarus and Ukraine that have recently acquired independence from Russia. Can they work together to design common policies and a joint approach without feeling they are compromising sovereignty?

In the autumn of 1997, I became convinced that the Organisation for Economic Co-operation and Development (OECD) offered a tested and proven method for negotiating policy among sovereign nations. Since 1947, OECD (originally OECE) members have been doing exactly that: negotiating, harmonizing, and ensuring compliance with new policies, without challenging existing sovereignty. Its distinctive approach is close to IDRC's practices: it rests on the principle of self-help, peer review, peer pressure, and the design of new policy based on the scientific search for facts. OECD's rigorous negotiating process adds the elements necessary to debate adaptations to local circumstances, and to arrive at joint regional policies.

In early 1998, the IDRC team for Eastern Europe transformed these disparate ideas into a single methodological package. This then became a central element in its proposal to Belarus, Russia, and Ukraine, who were seeking United Nations Development Programme/Global Environment Facility (UNDP/GEF) funds for the rehabilitation of the Dnieper River Basin.

The IDRC and OECD methodological approach is explored in this book, and answers are provided to the specific questions that were raised as we attempted to persuade various participants of the validity of this approach. It must be kept in mind that Ukraine and other former USSR countries were secluded for 70 years, and many ideas that characterized Western evolution during the 20th Century were and are still misunderstood and often ignored there. For example, the notion of win-win negotiation has yet to become practice within eastern bureaucracies. Also, the concept of cooperation among nations raises questions, doubts, and even suspicions.

The concepts and ideas are discussed in a sequence that should help the reader. The basis of our reflection rests on the premise that a major paradigm change took place after World War II as a means to reduce conflicts among traditionally war faring nations. The cooperation paradigm involved the creation of a multitude of international organizations and systems. It was a most innovative idea in 1947, one that went against all accepted ideas of the time, especially ideas that considered protectionism as central to the wealth of a nation. The creation of OECD was at the core of this new paradigm.

The relationship between market economy and democracy is perplexing to many, especially those who have spent their life under a socialist model of governance. Why does it work? Why are OECD countries richer than others? What is central to this success? I believe that good information is so central to wealth that we might argue that we have gone beyond freedom of the press (or information) as essential to protect democracy and human rights. Instead, I believe that the role of democracy is to guard the abundance, availability, and quality of information, without which development will simply not take place.

Secondly, development and growth has become dependent on the proliferation of networks: small and informal networks, structured and somewhat more formal scientific and technical networks and lastly, formal multinational networks. It is my view that managing networks, especially those that are made up of sovereign nations, is fundamentally different from managing companies, organizations, or ministries that fall under a single authority. In essence, the dominant management approach for companies and institutions rests on cybernetics, with the view of keeping communications and accountability simple and clear. Managing methods that are successful in such a context is counterproductive when managing networks. Networks by definition must retain the same level of flexibility and ambiguity that characterize the behaviour of its members. Network management, based on IDRC, is discussed in the following chapter.

In chapters 3 and 4, the praxis of OECD is discussed. How are things done in this unique organization? How were the traditions that govern its internal relations created? The practical application of fundamental values (democracy, market economy, and cooperation) is discussed in Chapter 3 in an historical context. From this, we conclude how these factors have led to specifics for conducting business. In essence, what is the etiquette prevalent in this institution? What are the unwritten rules of conduct? Why is it so? The chapter contains explanations and demonstrations of how a network such as this has to organize according to principles that are profoundly different from those that structure traditional organizations, such as ministries, large corporations, or even other international organizations.

Tools and skills necessary to arrive at consensus among various cultures to foster harmonized policy changes are discussed in Chapter 4. We go into not-so-trivial details, such as how to preside over committee meetings, how to draft persuasive documents, and how to manage the iterative process leading to agreements and to their applications by members.

In Chapter 5, answers are given to the confounding question: why does it work? In my view, the ever-increasing complexity of international exchanges that marked the turn of the 20$^{th}$ Century demanded the injection of simplification, the increase of our collective intelligence, and our capacity to deal with complicated and protracted common issues. OECD came as a response to this new problem: its mechanics are simple—search for consensus using peer pressure, and provide clarity and intelligence on many obscure problems. The chapter demonstrates this thesis through examples of clear successes as well as illustrative failures.

The final section contains a set of definitions to help readers from other parts of the world who are less familiar with concepts, ideas, conventions, and references that have become common usage in OECD member countries.

Planners, policymakers, and researchers in Russia, Belarus, and Ukraine may benefit most from this material. Their counterparts in industrial and developing countries will hopefully find the book instructive and revealing, particularly for those people in the countries that may soon become members of OECD, or for those groups, such as the New Partnership for Africa's Development (NEPAD), who are attempting to introduce Peer Review as a means to improve national governance. Hopefully, this book will also attract a broad audience, in industrial countries and in the emerging economies of Eastern Europe and elsewhere. It is written in a style that may be helpful to readers unfamiliar with some of the concepts and ideas. I have made generous use of metaphors, examples, and definitions in the hope this will improve both readability and understanding of the text.

The governance and internal functioning systems of OECD have not been described thus far. We were unable to find formal publications on the subject, other than two books in French, one written by Jean Bonvin, 1998, former President of OECD's Development Centre, and the other by Henri Chavranski, 1997, a former representative of France on the Economic Committee.

# Acknowledgements

I have borrowed heavily from the two authors who have published papers on OECD, Jean Bonvin and Henri Chavranski, and have translated sections of their material into English for inclusion in this book. I have had privileged access to a number of OECD internal reports, most importantly one key report prepared by Pierre Vinde, former Deputy Secretary General of OECD. Unfortunately, such reports are not part of the body of refereed literature. I have made liberal use of interviews with current and former staff of OECD. I have also used those sections from internal reports that can be communicated publicly without confidentiality problems; unfortunately, attribution is impossible in most cases. I have included in a set of References those papers and books that I believe will be of most direct relevance to my intended readers. Where possible, Internet website addresses are provided.

I wish to thank the following for their comments and contributions: Henri Chavranski, 1997, Derry Ormond and Pierre Vinde who reviewed the first draft of this text; Jean Bonvin, Anne de Lattre, Helmuth Fuhrer, Mark Pieth, Louis Sabourin, all former OECD senior executives, who provided sound advice; current OECD staff without whose help this text could not have been written: Christian Averous, André Barsony, Jim Carey, Jorgen Elmeskov, Vera Gündel, Raundi Halvorson-Quevedo, Jeremy W. Hurst, Peter Jarrett, Robert Ley, Alex Matheson, Hunter Mcgill, Fabrizio Pagani, Scott Wade, and Fredric Wehrle. I also acknowledge the comments and advice offered by colleagues on various drafts of this text: Ms. Carolyn Pestieau, then Vice-President of IDRC, and Ken Babcock, Fred Carden, Suzan Joekes, Kerry Franchuk, Carol Joling, Myron Lahola, and Réal Lavergne, of IDRC.

Chapters 1 and 2 have benefited immensely from Professor Martin Rudner's collaboration. A number of sections of these chapters were drafted by him. Professor Rudner teaches at Carleton University's Norman Patterson School of International Affairs and has authored more than 50 books and articles on international and development issues.

Caroline Bouchard provided valuable research and editing assistance. Elena Klimenko prepared the Definition of Terms and ensured the material is appropriate for readers in former Soviet Union countries. Reginald MacIntyre edited the text and provided advice on overall content and presentation. André Métivier provided many observations and suggestions. André Laplante and Laurier Trahan played a useful role in commenting on key chapters of this book.

I would be remiss if I did not underline the key role played by Maureen O'Neil, IDRC's President, who supported and defended the development of this project and gave me advice and encouragements throughout.

This being said, I take full responsibility for errors and omissions.

**Jean-H. Guilmette**

# Acronyms and Abbreviations

| | |
|---|---|
| ADB | African Development Bank |
| AIDS | Acquired Immunodeficiency Syndrome |
| APEC | Asia Pacific Economic Cooperation |
| ASEAN | Association of Southeast Asian Nations |
| CAP | Common Agricultural Policy |
| CGIAR | Consultative Group on International Agricultural Research |
| CIDA | Canadian International Development Agency |
| CILSS | Comité Inter-états de Lutte contre la Sécheresse au Sahel, Permanent Inter-State Committee for Drought Control in the Sahel |
| CIME | Committee on International Investment and Multinational Enterprises |
| CMIT | Committee on Capital Movements and Invisible Transactions |
| COMECON | Council for Mutual Economic Co-operation |
| CRTC | Canadian Radio-Television and Telecommunications Commission |
| CSE | Consumer Subsidy Equivalents |
| CSTP | Committee for Scientific and Technological Policy (OECD) |
| DAC | Development Assistance Committee |
| DG | Director General |
| EBRD | European Bank for Reconstruction and Development |
| EC | European Community |
| ECD | Economic Division within OECD |
| EDRC | Economic and Development Review Committee |
| ELSAC | Meeting of the Employment, Labour and Social Affairs Committee (OECD) |

| | |
|---|---|
| EMDU | Environment Management Development in Ukraine |
| EU | European Union |
| FAO | Food and Agriculture Organization (of the UN) |
| FDI | Foreign Direct Investment |
| GATT | General Agreement on Tariffs and Trade |
| GDP | Gross Domestic Product |
| GDR | German Democratic Republic |
| GEF | Global Environment Facility |
| ICAO | International Civil Aeronautics (Aviation) Organisation |
| ICARDA | International Centre for Agricultural Research in the Dry Areas |
| ICLARM | International Centre for Living Aquatic Resources Management |
| ICRAF | International Centre for Research in Agroforestry |
| ICRISAT | International Crops Research Institute for the Semi-Arid Tropics |
| IDA | International Development Association |
| IDRC | International Development Research Centre |
| IEA | International Energy Agency |
| IFAD | International Forum on Accountancy Development |
| IFPRI | International Food Policy Research Institute |
| IFRI | Institut français des relations internationales |
| ILO | International Labour Organization |
| ILRI | International Livestock Research Institute |
| IMF | International Monetary Fund |
| IMHE | Programme on Institutional Management in Higher Education (OECD) |
| IMO | International Meteorological Organization or International Miners' Organization |
| INTERPOL | International Criminal Police Organization |
| IPGRI | International Plant Genetic Resources Institute |
| IRRI | International Rice Research Institute |

| | |
|---|---|
| ISO | International Standards Organization |
| ITU | International Telecommunication Union |
| MAI | Multilateral Agreement on Investment |
| MAP | Millennium Partnership for the African Recovery Programme |
| NASA | National Aeronautics and Space Administration |
| NATO | North Atlantic Treaty Organization |
| NEPAD | New Partnership for Africa's Development |
| NGO | Non-governmental Organizations |
| NIS | Newly Independent States |
| OCEEI | Office for Central and Eastern Europe Initiatives |
| ODA | Official Development Assistance (Aid) |
| OECD/DAC | Development Assistance Committee (OECD) |
| OECE | L'Organisation Européenne de Coopération Économique |
| OEEC | Organization for European Economic Co-operation |
| OPEC | Organization of Petroleum Exporting Countries |
| POP | Persistent Organic Pollutants |
| PPP | Purchasing Power Parity |
| PRMC | Programme de restructuration des marchés céréaliers (Programme for Restructuring of the Cereal Markets) |
| PSE | Producer Subsidy Equivalents |
| PUMA | Public Management Services (OECD) |
| SARS | Severe Acute Respiratory Syndrome |
| UMC | Ukrainian Management Committee |
| UNDP | United Nations Development Programme |
| UNDP/GEF | United Nations Development Programme/Global National Environmental Facility |
| UNEP | United Nations Environment Programme |
| UNESCO | United Nations Educational, Scientific and Cultural Organization |
| UNICEF | United Nations Children's Fund |
| UNIDO | United Nations Industrial Development Organization |

| WHO | World Health Organization |
| WMO | World Meteorological Organization |
| WTO | Word Trade Organization |

# 1

# The Conceptual Framework

*Cooperation: A New Paradigm for Development and for Peaceful International Relations*

*"Build it, they will come..."*
In the movie "Field of Dreams"

## SECTION 1
## ALLIANCES AND COOPERATION: EMERGENCE OF A NEW POST-WAR PARADIGM

### 1.1 Fifteen Hundred Years of War

Since the time of Pax Romana in the 5<sup>th</sup> Century, European societies have experienced recurrent war. The causes of war may be found in the pathology of nations, leaders, and communities. Wars were fought for political or strategic reasons, for religious motives, and for commercial advantage. In pre-industrial Europe, the economic doctrine of mercantilism that guided the policies of most trading countries transformed, in effect, commercial competition into state rivalries to control access to markets and/or sources of supply. The emphasis in mercantilism on the possession and accumulation of gold and silver, as the prime indicator of national wealth and well-being had far-reaching implications for conduct of states. Countries tended to focus their efforts and energies on maximizing the accumulation of coinage through conquest and protectionism at the expense of genuine trade and international cooperation. International relations were shaped by temporary alliances designed to foment coalition warfare against commercial rivals, with the victors winning the spoils. War represented, in that context, mercantilism by violent means.

For almost 15 centuries European countries demonstrated their affinities for warfare and commercial jousting, which reached its most destructive levels in 1939-1945 (though historians would properly date the beginnings of German, Italian, Japanese, and Soviet aggression to the early 1930s).

## Box 1.1

### Using Traditional Games to Improve Understanding

In an attempt to understand better the dynamics of inter-state conflict, two high-ranking French civil servants, Pingaud and Reysset (1995), wrote an insightful book comparing alternative approaches to what we might call "strategic games." Their analysis compares the Asian game of Go and the European game of Chess in terms of their implications for strategic behaviour. They argue that these games exemplify the values, goals and behavioural patterns that characterize the strategic cultures of the societies whence they emerged. They further maintain that the ensuing "game strategies" feed back into and inform a strategic mind-set that prescribes the behavioural propensities of the countries concerned, thus further reinforcing their characteristic strategic cultures. As Pingaud and Reysset point out, the objective of the game of chess is to capture ("kill") the rival King. The game has a single, supreme goal: to eliminate the opposing King and thus to destroy the rival side. There is no ambiguity in purpose, values or ends. The strategic consequences are daunting: pawns and other chess pieces (except the King) are expendable if and when their sacrifice can confer a tactical advantage. A null, or a compromise, may be sought to avoid a humiliating outcome. However, in the last analysis, in chess victory for one side is absolute, and defeat for the other is total. By way of contrast, Pingaud and Reysset call attention to the more ambiguous, synergetic interplay associated with the Japanese game of Go. The object of this game is to enlarge one's vital space by gaining territory. However, the goal is not to kill or avoid being killed, but rather to live and to construct. The strategic dynamics of Go reflect this constructive thrust. Thus, pawns, if surrounded, become the possession of the adversary; they are not "eliminated" but rather are taken over, or subjugated. Because this may imply a certain ambiguity in relative strength, victory in Go is determined by agreement among the players following a general count of all points. Victory or defeat is often relative and reaching equality is a good omen rather than a null outcome. As compared to chess, where the loser is defeated and humbled, Go players are predisposed to try not to humiliate the adversary but rather to share an experience and comment upon it. Pingaud and Reysset claim that societies define their approaches to strategy and conflict, their societal relations and national goals, according to some fundamental, overarching paradigm. For Europe, the governing paradigm for international relationships between Pax Romana of the 5$^{th}$ Century and the end of World War II in 1945 clearly parallels the game of Chess.

In 1947, the 'Western' countries that allied together to form what later became known as the Organisation for Economic Co-operation and Development (OECD), underwent a major shift in favour of a fundamentally new paradigm for cooperative internationalism. Some might argue that the assumptions implicit in the traditional 'chess paradigm' were so widely entrenched by that time that the emergence of a 'cooperation paradigm' denoted something of a utopian counterintuitive fantasy. Be that as it may, the emergent post-war cooperation paradigm inspired and gave expression to the new pattern of cooperative international relations involving Western Europe and North America. This culminated, institutionally, in the formation of

OECD, the North Atlantic Treaty Organization (NATO), and the European Economic Community (now the European Union).

The cooperation paradigm differs in its essentials from the conventional treaty alliances and coalition arrangements entered into by states. In the chess paradigm, alliances form an integral part of the game strategy, where powerful states seek pawns to deploy, and weak states seek the protection of mighty kings. European monarchs were prone to sign all manner of treaties, secret and open, to bolster their relative power. These treaties and coalitions did not, however, alter the essentially predatory rules of international behaviour, unlike the cooperation paradigm, which is predicated on the synergy of partnering and embraces connectivity, networking, and information sharing. The use of the term 'alliance' to describe an arrangement like OECD, NATO, or EU would be misleading in the sense that it trivializes the scope and depth of the cooperation they embody. By contrast, the arrangements put in place by the USSR and its Eastern European neighbours were more akin to traditional alliance architecture, though subject to powerful ideological control.

## 1.2 Five Characteristics of the New Paradigm

The cooperation paradigm has several characteristics that distinguish it from the traditional chess-related strategy, and which seem to be more broadly consistent with synergetic strategic outlook associated with the game of Go. Four factors are especially significant in this respect:

(1) The cooperation paradigm suggests that synergetic partnering among countries offers a more effective, more efficient, and more resilient approach to enhancing the wealth of each and all countries. This is a radical departure from the earlier assumption that the wealth of nations derives from possession and control of territories, people, and resources, which promoted policies of conquest and protectionism.

It is important, however, to note that cooperation among countries may, in certain circumstances, itself give rise to perverse attempts to control the new wider markets by fostering monopolies and oligopolies or regional protectionist blocs. For cooperation to be effective in improving economic efficiency, therefore, any tendency toward market control must be counterbalanced by measures designed to stimulate competition among individuals and commercial organizations.

(2) The paradigm for international cooperation considers information to be the life-blood of the new, wider economic system, and indeed it requires that information flow freely, openly, and according to the highest standards of reliability to all prospective users. From the outset, OECD

has been tasked with maintaining for its member countries a flow of economic information, of safeguarding the reliability of its data even from distortions from members' own inclinations. This approach to information in the cooperation paradigm may be contrasted with the concealed treatment of information in mercantilist-type regimes, where economic or industrial data were usually deemed to have strategic value and were therefore protected as state secrets. Information was certainly not to be shared with competing countries.

The open approach to economic information in the cooperation paradigm also necessitates some measures for protection of personal rights and of privately owned information such as patents and copyrights. Otherwise, cooperation in sharing information could have the perverse consequence of deterring the creation and development of new knowledge. For cooperation to be effective and efficient, the state must ensure that the ownership of intellectual property is protected with as much care and firmness as was the physical property of, say, landlords in times past.

(3) It is implicit in the cooperation paradigm that a sense of confidence is a prerequisite for human creativity and development in an open, international system. The concept of confidence for present purposes covers a wide range of attributes to personal security, including: confidence in one's society; self-esteem; openness of mind; tolerance of others and of new ideas; accountability for one's actions; responsibility; confidence in the value of scientific and technical innovation; and acceptance of diffusion of one's culture.

The Peyrefitte (1995) essay on the source of wealth and development demonstrates the central role of confidence. Confidence is a generic term that refers to a general attitude toward things that seem foreign. A positive attitude of confidence allows for a faster acceptance of new ideas, new techniques and new values. In the context of a changing world, with scientific and technological progress moving at a very high speed, a high tolerance to new ideas is the most effective attitude in adapting to changes in a viable and sustainable manner. No society is totally confident or completely tolerant to change; resistance always exists. The significant question is: "Is the attitude of a society generally negative with respect to foreign or new ideas, values, products or peoples, or is it on average positive?" Countries that adopt a more open attitude have consistently been better performers economically. Conversely, countries where protectionist measures run high, which are hostile to things foreign, which consistently deny progress and new ideas because they do not fit with traditions, have demonstrated throughout history sluggish growth and increasing pauperization of their people.

It is clear that within OECD, levels of confidence in and among the member countries have heightened exponentially during the past 40 years along with, and contributing to, their economic expansion.

(4) Connectivity complements confidence, and provides the pathways and linkages for the transmission and dissemination of knowledge and information pertaining to cooperation for development and growth. It is connectivity that enables the flow of ideas and of goods and services within the framework of cooperation, and this in turn bolsters confidence and is itself the result of increased confidence. Without connectivity, ideas cannot circulate and function as equalizing agents. Ideas, in the form of knowledge, may be embodied in material products, in technical services, in cultural artefacts, in books, film and electronic media. Increasingly they are being circulated via computerized telecommunication networks like the World Wide Web.

The international dissemination of knowledge is intimately wrapped up with the flow of trade and investment. Given the increasing value attributed to knowledge as a factor of production, as demonstrated by the heightened attention to intellectual property rights, trade patterns and investment flows are increasingly tending to reflect differences in knowledge endowments and knowledge capabilities among countries. Countries that invest in knowledge creation and dissemination acquire important competitive advantages over those that lag behind in developing knowledge-based economies. Countries with otherwise poor natural resource endowments like Japan, the Netherlands, Singapore, and Israel have built up a strong capacity for trade based on knowledge-intensive industries. Even large, resource-abundant economies like Canada and the United States saw their traditional areas of comparative advantage enhanced and new globally competitive industries emerge as a result of knowledge-based developments.

Knowledge is the ultimate product of human resource development. The capacity for knowledge creation can move with human migrations, as countries gain and lose people with potential for new ideas. The global web of communications infrastructure facilitates exchanges and transfers of knowledge and ideas. If infrastructure for communications is low-cost and easy to access, this could help countries and communities that have a knowledge deficit to access the resources of knowledge-intensive societies, and thus facilitate their own creative efforts and development potential.

Information, in the cooperation paradigm, is shared through networks that connect people, institutions, and/or operations. Connectivity through these networks has become an extremely efficient means to disseminate ideas and knowledge about technological development and transfers of technology. Networks thus sustain and accelerate economic growth.

(5) Closely related to information networking are the standards, the documented agreements on technical specifications or other precise criteria to be used consistently as rules, guidelines, or characteristics, to ensure that materials, products, processes and services are suitable for their purpose. Agreement on standards creates confidence in the reliability and effectiveness of the goods and services concerned. By ensuring the quality of information flowing through these networks, confidence can be built up among trading partners, whether countries or between producers and consumers, in a way that nurtures connectivity and supports trade expansion and economic growth. For cooperation to be effective, networks and quality standards are needed to bridge the information and knowledge gaps between partners, and thus they play an instrumental role in the promotion of development efforts. (see *http://www.idrc.ca/en/ev-27997-201-1-DO_TOPIC.html*)[1]

## 1.3 Overall Impact of the New Paradigm

The post-1945 shift to a cooperation paradigm served to open up new opportunities for economic and technological innovation by liberating and facilitating human creativity. The most valuable resource of the human mind is its capacity for creativity. Through the synergy associated with international cooperation and its elements of confidence, information openness, connectivity, networks, and quality standards, the cooperation paradigm can widen the horizons of creativity and facilitate the spread of knowledge products broadly among trading partners, and even beyond, to a lesser degree. In other words, the cooperation paradigm yields economies of scope and scale for creativity and innovation. These economies of scope and scale for their emergent knowledge sectors contributed substantially to the sustained growth of OECD economies since 1945.

---

1. These ideas are fully developed in a text available on the Internet: www.idrc.ca/oceei/standards.html

Countries that did not participate in this cooperative effort incurred significant opportunity costs in terms of the development that was foregone. Once the cooperation paradigm shift occurred, so substantial was its developmental momentum that other countries could not be indifferent to its potential. Some, like the developing countries of East and Southeast Asia, realigned themselves by opening up to certain elements of the cooperation paradigm, though not all. To that extent these countries were able to participate in the upsurge of developmental cooperation. Other countries in Africa, the Middle East, and Eastern Europe remained more-or-less closed, and therefore found themselves excluded from the synergy of international cooperation. Not only did these countries forego opportunities for a knowledge-based developmental transformation, but their lagging economies actually degenerated into an anti-development syndrome, as they lagged farther and farther behind. In the USSR, for example, this process of anti-development was associated with a worsening failure of confidence, inadequate connectivity (even internal), ambiguous quality standards that were never universally applied, and networks that were structured vertically rather than horizontally, thus militating against the spread of creativity and innovation.

Paradigm shifts, it should be noted, do not necessarily occur immediately, coherently, or holistically. Behavioural patterns and attitudes change slowly and gradually, and sometimes even partially and incrementally. Every society faces a complex variety of individuals, groups, and attitudes, some flexible, others rigid; some outward-oriented, others inward-oriented; some amenable to innovation and progress, others resistant to change. Most modern societies tend to respond to this complexity of expectations by simultaneously promoting developmental change and encouraging stability, pushing on both the accelerator and the brake, as it were. This perceived ambiguity could sometimes complicate the observation of paradigm shifts. In such cases, the extent of the paradigm shift may only be fully revealed over time.

The operation of many cooperation mechanisms enabled OECD countries to attain progressively higher levels of confidence. This, in turn, encouraged more human creativity touching most areas of life: new solutions were found to old problems, and new challenges were addressed and solutions found. Along with creativity came new employment opportunities. This nexus between cooperation, creativity and employment led to increases in both levels of income and social equity in OECD member countries that are unparalleled historically.

## 1.4 Role of Human Rights and Democratic Governance in Functioning of OECD Methodologies

The OECD process for promoting international economic cooperation is predicated on a consensus with respect to basic political values, most notably human rights, multiparty democracy, transparency in government, freedom of expression, and reliance on market rules for management of the economy. These values were highlighted in clear and unambiguous language in the opening paragraphs of the OECD Convention signed in 1961. (See Statement of Preliminaries table). OECD partners are expected to accept and implement these core values in order for the process of international cooperation to succeed and to become effective.

Several factors account for the prominence of human rights among OECD member countries. First, shared memories of the Second World War, in which hundreds of thousands fought and died in the defence of freedom and liberty reinforced the urgency of human rights and democracy in the public mind. Moreover, there emerged a widespread belief in public and official circles that the harmonization of human rights practices among member countries and their being anchored in the day-to-day operations of governmental and intergovernmental institutions would empower the international community to deal with the prevention and resolution of future conflicts. Human rights acquired ethical primacy in international affairs, wherein civil liberties and democracy have come to be generally associated with the principles of a just society and good governance. In essence, human rights represent a moral imperative in western political culture.

The universality of human rights principles has become a core value and expectation for the global agenda for the 21$^{st}$ Century. As will be explained, it would be a profound error to assume that human rights represent a western artifice and are, in some sense, alien to the political cultures of other societies. Likewise, it would be folly to conclude that human rights are a luxury that poorer countries cannot afford. A shifting competitive advantage in favour of information-intensive industrial and marketing processes gives renewed emphasis to human rights as a key component of an emergent knowledge-based economy.

Why is information, the specific application of knowledge, important for economic policy and enterprise? Information is vital to economic managers because it enables them to assess past and present performance and therefore to anticipate better the future and to exercise improved control over prospective policy options. In some ways, knowledge and information are like commodities: they are costly to produce and have market value, in that others may be willing to pay for them. However, knowledge and information also have two other distinctive qualities: they can be transmitted to others yet still remain entirely in the possession of the producers, and they can be utilized over and over again without being diminished.

Several types of knowledge can be distinguished in terms of economic utility: technical knowledge, used in the production of goods and services; knowledge relating to the management of economic systems, such as identifying markets and routine information like the gathering and sorting of statistical data. There is, as well, intuitive knowledge, which derives from accumulated experience, learning-by-doing and the personal evaluation of lessons learned from practice: it is not readily transmittable. In an economy, the demand for knowledge will reflect the actual capacity of producers to utilize information efficiently in their productive and marketing processes. Those who know how to benefit from this knowledge will invest in its acquisition and utilization and, in turn, will gain improved control over their economic future. Knowledge-based industries and organizations will thus tend to outperform others, just as knowledge-based economies will demonstrate competitive advantages over those lagging behind in the acquisition and utilization of knowledge.

In a knowledge-based economy, the highest value-added in production is attributable to human creativity. Many high-value tradable goods are products of intellectual creativity, among them music, films and videos, books, and computer software. Moreover, many other products, which were once considered to be merely land- or labour-intensive, are today produced with significant technological or scientific inputs. Knowledge embedded in the human mind has now become of prime economic significance in determining the competitiveness of firms and industries, the wealth of nations and even the security of countries.

Societies that are able to draw out the best of their knowledge resources by releasing the creativity of all individuals without exclusion for extraneous reasons like race, religion, ethnicity, age, gender or sexual orientation, will tend to perform better as knowledge-based economies than societies that discriminate. Societies that demonstrate superior performance as knowledge-based economies tend to be those that ensure universal access to knowledge while stimulating the pursuit of excellence. This provides for the free pursuit of research and creation with all of its ramifications, which put in place the infrastructure for wide-ranging and openly accessible communications networks, and which protect private property and personal rights while encouraging population mobility, since physical mobility often embodies intellectual agility.

In the ordinary course of actions within OECD, human rights and democratization issues are for the most part unspoken and essentially implicit notions. Most OECD procedures and processes emphasize mainly empirical and practical matters and tend to adapt to the circumstances of the group and its ability to sustain changes.

OECD involvement in human rights concerns is usually subsumed into governance issues, tending to focus primarily on operational matters such as the transparency of government operations, rather than on ideological or normative questions.

Some may argue that OECD has not been entirely consistent in observing human rights standards for membership, especially during the Cold War period. For example, Spain and Portugal were allowed to join when they were still governed by dictators. Greece was not suspended during its Colonels' regime. However, others would respond that the OECD approach was incrementally goal oriented, that respect for human rights was promoted progressively and indirectly as is spelled out in the first sentence of the OECD preliminaries: "Considering that economic strength and prosperity are essential for the attainment of the purposes of the United Nations, the preservation of individual liberty and the increase of general well-being." It was deemed more critical to adhere to market economy and free trade. OECD members' behaviour was dictated by practical considerations, in particular the Cold War, which pitted its members against the Soviet Bloc and its regime of state control and 'proletarian dictatorship.'

Discussions with OECD colleagues and former delegates have revealed that the willingness to tolerate these three transitionally delinquent member countries was *"geo-strategically mandatory and politically convenient,"* and hinged on the commanding hypothesis that OECD membership would in itself facilitate and expedite the process of democratization. OECD members were apparently prepared to be tolerant of some deviations, implicitly believing that, over time, the OECD general philosophy would prevail. History proved them right when in the 1970s all three countries moved toward democracy. Since the fall of the Berlin Wall, OECD members have become increasingly confident, in some cases overconfident, in their approach and more open about their commitment to human rights and democracy.

## Box 1.2

### *Human Rights and Progress*

Given the value placed on human rights in public discourse, it may seem paradoxical that people and governments in OECD countries may sometimes appear to be ambivalent about human rights concerns relating to other non-OECD countries. When efforts to promote economic, political, or security objectives come up against concerns for the defence of human rights, the support for the latter is sometimes compromised. In particular, most governments and firms are unwilling to forego the promotion of commercial opportunities even in countries with a poor human rights record. Some may even attempt to rationalize their ambivalence by arguing that human rights principles are moral matters with little direct relevance to economic performance. In pre- and early industrial periods, economic advantages accrued to those who controlled physical resources, land or minerals. Human beings were considered a labour resource; and in some countries, they were regarded only slightly better than animal labour. Hierarchical social structures were generally embedded in coercive force; inequality and privilege were the concomitant of governance. Since physical resources were and still are essentially linked to land, landed property and its protection became the predominant factor in political and economic management. Thus feudalism was, in essence, an orderly pyramidal arrangement for empowering landed classes. To the extent that these land- and resource-based social systems succeeded in maintaining effective control over their physical resources, they were able to remain relatively stable for very long periods of time. Technology and knowledge evolved slowly in such circumstances and had merely a marginal, incremental impact on these closed traditional societies. Since populations tended to expand over time, large numbers of people had to be employed in marginal, often sub-economic, occupations, sometimes in conditions of serfdom or even slavery. Economic value-added was abysmally low and poverty was rife. The Renaissance marked a radical transformation of this pattern of political-economic organization, as Europeans began to rediscover the power of human creativity, the vitality of knowledge, and its ability to innovate. Steadily, progressively, knowledge and inventiveness came to be recognized as vital resources in the wealth of nations. It is this knowledge-based value-added environment that enables modern industrial economies to obtain competitive advantages in traditional agricultural and manufacturing products at high and rising levels of income. The competitive advantages provided by investment in knowledge resources are such that it can be argued that as basic a commodity as wheat, for example, produced with traditional methods would have to price labour at zero or close to zero in order to be tradable internationally. Physical resources are still important for human survival and wealth, of course. Computers need plastic and other materials; data communications are often printed out on paper; people require physical shelter; social identity is often represented in concrete landmarks, whether edifices, monuments, or physical infrastructure. A socially just system of land tenure remains an important ingredient in good governance. However, it is the knowledge embodied in the human mind that today determines the wealth of nations, enabling societies to achieve material and cultural progress and even to defend themselves: even warfare has become knowledge-intensive, as demonstrated by the 'Desert Storm' campaign in the 1991 Gulf War. Human beings who suffer enslavement, imprisonment or discrimination are typically deprived of access to knowledge creation. Arguably, denying people access to markets—as happens with women, for example, in some countries—will constrain their potential contribution to knowledge development. In order to optimize their human capacity for knowledge development, communities must ensure and protect the rights of all individuals—without discrimination—to access existing knowledge resources so as to develop and enhance their potential for creativity and innovation. Investments that stimulate and protect the creativity of the human mind will help reinforce the elements of confidence and connectivity, which are deemed vital for the new co-operative approach to international relations. Moreover, competition between countries and regional country groupings will, in turn, tend to stimulate the dissemination of these ideas and values more or less broadly throughout the connected domain. However, societies that fail to uphold these rights and values could find themselves lagging increasingly behind the leading innovators, and will likely form the next bloc of "underdeveloped countries" in the new millennium.

## SECTION 2

## FROM PARADIGM SHIFT TO INSTITUTIONAL ACTIVITIES

Implementation of the new post-war cooperation paradigm involved the establishment of various kinds of institutional mechanisms and policy regimes at different levels of partnering and for various purposes. These may be grouped together in terms of the following typologies:

### 2.1 Multilateral Organizations with Universal Membership

*The United Nations Specialized Agencies*

The specialized agencies of the United Nations are open to all member states and even non-members, in certain cases. Among these are UNDP, FAO, WHO, UNIDO, UNESCO, IFAD, ITU, ILO, ICAO, IMO, UNICEF, UNEP, and WMO. Most of these multilateral agencies have specialized, sector-specific mandates. Each has its own governing body, composed of delegates from member countries, which meet annually, to adopt policies and programs and approve budgets. Member states have one vote in the governance of these multilateral organizations, irrespective of country size, population, income level or financial contribution. Executive responsibilities are vested in a chief executive and are administered by a professional secretariat. Staffing of these bureaucracies is typically representative of the diversity of the membership. Operating and program costs are shared according to some burden-sharing formula based on relative affluence.

*The Bretton Woods Financial Institutions*

Although the World Bank Group and International Monetary Fund are also specialized agencies of the United Nations, their structure differs in that membership is open only to those countries willing to pay subscriptions and purchase shares. The USSR declined to join initially. Governance of the World Bank and IMF is vested in their respective annual meetings of Governors (usually the Ministers of Finance of member countries). Voting is weighted in proportion to the number of shares held by each country, with the United States obtaining the largest number of shares and votes and other countries getting shares/votes according to a burden-sharing formula based on their relative economic attainments. Each multilateral institution has a Board of Directors to supervise the flow of programs and activities. Since there are a limited number of Executive Directors (15 to 25), each Director represents several countries, which become their 'constituencies.'

The multilateral financial institutions are managed like banking organizations, which is how they define themselves. Each institution must remain financially viable in its own right, since it operates as a financial intermediary raising funds in world capital markets for on-lending on favourable terms to client countries. Their programs, and especially their lending, are expected to be disciplined and adhere to sound financial and risk-management criteria. In principle, loan approval decisions should be free of political considerations, though some important shareholding countries have occasionally breached this principle. The loans they issue are repayable, with interest. Borrowers must repay real cost of the loans plus a fee for administration. Defaults would carry severe sanctions, and there have been none.

To address the economic development requirements of poor countries, the International Development Association (IDA) was set up in conjunction with, and complementary to, the World Bank. IDA does not have staff of its own, but operates through the World Bank, which receives a management fee in compensation. This arrangement ensures that IDA-supported programs and projects are subject to the same rigorous standards as World Bank-financed activities. Like the Bank itself, IDA is also a financial intermediary, mobilizing grants ('replenishments') from donor countries for on-lending. Eligibility for IDA concessional credits (0 interest, but with a service charge of 0.75% annually) is restricted to the poorest and least creditworthy developing countries, and is reviewed periodically.

IDA funding is allocated to eligible countries in accordance with criteria that are laid down at each tri-annual replenishment. Current criteria emphasize poverty reduction in an environmentally sustainable manner and per capita income. There are also guidelines for the geographic distribution of IDA resources. Southern Africa is targeted for 45-50% of IDA funding, and so-called blend countries (countries that are IDA eligible but also borrow from the World Bank) 30-35%. Until the mid 1980s, IDA credits were repayable over 50 years with a 10-year grace period; currently the maturity period is 40 years for the poorest countries and 35 years for others.

The IDA replenishment process also provides a mechanism for donor countries to achieve consensus on the overall thrust of IDA programming for the upcoming three-year funding cycle. The consensus that poverty reduction should have priority has been translated into a strengthened operational focus on basic human resource development and social services, while emphasizing the importance of policy developments that encourage broad-based economic growth.

## 2.2 International and Regional Organizations with Limited Membership

*Regional Financial Institutions*

Regional development banks have been set up for Asia (Asian Development Bank), Africa (African Development Bank), the Americas (Inter-American Development Bank), the Caribbean (Caribbean Development Bank), and most recently Central and Eastern Europe (European Bank for Reconstruction and Development), and are modelled broadly on the World Bank. All engage in financial intermediation to mobilize funding for on-lending to regional members. Except for the EBRD, all have a concessionary financing facility funded by grants from donor member countries.

*Regional Cooperation Institutions*

Various regions have experienced the emergence of regional organizations designed to promote more-or-less comprehensive economic and social cooperation among countries in the grouping. Membership is typically limited to countries within defined geographic parameters, often by invitation from a core group. Prominent examples include the European Economic Community, now the European Union, and the Association of Southeast Asian Nations (ASEAN). These organizations are typically mandated to facilitate a broad range of interactions and to foster closer collaboration in policy and outlook.

Some regional groupings may tend to focus mainly, if not exclusively, on particular issues or sectors of shared interest or concern, like the Club du Sahel, and may thus function more like sector-specific organizations.

## Specialized Sector-specific Regional Institutions

There are specialized international institutions whose mandate was determined by some specific concern, interest, or agenda. Membership is typically plurilateral, embracing countries that have a shared interest or concern regarding the issue(s) at stake. Examples include Asia Pacific Economic Cooperation (APEC), which largely limits itself to certain defined areas of activity pertaining to economic cooperation, or the Organization of Petroleum Exporting Countries (OPEC). These sector-specific types of international or regional organizations may form around any issue that countries deem appropriate for collaborative efforts, and where plurilateral synergy and financial support can yield advantages that exceed what might be expected from unilateral action.

## 2.3 The North Atlantic Treaty Organization (NATO)

NATO was originally established as an instrument of traditional alliance politics to deal collectively with the defence of Western Europe. Gradually, however, it evolved into a security component of the new post-war cooperation paradigm. In keeping with this transformation, NATO military officers, defence planners, and strategic thinkers were gradually but systematically co-opted into this new way of managing security policy. Signed on April 4, 1949, it comprises 19 West European and North American countries. In accordance with the Treaty, the fundamental role of NATO is to safeguard the freedom and security of its member countries by political and military means. During the last 15 years, NATO has also played an increasingly important role in crisis management and peacekeeping partially as a result of the end of the Cold War, and the creation of a stronger compact of European Nations under EU. These modifications of the international environment have opened up many possibilities for the future of NATO, which I don't feel is essential to discuss in this book.

## 2.4 International Policy Regimes and Coordinating Institutions

Implementation of the cooperation paradigm has been accompanied by the creation of new types of international institutions designed to promote closer coordination and even harmonization of national policies in areas where international synergy is sought. In the past, powerful countries attempted to impose on others the same policy standards it took upon itself. During the post-war period, the Western democracies initiated new forms of policy coordination through the establishment of policy 'regimes,' such as the General Agreement on Tariffs and Trade (GATT), providing agreed rules-based frameworks for the conduct of international activities. The development and enforcement of these international regimes through the coordinated policy efforts of the countries concerned has militated against arbitrary actions by individual states, on the one hand, and anomalous double standards, on the other. Dedicated organizations were established to help service and enforce the application of these international regimes. The operations of rules-based policy regimes served to create balance and equity among partner countries of varying sizes, populations, and economic capabilities, while reinforcing the value of international cooperation.

These new types of policy arrangements played an important part in making the post-war peace sustainable. By promoting the equal application of agreed rules to international activities, they helped construct a congenial post-war environment that was conducive to transforming former enemies into partners in international cooperation.

## The Organisation for Economic Co-operation and Development (OECD)

The establishment of the predecessor to OECD in 1948 proved to be a landmark event in the development and application of the cooperation paradigm. The Organisation for European Economic Co-operation (OEEC) was set up to manage the Marshall Plan, with membership limited to the countries concerned, and by 1961 this had evolved into the somewhat broader-based OECD.

OECD groups together countries that share the same political outlook (democracy), economic system (market economy), and level of industrial development. Its purpose has been and is to facilitate policy dialogue and coordination among its members, with a view to creating common frameworks for economic and social policies, common definitions for national accounting purposes, and common standards for assessing performance. It conducts studies and proposes policy designs intended to improve the quality of economic management, or to derive lessons learned from comparisons of sector performance (e.g. agriculture, transportation) across different countries. OECD does not disburse funds and does not engage in programming for specific sectors of concentration. OECD member countries are themselves expected to adhere to mutually agreed principles, policy norms, and definitions.

For most observers of international affairs, OECD is both a paradox and a mystery. Although many are familiar with the initials OECD, few understand the influence the organization has had in good governance and on economic progress. Its actual role is opaque, since a significant portion of its activities and deliberations take place behind closed doors and are limited to senior civil servants representing member countries. Often the outcome of these sometimes protracted processes appear so prosaic or even trivial that they are not covered by media reports. The *modus operandi* of OECD, of conducting complex negotiations over years rather than months, has not been described fully in the past, and very little has been published about its management systems. Scholars have rarely attempted to analyze and document its achievements. After 50 years of effort, and judging from the achievements of its member countries, OECD must be doing something right.

In conceptual terms, OECD may be best described as one of the central institutions forming the international policy 'regime' that governs the policy dialogue amongst the 'Western' industrial democracies (including, of course, non-European/American members). A substantial portion of the policy dialogue that constitutes this international regime takes place within the framework of OECD. A policy 'regime' may be defined as, "sets of implicit or explicit principles, norms, rules and decision-making procedures around which actors, i.e. 'states' or 'governments,' expectations converge in a given area of international relations" (Koehane, 1989: 57), including subjects such as regional economic cooperation. Ruggie (1982) offers a slightly different definition: "a set of mutual expectations, rules and regulations, plans, organizational energies and financial commitments, which have been accepted by a group of states." These definitions help characterize OECD as an international policy regime. This concept of regime reflects the notion of the paradigm shift, highlighted in Chapter 1. Movement toward a new cooperation paradigm in international affairs implies that some of the attributes of sovereignty be sacrificed voluntarily in order to reach a new type of consensual discipline.

I will demonstrate throughout this book how OECD has played a catalytic role in the creation of wealth among its member countries. Such is the power of information as a public good, and such is the significance of international policy regimes.

## International Policy Enforcement Mechanisms

The Economic Division of OECD (ECD) has established certain mechanisms to help address the challenges of enforcing international policy regimes in the absence of more formal systems of global governance. These mechanisms functioned within the consensus arrangements of OECD, and were managed through OECD itself, without permanent staffing or administrative systems of their own. For delinquent borrowers of official loans the mechanism was the so-called "Club of Paris," an ad hoc arrangement of the OECD; for unfair trade subsidies the mechanism was the OECD "consensus arrangement"; for matters concerning aid policy and criteria it was the Development Assistance Committee of OECD. This approach to enforcement enabled OECD to achieve a fair measure of coherence and consistency (if not participatory universality) in the making and application of its international policy regime.

## SECTION 3

## INTERNATIONAL DEVELOPMENT COOPERATION

The initiation of international cooperation for post-war reconstruction and development represented a conceptual watershed in the formulation and application of the cooperation paradigm. Beginning with the Marshall Plan for European reconstruction and continuing through the evolution of development assistance, aid was to play a crucial enabling role in the renewal of international economic relationships in post-war Western Europe, and in developing countries after independence. The establishment of programs and mechanisms for the transfer of assistance from better-off donors to needy recipient countries was not merely complementary to commercial flows, but also in many instances aid actually led the rehabilitation of trade and investment. Aid was not a substitute for trade and investment; rather it exemplified a shift from traditional mercantilist precepts to a new perspective that situated commercial relations within the cooperation paradigm. Moreover, the precedent of economic cooperation helped almost everywhere to bolster the political sense of confidence and institutional capabilities. The structural symmetry thus induced, facilitated, and stimulated the expansion of international economic linkages.

### 3.1 The Marshall Plan

The principles of aid were initially formulated in conjunction with the Marshall Plan for post-war European reconstruction. This transfer mechanism was designed to provide American capital goods, equipment, and resources on concessional terms to war-damaged Europe, to help accelerate the rehabilitation of their production systems. Though invited to participate, the Soviet Union refused to take part and even prevented its satellites in Eastern Europe from doing so. Not only did this act of denial deprive these countries of economic assistance, it effectively severed Eastern Europe and the USSR from the newly emergent patterns of cooperation that were reshaping the economies and societies of Western Europe and North America.

Meanwhile, the Marshall Plan helped restore the productive capacity of Western Europe in a relatively short time, and paved the way for closer regional cooperation within Western Europe, starting with the European Coal and Steel Community and culminating in the European Communities/ European Union. Europe repaid its debt to the Marshall Plan both financially and through its subsequent achievements in sustained economic growth.

## 3.2 The Colombo Plan

The Colombo Plan had its conceptual origins in the British Colonial Welfare and Development Acts of 1940 and 1945. Encouraged by the Marshall Plan, but constrained by the chronic weakness of the post-war British economy, countries of the Commonwealth (including Canada) grouped together to formulate a plurilateral framework for transferring resources from richer Commonwealth countries to Asian developing countries, based on the same principles of international assistance. This became the Colombo Plan, inaugurated in 1950. Transfers of assistance through the Colombo Plan emphasized capital goods, equipment, and industrial raw materials deemed necessary to help the developing economies overcome infrastructural bottlenecks to their economic growth. The Colombo Plan, however, provided as well for food aid, technical assistance, and transfers of technology and knowledge, to help countries maintain social stability and advance to higher stages of development.

## 3.3 Official Development Assistance (ODA)

The evolution of ODA since the Colombo Plan and until the present has been guided by principles and rules adopted by the OECD Development Assistance Committee (DAC). These principles and rules are generally designed to enhance the elements of development cooperation inherent in aid, while mitigating the more mercantilist elements involved in procurements and deliveries.

Neo-mercantilism always looms in aid transfers, inasmuch as ODA involves subsidized procurements and deliveries of tradable resources—whether goods or services or knowledge—from donors to recipient countries. Early on, the donor community decided that it would be advantageous to them, for local political and economic reasons, to tie their respective aid contributions to procurements from domestic sources. This was known as 'tied aid.' When the subsidy element in tied aid threatened to undermine commercial trading relationships, the donor community through OECD/DAC decided to adopt rules to mitigate the deleterious effects of concessional funding on trade and investment. Thus the ethos of cooperation that had been built up within OECD enabled the donor community to constrain their own otherwise predatory, neo-mercantilist impulses. DAC likewise formulated rules and standards for areas where ODA could become ambiguous, such as aid quality and concessional requirements, eligibility, associated financing, and the principles underpinning various transfer mechanisms.

## 3.4 Aid and the International Projection of Ideas

ODA was involved from the outset, explicitly and implicitly, in the global ideological struggle with communism, and was envisaged by the Western donor community as a means of projecting the values of democracy and market economics to non-aligned developing countries. Certainly the Colombo Plan was, strategically, a Commonwealth-led effort to bolster the capacity of newly independent India, Pakistan, and Sri Lanka (followed later by other countries) to withstand communist subversion by promoting a more effective development model.

In this ideological struggle, the West saw itself as enjoying a clear competitive advantage in the use of ODA to project values, though it remains questionable whether any real leverage was obtained thereby. In response, the Soviet Union and certain Eastern European countries offered their own forms of assistance, with a strong military component, which was particularly effective in cultivating ties with Arab countries. Western ODA excluded military transfers from the definition, and instead deliberate emphasis was placed on the linkage between development assistance and stability and peace. Indeed, ODA was officially conceptualized in OECD/DAC as "development cooperation," expressing the notion that aid ought to project the ethos of a cooperation paradigm onto the developing countries.

The notion of development cooperation carries with it the idea of connectivity, linking people and institutions horizontally and vertically. Aid has thus tended to emphasize the strengthening of communication linkages between and among institutions and communities. There has been aid support for regional cooperation, in South and Southeast Asia, Southern Africa, Latin America and the Caribbean, as an intermediate step toward more widely based, global economic and political arrangements. Innovative aid instruments were introduced to encourage the sharing of resources and knowledge to demonstrate the power of sharing ideas to developing countries. This has contributed to the emergence of a wide array of new communications networks between 'North' and 'South,' between OECD countries and developing countries.

Along with information sharing has come the related idea of sharing standards and measurement norms for economic and social development. The availability of standard performance indicators for economic and social development was critical for multinational companies seeking to invest in unfamiliar new markets. Direct foreign investment by multinational countries in developing economies provided significant inflows of capital and technology transfers that combined with local labour and newly created infrastructure (often financed with ODA) to diversify and expand local production capacity. This has resulted in increased employment opportunities and higher levels of economic activity in the developing countries concerned, and an expanding supply of labour-intensive products from developing economies to world markets. Linkages between industrial and developing countries, between multinational enterprises and host economies, between direct foreign investment flows and aid-financed infrastructure, between productive sector activities and public sector concern for good governance, social development, and environmental sustainability, have become increasingly pronounced as part of this globalization trend.

The Marshall Plan was formulated in unique post-war circumstances. The Allied War Crimes Tribunal at Nuremberg, and the imposition of a new democratic Constitution onto post-war Japan, signalled clearly that victorious powers intended to promulgate human rights and democratic values into recently liberated Western Europe and Japan. The founding of OECD was seen as instrumental to the propagation of these values, and to the harmonization of their practices among its member countries. Key partners shared this perspective, including the US, UK, France, and Canada, and all were prepared to face the challenges of democratization for post-war Europe and Japan.

The times and circumstances were strikingly different with respect to aid to post-colonial emerging nations. In response to the spread of the Cold War to the emergent Third World, western donor countries chose to focus on the economic and social dimensions of the post-war paradigm shift in addressing the challenges of development in post-colonial Asia and Africa. Western aid was thus directed mainly at infrastructure development, agriculture, education, and health, a predilection that was shared also by nongovernmental organizations (NGOs) operating at the so-called 'grass-roots' level. By contrast, there was little, if any, aid involvement in the more politicized dimensions of the new post-war paradigm: in matters of human rights, personal liberties, governance, and democratization.

This bias toward economic and social development, to the neglect of political development, reflected the ambivalence and ambiguity of Western donor and developing country objectives. Developing country governments invoked the high principle of National Sovereignty to exclude external donor interventions in politically or culturally sensitive domestic affairs. Multilateral and bilateral donor agencies were prepared to accept this exclusion, as did most of the NGO community. Aid donors were, in general, willing to rationalize their activities in countries ruled by dictators, where human rights were abused, or where governmental transparency was absent. It would seem that a considerable degree of complacency accompanied this attitude on the part of donor governments and NGOs. Thus, Jacques Chirac, then a former Prime Minister and candidate for President of France, declared in 1991 that, in his opinion, "...Africans were not ready yet for multi-party democracy." That perspective, which prescribed democracy as pertaining solely to the more sophisticated industrial countries, was widely held both in the donor community and in the developing countries.

Progressively, the past 20 years have seen heightened attention being devoted to environmental and governance issues in aid discussions within OECD/Development Assistance Committee, and beyond. Renewed attention has been given to human rights and democratization and to promoting ecologically sustainable developments consistent with the principles of market economies. Among the considerations that prompted this sensitivity to governance and environmental matters was the manifest failure of the centrally planned economies, compared to accelerated growth and improved social equity attained by OECD countries. A conclusion was reached, in OECD circles at least, that its model was working better than any available alternative.

## 3.5 Aid Volumes and Impact

In assessing the developmental impact of aid, I believe far too much emphasis has been placed on the sheer volume of ODA. It has often been argued, in both donor and recipient country circles, that the high overall levels of ODA commitment, which peaked at US$70 billion in 1994, could offer almost interminable support for large-scale infrastructure and social program development in recipient countries. In fact, ODA never represented more than one-third of total financial flows to developing countries. Even for lower-income developing countries, ODA disbursements averaged only about 5% of their gross national product, or about one-sixth of gross domestic investment. For some very small, poor countries, the share of ODA may be larger, since other resource flows were scarce. However, the proportional contribution of aid tended to shrink relative to the actual requirements of larger, more populous economies. It is necessary to adopt a realistic perspective on aid resource availability in order to avoid reaching misleading conclusions or raising unrealistic expectations.

From my perspective, the essential purpose and role of ODA is to test ideas relating to development in a large scale, and in a relevant, developmental context. Thus, the ultimate significance of aid can only be evaluated with reference to ideas embodied in the project/program design and their developmental implications; for example, a hydroelectric dam and its economic utility; a telecommunications facility and its effects on connectivity; universal primary schooling and its consequences for increased income distribution and growth; a particular technology transfer and its ramifications on employment creation. It is the responsibility and benefit to the recipient country to make appropriate use of this evaluation. The information yielded should help define future development strategies, investment priorities, technological choices, and—very importantly—management models.

## SECTION 4

## THE COOPERATION PARADIGM AND THE FORMER EASTERN BLOC

In the heady aftermath of the destruction of the Berlin Wall, OECD countries found themselves confronting a dramatic and unprecedented challenge: what to do to assist the USSR and its Eastern European satellite countries achieve a peaceful, stable transition to democratization. Some maintained that the task of political and economic reform was of such magnitude that OECD countries would be called upon to offer a full array of ODA instruments to help these countries overcome their lagging development, while others responded that average real income levels in Eastern Europe and the former Soviet Union exceeded the eligibility criteria for ODA.

### 4.1 The 'Magic' of the Market

One of the key arguments was that most of the countries of East and Central Europe and the Newly Independent States (NIS) already possessed, in fact, the human resource and technological endowments necessary to achieve considerably higher levels of economic performance. Accordingly, they insisted that these countries required only certain elements of market 'know-how,' which arguably could be transferred through normal commercial mechanisms and bank loans. To this end, the European Bank for Reconstruction and Development was established as a regional financial institution, albeit without an aid facility analogous to IDA. The 'magic of the market' was expected to do the rest.

## 4.2 Reform: A Complex, Multifaceted Process

If one accepts the premise of this paper concerning the emergence of a cooperation paradigm, then it becomes clear that the extent of the transformation required in order to bring about the reforms called for in East and Central Europe are overarching and all-embracing in scope and purpose. There are three considerations that ought to be taken into account in this regard:

- Paradigm shifts can range in significance from a comprehensive transfiguration of the conceptual mindset to more singular changes in intellectual method. Be that as it may, they reflect, at once, a reoriented perception of the realities in one's environment, and indeed a new perspective of oneself in that reality. A paradigm shift may take hours, days or even years for the new perceptions of reality and changed perspectives of self in that reality to become internalized.

- A decision to reform a part of a social system usually invokes corresponding changes in other related parts of the system. For example, transforming a Russian collective farm ("kolkhoz") into a market-oriented enterprise involves substantial changes in the lifestyle, corporate identity, leadership, hierarchy, and incentives framework in the organization. It is just not possible to simplify and reduce this to merely changing the method of production, or even the ownership structure, as some have suggested.

- A stable market economy is neither the outcome of some 'Hobbesian' solution to social disorder, nor is it the product of relentless, unfettered acquisitive individualism. Markets, to function efficiently and effectively, require the rules and structure of civil society, and must be subject to surveillance and controls by a civil authority to keep them honest, to enforce contractual relationships, to sustain competition, and to mitigate socially unjust outcomes. Market economies thus involve a balanced, dynamic tension between entrepreneurial initiative and the societal precepts of cooperation. This balance can operate through law or custom, and in a modern market economy they will be administered by government and enforced by the courts. Governments, in turn, have their propensity to control kept in check by balancing mechanisms in their political and economic systems, and in particular their desire for markets to create and grow wealth.

The challenge confronting advocates of structural reform is how to bring about a transformation away from an equilibrium situation that exists, and which offers some sense of stability and familiarity, even if the outcome—in economic terms—is not satisfactory, and move to a more dynamic yet orderly equilibrium that would offer improved prospects for economic and social development. The impulse to reform is simple to comprehend but extraordinarily difficult to implement. Its processes are poorly understood, and the path to change is uncharted. It is a question in search of an empirical answer.

## 4.3 Need for New and Relevant Aid Instruments

When the donor community focused on aid for newly independent emerging economies in the 1950s, it was necessary for donors to design new and relevant concepts of development cooperation and invent new instruments for the transfer of assistance. Today, conditions in the NIS region are substantially different from previous situations in either post-war Europe or the Third World. One would assume that an array of new instruments for cooperation and assistance would have been designed to respond to this dramatically new situation. In fact, except for the establishment of the EBRD, which had few innovative qualities, little new has been attempted to date. The conjunction between the need for new instruments for the transfer of appropriate types of assistance, and support for a paradigm shift that must accompany effective reform, remains by and large unrecognized among Western donor agencies.

This gap, and the imperative for innovation in the development of new and appropriate forms of assistance, seems likely to become increasingly salient issues in the policy dialogue between Western aid donors and the NIS.

The challenge of creating a relevant new transfer mechanism will be addressed later in this book.

## SECTION 5

## RELEVANCE OF THE IDRC AND OECD EXPERIENCE TO EASTERN EUROPEAN COUNTRIES

The challenge of systemic reform is not unprecedented historically. Indeed, the countries of Western Europe and Japan also underwent sweeping reforms of their institutional and policy frameworks after the Second World War. At the heart of these reforms lay the adoption of a common definition of human rights and the introduction of democratic forms of governance within the context of a market economy. Previously, the political systems of Germany and Japan, and also of other countries such as Austria, Greece, Portugal, and Spain, were volatile and repressive. This rendered Europe chronically vulnerable to internal and external conflict. The situation of Western Europe after World War II was in some ways analogous to that of Eastern Europe following the collapse of communism.

Certain OECD methods have been introduced into some central European countries since 1982, and have contributed to the revitalized connectivity between Poland, Hungary, the Czech Republic, and Slovakia and Western Europe. The acceptance of OECD procedures helped to create an enabling regime that expedited the adoption and adaptation of new policy designs, institutional norms, and principles of governance in these countries. Today, most if not all of the countries of the former Soviet Union are becoming, to a greater or lesser degree, integrated into the global economy. The 1998 ruble crisis is indicative of this, in a perverse way: The monetary shock of the collapse of the ruble highlighted the need to strengthen the capabilities of these countries to manage their economic systems in a manner consistent with the OECD policy regime, which in turn would enable them to participate effectively in the world economy.

It is important to emphasize the empirical character of the OECD negotiation process. The OECD approach to negotiations is designed to lead incrementally and over time to consensus-based policies and structures, which may be implemented by all member countries. In essence, the OECD process produces outcomes that are seen—by member countries—to be reasonable and acceptable. These policy outcomes are generally considered relevant and timely, and can be readily adapted to the specific needs of the member countries concerned.

Some commentators and observers of the transformation of Russia and of other ex-USSR countries are coming to the conclusion that excessive emphasis was being given in policy development to World Bank and IMF prescriptions and interventions. The policy recommendations of these two multilateral institutions, perceived at times as externally imposed "diktats," usually reflect their repertoires of knowledge and experience, and are neither malevolent nor irrelevant *per se*. Their actual appropriateness and adaptability to local circumstances, however, can depend on whether they demonstrate an understanding of the premises explained previously, especially the central role of information in building a strong and modern economy.

For example, some IMF critics may fail to understand the significance of maintaining a market-sensitive exchange rate, a cornerstone of international financial discipline, if they do not appreciate the role of exchange rates as a significant piece of information required by economic enterprises in making sound investment, production, and marketing decisions. Exchange rate information is one of a wide range of market-related data that must be kept current, reliable, and transparent at all times. Similarly, now that a significant and growing share of international trade is subject to ISO standards, which in essence is another form of information, individual enterprises find themselves compelled to adopt these standards in order to participate in and benefit from this new, standardized international trading environment. No modern market economy can be run with multiple standards, as occurred, for instance, in the USSR, where standards were generally high in the military, science, culture and sports, but for consumer goods and for basic infrastructure were relatively low. Therefore, a significant change of attitude is required with respect to availability and transparency of information. However, recent debates in the Russian and Ukrainian parliaments about curtailing access to the World Wide Web indicate how problematic it can be to internalize the concept of information as a resource for economic development and good governance.

The rehabilitation of the Dnieper River Basin will require international cooperation, knowledge and information in development processes at the level of enterprise and municipal management, as well as for whole economic sectors like agriculture and mining. In all of these sectors of production, sound practices are called for to achieve high-quality production and, at the level of policy management, well-designed policies have to be drafted and rigorously enforced internationally. From our perspective, there are significant parallels and similarities between the project for restructuring the Sahel ecological situation and the present challenge of cleaning up the Dnieper River Basin. In the mid 1970s, the entire Sahelian region comprising nine countries, was faced with a devastating famine. This food crisis was inextricably linked with desertification and soil erosion. To resolve this problem, a well conceived collective effort was required. The consistent involvement of donors rested on them being confident that things could change and that Sahelian countries were prepared to do what was necessary to resolve this massive problem. Sahelian representatives, for their part, needed to be reassured that donors were really there to help and were determined to 'go the distance' with them. This dual predicament rested on fears. To surmount this obstacle, an entirely new form of dialogue between potential partners as well as a new way of gathering knowledge in order to establish agreed upon policies were required. This is what the Club undertook to do.

The task ahead with respect to the Dnieper River is critical for humankind as scarce water resources are going to become increasingly vital to ensure world peace in the coming years: currently up to 50 million people depend on the waters of this river for their day-to-day survival. This complex task is likely to span a 30 to 40 year period and will be an immensely costly undertaking. The best international cooperation practices will be called for in order to reach such goals.

We are confident that 'policy-driven coordination' can be a more durable and resilient means of intergovernmental collaboration than any other form of cooperative endeavour. A 'virtuous cycle' can be initiated by building on a combination of interrelated instruments as developed within OECD and IDRC. The IDRC methodology favours research implemented by those immediately concerned with the problem rather than by spending on costly and often irrelevant foreign expertise. This approach prepares the basis for informed policy dialogues among riparian countries, as well as with international partners. The result will be not just a better plan of action in the technical sense, but also synergy arising from the subtle interplay of peer pressure to follow up with implementation. National policies that are built on consensus have a greater chance of being implemented, and this in turn builds confidence among the various sources of external grants, loans, and investments. Project compliance follows naturally.

IDRC's relevant experience, especially its seven-year involvement in the rehabilitation of the Dnieper in Ukraine, is discussed in Chapter 2. The basic elements of what we believe to be an efficient overall management system to attain complex goals involving many different partners is also discussed.

# 2

## Development and Networks as Instruments for Change

### SECTION 1

### EXPERIENCES IN DEVELOPMENT

The 20$^{th}$ Century saw a large number of experiments concerning governance systems. Various forms of fascism in Italy, Germany, Spain, and Portugal, and socialism in the USSR, Central Europe, Vietnam, Korea, and China, replaced the 19$^{th}$ Century evolution toward liberal economies and the emergence of democracies. By 1945, fascism was more or less a defunct ideology, but Soviet-style socialism remained as an alternative to market economy and democracy until the early 1990s. In contrast to previous centuries, which operated more or less in accordance with only a few ideologies and governance systems, the second half of the 20$^{th}$ Century was marked by a great diversity of social and economic experiments. Even within Western style market economies, economists of all schools of thought had a field day as successive governments tried various ways to generate wealth, and to promote their development. Even the notion of development gave rise to an abundant literature and to various definitions and practices. All these ideas were exported in some form or another to developing countries. Successes were as diversified as the recipes, so to speak.

In the final analysis, development seems to be the attributes of governments that adopted sound policies. Successful governments fostered the following basic conditions. They created a state of law and adopted rules that correspond well to their population's aspirations, and dealt appropriately with existing cultural constraints and imbedded reflexes. Fundamental laws of economics must prevail for creativity, innovation, and freedom to thrive. At the same time, major social conflicts are averted and individuals are capable of getting justice. Governments, in turn, have their propensity to control kept in line through checks and balance mechanisms in their political and economic systems.

This being said, it leaves a most haunting question unanswered: "Which policy or set of policies are likely to foster economic growth with a real measure of human satisfaction, as well as fostering long-term sustainable development?"

In the following chapters, we will argue that some very broad policies seemed to work better than others, and have rallied a consensus as to their likelihood of achieving development goals. However, the devil is in the details. Democracy is multiform and so are market economy rules of conduct and know-how. Faced with a multitude of choices, governments must exercise clever judgement and appropriateness. Which management of public dialogue process is most likely to help in this task?

## 1.1 Lessons Learned from the Japanese Experience

Comparing many types of experiments, we have come to the conclusion that all things considered, the most pertinent example of an effective approach to development is probably to be found in the hearth of the Meiji restoration, more specifically in the 'Iwakura mission'.

From 1630 onward, Japan closed itself from all outside influence. It closed all ports and barred all trade, except for a very limited amount of luxury goods that Dutch merchants were allowed to bring in through Nagasaki, under strict government control. Thus, for a period of two centuries, Japan avoided all cultural influence from abroad. It also missed out on the European technological revolution that started to gather speed and momentum in the 17th and 18th Century. In 1843, Britain defeated the almighty Chinese army in order to gain trade access to China. In 1853-54, the American Commodore M.C. Perry, heading a fleet of eight ships, forced Japan to sign a trade treaty and open its ports to American and European goods. The combination of those two shows of strength on the part of 'distant foreigners' had the effect of altering Japan's foreign policy, and it shook the entire country. In 1868, the young Emperor Meiji, with the help of a cadre of progressive samurais, stripped the Shogun of its power and embarked Japan into massive changes and modernization of all aspects of its economy and political systems.

In December 1871, the Emperor of Japan sent a large diplomatic mission (up to 50 delegates) to America and Europe with the mandate of renegotiating treaties signed in the 1850s. A number of officials who accompanied the mission had been "tasked to study Western political, economic, and military institutions, with a view of identifying those that could most usefully be transplanted to Japan (Beesly, 1992: 116). The mission was advised by American, British, and German ministries of Foreign Affairs, that Western nations were reluctant to renegotiate former treaties unless a variety of reforms, including a complete revision of Japan's legal system, were carried out. Only then would the powers accept to enter into a new relationship with Japan. Furthermore, "the envoys had the evidence of their own eyes to show them that Japan had far to go before she would be in a position to negotiate on equal terms" (Ibid: 114).

One can only surmise that the members of the Iwakura mission were astute and remarkable observers of Western knowledge and know-how. As a result of an "18 month worldwide search for best developmental practices," the Iwakura Mission identified the following best applications: "at first a contract was passed with the Dutch to learn about their industrial and military technology. A Prussian military organization was soon retained with a general staff, a general college and a divisional structure. In 1869, the Japanese constitution, based on a Prussian model, was promulgated. Codes of law, based on the French and Prussian model, were adopted. A program of translation of Western scientific works was initiated, and as early as 1870, students were sent abroad to study sciences and Western science teachers were imported. A massive program of patenting and licensing was developed" (Ibid: 138). One should add that Japanese experts identified that England had the best or most appropriate manner of managing a navy, and it also proceeded to copy its organization. The result was that 30 years later, a country, which had not had a navy for two centuries, was able to defeat the somewhat powerful Russian navy in the Bay of Kamchatka in the war of 1905.

Many analysts have regretted that the Japanese development model took the path of regional imperialism that was fostered by a military compact. On the other hand, hardly anyone can deny that the Japanese approach was extremely efficient to bring about modernity into a technologically and economically backward nation. Many lessons can be learned from that development process.

First, Japan was informed without any ambiguity that its archaic (and perceived as barbaric) legal system was an obstacle to becoming a full member in the concert of nations. This forced an awakening within Japan's governing body, leading to the adoption of a constitution, but equally and most importantly to drafting a civil code, a modern land tenure system, as well as a more liberal criminal code. Japan also introduced a great variety of modifications to its old ways of doing things; all of these were inspired in one form or another by what they saw and learned from the West. In essence, powerful peer pressure from other sovereign nations was exercised. Peer pressure and peer review are central to progress and change and will be discussed at length in the following chapters.

Second, what stands out in the Meiji development process is the discriminative analysis leading to the selection of western management systems. In other words, officials of the Iwakura mission studied and compared various organizational systems and selected from among all those the one that corresponded best to Japan's tradition, culture, and developmental goals. It preferred, for example, the French Civil code to that of other European nations; it selected the British management of its navy, or Germany's commercial code. And once these choices were made, Japan's own trained specialists proceeded to adapt them within its tradition and culture. In essence, appropriation took place at the very early stages of development. It is my view that appropriation is not the result of foreign transfer of technology, but is, as demonstrated by the Meiji Restoration process, at the very core and at the beginning of any change process.

In contrast, Development Assistance or Foreign Aid is premised on the belief that ideas coming from any industrial country are in the best interests of the recipient. In this way, each donor feels empowered to insist on exporting its own way of doing things, even if this means that different value systems will have to co-exist and contradict each other, thus generating discomfort and cynicism. Contrary to the Japanese restoration process, recipients of aid are often disenfranchised from developing activities. They do not take part in program frameworks, in the project design, nor in its implementation, and are seldom part of the post-facto evaluation team. Donors often moan about the absence of appropriation by recipients. Development is not something that is done to others, but something that must come from the inside. In other words, the acquisition of knowledge and technology must be internalized from the outset, not hoped for as an end result. If we were to draw lessons from the Iwakura mission, donors would open a dialogue with would-be (and presumably cooperative) recipients, help them identify which system best fits their own traditions, culture, and goals, and from then on, follow the lead from each recipient. The reverse, that is defining an 'agenda for change' in donor capitals, is unlikely to breed the results one would hope for.

## SECTION 2

## ERA OF COOPERATIVE UNDERTAKINGS

From 1870 onward, Japan made tremendous achievements all by itself. Today's world has changed; no country would go at it alone. The aftermath of the Second World War saw the creation of Interpol, NATO, and a number of scientific networks. These helped to promote research, innovation, and generally speaking, change. The creation of OECD to manage the Marshall Plan and to improve policies in Europe is a key example. Networks more or less happened, and became a fixture of everyday life. People such as Robert Lattès, one of the founders of the Club of Rome, have very aptly demonstrated the tremendous power of networks in the context of scientific and technological progress that have propelled our economies after the Second World War and still do. Lattes (1998: 28) argues that scientific and technological progress as well as the ensuing economic growth have been accelerated significantly by networks, formal and informal. In his mind the West would not have experienced the technological boom experienced in the 1950s, 1960s, and 1970s were it not for this key factor.

## Box 2.1

### *Organizational Forms*

"Standard organizations have a defined functional purpose, a clear domain of operation. It may provide a particular kind of service to a certain group of client." For that purpose, it is organized in a very structured way. To ensure clear communications between the top echelons and the lower ones, as well as to minimize redundancies and conflicts, most standard organizations rest on a simple organizational chart where hierarchy prevails, as the guiding principle. The typical organizational structure of a firm or a ministry essentially replicates cybernetic arrangements, whose characteristics are simplicity and clarity. Such arrangements also provide a clear and succinct road map for everyone to see who does what in the organization. For that reason, it fits well with the principle of accountability. Evaluation is possible and attribution easy to track and demonstrate. Lusthaus *et al.* have noted that networks are collaborative organizations between free entities such as researchers, universities, institutions, or a combination of these. It may also gather government representatives, as is the case in OECD. The needs of the group may not necessarily be very well defined at the onset, or they may change as the network progresses. Furthermore, it may not be clear as to who is doing what in the partnership; here again, this may change over time. They may or may not have legal existence. Instead, they are built around shared interests and business relationships. They are not clearly owned by one individual or one organization. Ownership is spread across the group. Because members may have multiple loyalties, they may adopt ambiguous behaviour depending on time and circumstances and multiple boundaries, the boundaries themselves being somewhat fuzzy. Because boundaries are fuzzy, performance assessment that is concerned with efficiency is problematic and attribution elusive (Lusthaus *et al.*: 169-170).

## 2.1 Informal Networks

Networks are increasingly recognized as key instruments for knowledge acquisition and as sources of innovation. They are also heralded as central instruments for policy changes, because policy is often the product of better knowledge and wider citizen's and civil society's commitment. In various departments of the American Government, for example, the ability "to network" is part of the standard annual appraisal form. Employee performance is measured by one's ability to manage and/or expand his/her specific network.

There are many types of networks, including informal ones, such as we find among scientists in any specialized or multidisciplinary domain. There will be a few researchers who know each other, get together regularly at international symposia, and are used to exchanging views, ideas, and even their discoveries. There is no one officially in charge of making such a network operate. It runs by itself, in a sense, and its cost is small. It can be argued that, relative to its cost, it is a most efficient model: it can lead to great advantages, pecuniary and otherwise, while its operating costs are negligible. Such informal networks play a recognized role in the creation of knowledge and are often associated with new inventions.

## Box 2.2
### *The Power of Informal Networks*

The dissemination of scientific and technical information does not come free. The key to the game is the rule of reciprocity. Trading information enhances and speeds up everyone's work. Robert Lattès tells the following story to illustrate the importance of those points. Back in the 1950s, when he was working at the Atomic Studies Centre of France, he had to deal with a tricky problem. Atomic research was then clouded in secrecy, for obvious security and commercial reasons. Nevertheless, scientists who met at international conferences had developed the habit of sharing discoveries. In one particular instance, British researchers had given to their French counterparts their plans for a new reactor being built in England. Reviewing the British calculations, French mathematicians and physicists were puzzled: their calculations suggested that the designs they had in mind should pose no risk of melting nuclear fuel cartridges, but when they tested these calculations on the British model, they discovered that there were in fact serious risks inherent in that model: they prepared a report on it. By coincidence, the very afternoon that they finished their calculations, they learned that some of the fuel bundles in the British reactor had melted, forcing them to shut the reactor down for several weeks. Needless to say, the French experts fired off their report to the British scientists as quickly as possible. Lattès marvels at the costs that were thus saved by the British and by the French atomic industries through this simple exchange. Speed in technical and industrial development was enhanced for the benefit of both countries. I would also argue that a measure of confidence was added to the confidence level of those trading partners. (Lattès, 1998: 133-134, translated from French by the author)

## 2.2 Multinational and Formal Networks

At the end of a highly diversified range of types of networks, there are formal international networks, with imposing secretariats and structures and a respected identity. OECD and INTERPOL are two examples. They generally have legal existence in the country where the network has its secretariat; they may also enjoy international recognition. Furthermore, the Head of the Organization and the staff enjoy diplomatic status and privileges similar to those granted to country representatives. Members are representatives of sovereign nations, and they themselves are part of highly formalized and structured systems. Because of that, such networks may have the appearance of a standard organization. Appearances, however, are deceptive. These are networks with all the characteristics of networks as described earlier.

Thus, the internal governance systems remain structurally different from those of a standard organization and should never be confused. Methods that are useful in standard organizations are destructive in any network arrangement. Because members retain sovereignty attributes throughout, command and control mechanisms and management approaches are the antithesis of network management. Because national representatives cannot adopt unambiguous behaviour, the organization itself must be able to retain ambiguity in its midst. Finally, because they wish to maintain flexibility and multicultural attributes are characteristics of the group, it follows that redundancies are an integral part of network adaptation. The attributes of productivity characterized in standard organizations are unlikely to work in networks, either informal or formal.

Networks have to invent their own forms of productivity that are best related to their goals and membership. For instance, 'standard organizations' strive to maximize efficiency by ensuring that the goals of the organization are well understood by everyone and enforcing those through corporate discipline. Redundancies can thus be reduced to a minimum. Networks on the other hand must encourage voluntary participation and ownership. In so doing members taking initiatives may not necessarily act in a timely manner, but nobody can or may enforce discipline. Secondly, as members retain their capacity to change their goals it follows that no network can have well-defined goals in a manner equivalent to those that characterize a well-run 'standard organization.' Thirdly, country representatives constantly change as they are promoted or moved within their own bureaucracy. This creates discontinuities and needs for constantly re-explaining things to newcomers. Thus more time is needed to bind the group together, to define a typical style for the group so that members learn gradually how to behave and how and when to take initiatives. Two meetings per year might be needed instead of one. More documentation may have to be produced and the staff of the secretariat might have to work longer hours to ensure the proper functioning of a given network. In other words, a network feeds on redundancies.

An interesting knowledge deficit has appeared in IDRC's literature review on knowledge utilization and public policy processes. None of the various authors surveyed, at least before December 2001 when IDRC's Study on Public Policy was published, were aware of the role played by OECD in policy formulation. Hopefully, this book will help reduce this gap.

## SECTION 3

## THE CASE OF FORMER SOVIET COUNTRIES

Networks existed under Soviet regimes, at the national and international levels. The COMECON acted as a regrouping of Eastern and Central European economies. Internally, the Communist party was itself a major network, and a network of networks as well. However, a position of monopoly, it behaved as monopolies generally do: it worked hard at eliminating competition, or at enslaving nascent networks. In this manner, creation, innovation, and the emergence of new ideas were stifled. In all its doings, the Soviet system rested primarily on 'command and control' techniques and methods of management. This is a Russian tradition that runs deep in its history. Under Stalin, this was pushed to caricatured extremes with devastating human and economic effects. But even after Stalin was discredited, soviet-style bureaucracy continued to run things in a highly centralized and authoritarian way.

Perestroika introduced the dual desires to move toward democracy and market economy at the same time. It did little, however, to change ingrained bureaucratic reflexes. As a matter of fact, the ill-planned economic liberalization that ensued gave rise to perverse forms of anarchy. This compounded the fear of bureaucrats who still are not sure how to liberalize while maintaining law and order. In the Ukraine, independence created another series of related problems. In the past, all scientific or commercial networks were coordinated in Moscow. Once that link was severed, institutions and nascent ministries stood erect and alone like freshly cut straw. They instantly became stove-piped to the extreme. Horizontal cooperation between them did not exist. This became the first challenge of IDRC.

## SECTION 4

## SCIENTIFIC NETWORKS: IDRC EXPERIENCE

### *Part 1*

### *IDRC and Scientific Networks*

### 4.1.1 Background

A third category of networks can also be identified that may be no less effective. It blends informality within a structured arrangement: these form a significant portion of IDRC's research grants recipients.

The promotion of networks to foster quality research, to build capacity, and to induce knowledge-based policy changes has been IDRC's approach since its creation. Participants may include groups of individuals and organizations around a well-defined theme. This was the case, for example, of the Consultative Group on International Agricultural Research (CGIAR) (see box 2.3). A network might evolve or give birth to even more structured knowledge networks, where the purpose is clearly to further the application of the knowledge generated, and to influence the drafting of national or state policy through participatory research and advocacy. These types of networks might enjoy legal existence, and a formal constitution. They usually generated their own governance systems in the form of a council, a board, or a governing committee. They might have a secretariat that is generally kept small.

---

**Box 2.3**

*IDRC and CGIAR*

IDRC's association with the CGIAR is typical of IDRC's modus operandi. The CGIAR, established in 1971, is an informal association of 58 public and private sector members that supports a network of 16 international agricultural research centres. CGIAR's mission is to contribute to food security and poverty eradication in developing countries through research, partnership, capacity building, and policy support. In 2002, it was accountable for funded research programs valued at US$ 331 million. IDRC was one of the founding members of CGIAR. Nine of the current 16 member research centres were either co-creations of IDRC (ICARDA, ICRAF, ICRISAT, IFPRI), were derived from IDRC existing networks (ICLARM, ILRI, IPGRI), or received substantial support during their critical early years (IRRI, WARDA). Supporting local research networks rather than relying on foreign expertise and technical assistance was based on the profound conviction that developing countries could do more for themselves than any other form of assistance. As the CGIAR illustrates, investing in networks and networks of networks can lead to resilient and durable instruments for development (Hulse, 1981).

But first, I must introduce IDRC to the reader.

## 4.1.2 IDRC's Legal Foundation

The International Development Research Centre (IDRC) is a public corporation created by an Act of the Parliament of Canada in 1970. The main elements of the Act provide IDRC with its legal mandate, "...to initiate, encourage, support and conduct research into the problems of the developing regions of the world and into the means for applying and adapting knowledge to the economic and social advancement of those regions."

To enable IDRC to meet the challenges of its mandate, the Parliament of Canada determined that the Centre would benefit from an extraordinary degree of autonomy. It is not an agent in law of the government, nor are its employees government employees. Yet, despite this measure of political autonomy, IDRC remains accountable to the Parliament of Canada and the Office of the Auditor General audits its operations annually. Unique to IDRC as well is its governance structure. A 21-member international Board of Governors leads it. The IDRC Act stipulates that a majority of members, including the Chair and Vice-Chair, must be Canadian. By tradition, 10 governors come from developing and other OECD countries.

The core of IDRC's funding is an annual appropriation from Parliament. While this funding is critical to IDRC's work, provisions in the Act allow the Centre to seek external funding. The Centre enters into strategic partnerships with like-minded donors, development agencies, and other institutions in Canada and worldwide. Over the years, 146 donors have co-funded Centre projects.

IDRC works with governments, universities, private businesses, remote communities, development organizations, and international agencies throughout the world. It has experience in consensus building and the development of multi-donor consortia for long-term support for research and training programs; for instance, it was named by Canada as a lead organization in the implementation of Agenda 21 at the UN Conference on Environment and Development in 1992.

IDRC was also chosen to incubate the Institute for Connectivity in the Americas, one of Canada's contributions to the 2001 Summit of the Americas. IDRC, in partnership with the United Nations Economic Commission for Africa, is also implementing Connectivity Africa, a Canadian response to the 2002 G8 Africa Action Plan.

The Centre hires staff from around the world, basing them in Ottawa and in regional offices located in Cairo, Dakar, Nairobi, New Delhi, Montevideo, and Singapore. It may also make use of project offices, like that in Kiev. It employs a multidisciplinary team of scientists, technicians, managers, and policymakers with broad experience in the physical, social, life, and information sciences, and is capable of administering large international projects. For support in its endeavours, IDRC draws upon a network of development experts from around the world. It has access to diverse networks of development thinkers and researchers, scientists, and policymakers worldwide and is unhampered by 'tied aid' issues in choosing or hiring partners.

Over 34 years, the Centre has provided more than CAD\$ 2 billion in support of over 6,800 research projects in 126 countries involving more than 20,000 researchers and 2,800 institutions.

### 4.1.3 IDRC's Vision

The Centre believes that sustainable and equitable human activity depends on people controlling their own social and economic progress, on commensurate access to knowledge of all kinds, and on an indigenous capacity to generate and apply knowledge. The mission of IDRC is 'empowerment through knowledge', i.e. helping to optimize the creation, adaptation, and ownership of the knowledge that the people of developing countries judge to be of greatest relevance to their own prosperity, security, and equity. This mission represents an essential contribution to redressing the imbalances in global prosperity and access to knowledge.

It is vital that the peoples of developing and transition countries be in a position to control their own 'knowledge-based' development. Therefore, strengthening capacity for research, independent policy analysis, and accessing knowledge are critical. Analytical capacity in these countries must be strengthened to ensure that they can contribute as informed participants in major international debates, e.g. WTO and intellectual property rights over genetic resources. They must be able to deal directly with issues of domestic concern, like governance and economic policy, where, in the absence of indigenous capacity, the analysis by external actors may be all that is available and will carry undue weight. These considerations influence the program choices that IDRC makes.

IDRC recognizes that respect for human rights and their promotion are integral parts of sustainable and equitable development, and are fundamental to research being carried out under conditions of intellectual liberty and unrestricted communication of results.

As written in the Parliamentary Act, IDRC is enjoined, "to enlist the talents of natural and social scientists and technologists of Canada and other countries," "to encourage generally the coordination of international development research," and "to foster cooperation in research on development problems between the developed and developing regions for their mutual benefit." These have all provided and will continue to provide direction to the activities of the Centre. The cornerstone of IDRC's future work will continue to be an ever stronger link to the aspirations and needs of the people in the developing and transition countries of the world. As stated in IDRC's Corporate Strategy and Program Framework 2000-2005, the Centre' strategic goals are to:

- Strengthen and to mobilize the indigenous research capacity of developing countries, especially directed to achieving greater social and economic equity, better management of the environment and natural resources, and more equitable access to information.

- Foster and to support the production, dissemination, and application of research results leading to policies and technologies that enhance the lives of people in developing countries.

### 4.1.4 IDRC's Methodology

Access to knowledge must be equitable. The ability to carry out analysis, to review options critically, and to write and to speak about them publicly—in short, to generate and to use knowledge—makes a vital contribution to social progress. This requires social innovation. There is no such thing as a technological fix. The technical ingenuity of humanity has far outstripped its ability to design and apply the policy, managerial, educational, governance, and institutional innovations required to improve well-being and to redress the stark inequities around us. Each society must devise its own solutions while learning what it can from the experience of others.

Organizations like IDRC must contribute to strengthening the scientific and analytical capacity of developing countries. In the Centre's case, this continues to mean creating opportunities for our developing and transition country partners to carry out research and to work as equals with their peers in the rest of the world. Developing and transition countries must be able to be full participants in the discussions and arrangements that are driving, and responding to, profound global changes.

In fulfilling its mission of "empowerment through knowledge," the Centre has concentrated on encouraging and supporting researchers in the developing countries to carry out their work in their own institutions and, in so doing, has assisted the developing regions, as stated in the Act of Parliament, "...to build up the research capabilities, the innovative skills, and the institutions required to solve their problems." Unlike most development agencies—this includes many NGOs as well, which hire outside consultants to study a problem, to conduct training, and to issue a report, IDRC's proven methodology utilizes local institutions to determine their own needs and to carry out the necessary work. By looking first to indigenous institutions when providing research grants, IDRC not only helps to build self-confidence in those institutions, but also strengthens those institutions' research and technical capacities. Moreover, because research is carried out by locals for locals, a greater measure of 'buy-in' is ensured than if the work, however valid and technically sound, were carried out by outside consultants. A risk in using local capacity is that output quality can suffer: IDRC therefore uses its in-house expertise and worldwide networks of researchers and experts to guide researchers and to provide input and to bridge knowledge or technology gaps as needed.

"For IDRC, the most significant decisions on how to convert the ideas into practice were taken during the Statement to the Inaugural Meeting of IDRC's Board of Governors, in October 1970. The following quote is taken from the statement made to the Board by IDRC's first President, David Hopper.

"In establishing the Centre's stance toward co-operating institutions and research workers, I hold that it must be founded on a confidence that they, not we, are the best judges of what is relevant to their circumstances. Until this confidence is proven misplaced, I will be content to leave the direct management of our support in the hands of our partners, reserving to ourselves only the rights of audit and periodic substantive review."

Hopper envisaged collaborative networks of researchers meeting and devising their own techniques for self-monitoring, so that a new style of international operation would emerge, "that can remove the stigma of charity and donor control from the support of research in development" (McConnell: 20-21).

From this initial "Statement of Intent," IDRC staff proceeded to develop 10 partnership principles that served to turn this into know-how and operational ways of doing things that now characterize the work of the Centre. These were outlined by P. McConnell in an internal paper he prepared for the IDRC Board of Governors in 1998 (see Box 2.4).

---

### Box 2.4

*Ten Partnership Principles*

IDRC's involvement in a partnership will be guided by the following 10 principles:

**1. A Shared Vision**

Effective collaboration entails much more than a transfer of funds. It requires a commonality of purpose and a full intellectual partnership. There must be a shared vision about the value of the research work, the intended objectives, the potential outcomes, and the soundness of the methodological approach. This will require a foundation of trust and mutual respect, in which both partners are aware of the risks as well as the anticipated benefits. IDRC will use all options open to it to ensure that the program of work adopted and the operational mechanisms are fully responsive to the needs, priorities, and aspirations of the developing countries. There will be substantive participation by the South in planning and decision-making on Centre policies, strategies, and program choices.

## 2. Joint Ownership

An essential characteristic of a partnership is that all parties share ownership of it, and thus seek to pursue it as a joint undertaking. There should be joint elaboration of the research protocol, with the division of tasks and responsibilities meeting the needs of both partners and clearly delineated. The relationship cannot be dominated by the financial transfer. Instead, the partnership must proceed equitably among compatible partners, giving full acknowledgment to the different strengths and particular roles that each one brings to the activity, and which are essential for its success.

## 3. Shared Control

The partnership must provide an environment that enables the developing country proponents to take responsibility, to innovate, experiment, and learn, thereby further developing local competence. Within the context of agreed objectives and shared accountability, maximum decision-making and operational authority will be exercised by the Southern partner for managing the project and its funds. In order further to reduce constraints, IDRC financial support will not be conditional on satisfying narrow or arbitrary procurement requirements. Indeed, IDRC will encourage the use of local resources wherever possible. Decentralized control may entail acceptance of higher risk by IDRC, but this is imperative for the creation of responsible partnerships and evolution of genuine empowerment.

## 4. Reciprocal Accountability

In a frank and confident relationship, where there is agreement over the rights and obligations of each partner, criticism and advice must flow both ways. Each partner should be willing and able to provide constructive criticism, and should also seek feedback on its own efforts. This joint monitoring of performance and mutual accountability provide a mechanism for ensuring quality control, and for identifying problems and their resolution. This process should be dynamic and ongoing, using formal and informal channels to ensure productive interaction.

## 5. Sustained Commitment

Sustained commitment means more continuity, less uncertainty for the research activity. Short-term grant allocations pose problems for research budgets and development plans. Adequate time is needed to build a strong relationship between partners, who will work together to resolve problems. Perseverance over an adequate time-frame is required in order to strengthen research capacity and achieve meaningful results. Partners must provide sustained support for the required duration, confirming their reliability and commitment.

## 6. Flexibility and Versatility

Each research initiative has many stages, facets, and components. Success can be compromised by the constraints of excessively rigid policies, slow response time, and piecemeal funding criteria. An effective partnership, based on shared objectives and mutual trust, will demonstrate the flexibility and versatility necessary to adapt to changing circumstances. It should also accommodate the full range of research support, covering, for example, training, international travel, capital equipment, library services, telecommunications, staffing, local overhead costs, etc.

This versatility is reflected in the eligibility of both individuals and institutions, broad geographical coverage, absence of 'country quotas', involvement of public and private sectors, no minimum or maximum grant size, etc.

### 7. Effective Communications

Effective partnerships are built on effective communications. A partnership is much more than a simple contractual relationship, and the interaction should reflect this. Partners must actively promote information-sharing in an open, timely, and collegial fashion. They must also respect the communication culture, resources, and perspectives of their partners. Opportunities should be sought to enhance communication through face-to-face meetings, as well as more frequently via the new electronic options. For its part, IDRC has aimed to build credibility and understanding by recruiting a competent and mobile international staff drawn from around the world.

### 8. Streamlined Administration

Many collaborative efforts encounter unnecessary administrative delays and other inefficiencies that decrease their value and effect. The problems can arise within any partner institution. Partners need to recognize this risk and constantly strive to simplify, reduce, update, and harmonize their administrative rules and regulations. Clarity of administrative procedures can be verified and improved by seeking input and feedback from partners. Performance in this area can be monitored through introduction of quality standards—e.g., extent of reporting requirements, tracking response times, availability of administrative instructions, etc.

### 9. Coordination of Efforts

Partners can strengthen international collaboration by communicating with other institutions (including donors) and coordinating their research efforts. Coordination can help reduce duplicate or conflicting demands on developing country research institutions. Alliances with other funding and development agencies can also help mobilize additional financial, policy, and program initiatives of practical assistance to the partnership.

### 10. Effective Follow-up

The work of a research partnership does not conclude with a set of research results. There is an onus on partners to ensure the dissemination of findings (through publications, conferences, electronic networks, and other channels) and to promote their adoption and use. In some cases, negotiation of intellectual property rights and licensing arrangements may be required. It is also possible that follow-up may involve building new institutional partnerships (South-South, South-North, Public-Private, Multilateral Consortium) to continue the next phase of work.

For comparison, here is an excerpt from a USAID policy statement:

"Partnership is a two-way street based upon shared rights and responsibilities. Each partner brings different but complementary skills, expertise, and experiences to a common objective. Each contributes to areas of comparative advantage that complement each other and are fundamentally compatible (USAID, 1995)." (McConnell: 8-10).

As an example of IDRC's method, the need to establish baseline data on water quality in the Dnieper River was identified in 1993 by local and international agencies as the most pressing need related to the management of the River. In order to carry out the study, IDRC brought together three Ukrainian institutions and granted them funding to perform the work. The institutions were the Institute of Hydro-biology, the Ukrainian Scientific Centre for the Protection of the Water (USCPW), and the Hydro-meteorology Institute. Interestingly, these three institutions had never worked together in the past. To add value to the contributions of the Ukrainian institutions, IDRC located and contracted expertise from two foreign research facilities, in this instance, two Canadian organizations well known for their proven capacity: The Canadian Centre for Inland Waters and the Fresh Water Institute of Winnipeg. Hands-on expert support was also provided through the purchase of specialized analytical equipment from the United States, Canada, and Germany.

The report on the condition of the River was first published in Ukraine by the Ministry of Environmental Protection and Nuclear Safety (MEPNS) and became the basis for the adoption by the Verhovna Rada (Parliament) of the National Policy for the Rehabilitation of the Dnieper. Bearing in mind this link, it can be argued that the report findings were immediately appropriated by local authorities and internalized. There was no need in fact for IDRC to sponsor intermediary policy papers. The findings of the study were eventually published in the Water Quality Research Journal of Canada.

Would-be recipients of IDRC grants, often introduce research projects that demand more capacity that they can put to the task. They may need specialized equipment or knowledge or technology they do not possess. IDRC philosophy is to look at the immediate region to see if another institution may complement the shortfalls of the recipient. In this fashion, IDRC has been responsible for the creation of a multitude of indigenous networks. Networks have the distinct advantage of being highly flexible, multidisciplinary, and less expensive than formal institutions. From the beginning of IDRC's history, networks have been perceived as ideal vehicles for innovations and creative thinking. Networks are the main features of IDRC funding, so much so they are in and of themselves direct outputs of research grants. It has been observed that up to 30% of IDRC's funds are expended in support of network arrangements (Bernard, 1996: 2).

### 4.1.5 Assessing IDRC Sponsored Networks

Networks are, in essence, 'social exchange arrangements', a process that needed to be better understood in order to manage and monitor this form of assistance with effectiveness and efficiency. Following years of experience in this area, IDRC has undertaken major studies to evaluate networks and networking. In 1995, the IDRC Evaluation Unit tasked Anne Bernard to answer three critical questions concerning networking "What are networks, how do they function, and with what effects? (Ibid.: 11).

## "What Makes Them Tick?"

### Defining Characteristics

The study found that networks are a mix of various defining characteristics.

Networks are clearly more than simply technical linkages. As social arrangements they depend for their success on durability on members who commit to one another on a personal level for joint exchange, action, and learning. One respondent of Bernard's study went as far as saying: "Networks are metaphors rather than clear-cut concepts. They are as old as mankind and have to do with communication, with intermediation between people so that things can happen; with doing things together. No one is self-sufficient. We all built our networks of help in order to survive." (Cariola quoted in Bernard, 1996: 14; Ibid.: 7).

Networks act as forums for social exchange and build shared ownership of ideas or products. They allow members and users to interact directly with one another, and to reconsider how they think or what they do as a consequence of this interaction. Networks that are considered effective were those in which by doing things together, members added value to what they would otherwise have done individually. The process of networking is important, including the development of a network culture in which members come to realize an awareness of themselves as part of the group, sharing a common purpose and mutual rights and responsibilities. Expressed another way, the issue is of establishing shared ownership (Ibid.: 7 or 15).

They also open opportunities, often by enabling a broader base for the generation of ideas and action. "Most networks can easily be described, in a positive sense, as opportunistic: either *ex post*, a number of initially separate projects linked eventually together in recognition of the complementarity or cumulative value of their work or of the potential for joint training; or *a priori*, a network put together as such to enable the respective advantages of participating agents collectively to serve a wider and better end" (Ibid.: 8, 15).

Networks have been found not only to sustain existing capacity but also to strengthen capacities over the long term. To achieve such results, a network requires "sufficient long time-lines and consistent mandates to allow staff to identify and adapt training needs, and create learning opportunities. The need to be involved for the long term, even up to twenty years, certainly presents problems for aid agencies faced with diminishing resources.

"One network member in Latin America referred to the value of informal referent-group networking as a critical means of "protecting against the abuse of our institutions" during repressive regimes" (Ibid.: 10, 17).

Networks enable creativity and risk taking, two essential commodities when fostering development.

"Providing the critical mass for moving beyond simply sharing, to be able to advocate, lobby and operationalize change. They allow cross-sectoral perspectives into the policy debate... give protection in expressing alternatives... provide a space within and for professionals and policymakers to move, explore and create together, within a context of suspended responsibilities. They're a venue to encourage lateral thinking, to develop new agenda which might eventually make it into the mainstream. They free members from institutional limitations." (quoted by Bernard, 1996: 10, 18, from a network review workshop in Singapore, Jan. 1994).

Networks play other essential roles such as providing an interface between indigenous groups and foreign donors, or providing access to a wide and loose configuration of actors, businesses, researchers, civil society, and bureaucrats. They might provide a means for scientists from closed societies, such as those that became opened to the West at the division of the USSR, to become exposed to international networks of scientists. This is quite important in hard sciences and essential in social sciences.

They might become platforms for action, and in this fashion, networks have become important in policy formulation. Bernard gives the case of the whole Philippine NGO community that is exemplary in that regard.

"As programming capacity, political and social analysis skills and management sophistication increase, domestic NGOs and people's organizations in that country are creating a vast array of networking arrangements—at national and local levels; across types and sectors; with government, donors and internationally. Though with a variety of specific objectives, the overarching goal of these networks is: to imagine a future and fashion it instead of waiting for things to happen...(This) demands the synthesis and synergy of a multitude of perspectives, to be able to create a vision...This is where networks are most useful because (they) facilitate the process of gathering people with different views and organizations with different expertise" (Polestico, 1995: 8 in Bernard, 1996: 12).

## Success Factors

IDRC's experience points to a few key factors associated with the success or failure of networks.

Networks are stronger and ultimately more sustainable when they simultaneously create solidarity around a shared purpose, and allow members to work together on a common task. For that, internal management must be kept flexible and internally driven. "Networks need to have a culture of informality, to maintain a family character...At the same time, task and professionalism are necessary. There needs to be a balance; a family, but with a structure of professionalism" (Branzuela in Bernard, 1996: 16). Ownership is key to network sustainability: it is both a condition and an outcome of a successful network. "While people and institutions may join a network because they expect to get something out of it, it appears they stay active when their goals, stated and/or unstated, remain coincident with those of other members and the network adds value to their own work" (Ibid.: 17). Successful networks function to best advantage when they are not rigid in organization or in functions, but are encouraged to evolve according to changing circumstances. Learning through diversity, that is the diversity of its membership, and creating shared agreements are two last but significant characteristics of solid and sustainable networks.

## Specific Problems

A number of specific problems are associated with networking. From the point of view of donors, networks are inevitably looser and more ambiguous in implementation than anticipated in initial plans. Networks tend to allow for only loose control over what is happening inside them. They are difficult to monitor, because they give few early warning signs of going off track (Ibid.: 19). In terms of money, time, and energy, the building of a network is costly, especially at the front end. Most networks require at least five to seven years to reach maturity, a longer period than donors can accept. Networks are labour intensive, which is another vanishing commodity among donor agencies. Donors, pressed for immediate results and with fewer resources, have created a new risk by "creating too much standardization; of stunting the chance of innovation and of new ideas coming out by gearing too much to the more conservative agenda of donors and senior institutions, and too rarely challenging the status quo in research questions and power alignments" (Ibid.: 20).

## Mitigating Risks

Risks can be mitigated through realizing effective balances in an explicitly recognized and effectively negotiated fashion. Networks generally operate at different levels: international, regional, and local. This breeds tension that successful networks surmount by balancing the needs of all parties. Often this is achieved through networks of networks arrangements, strengthening in this fashion the "think globally–act locally potential of networks" (Ibid.: 21). Secondly, a symbiosis or balance is needed between different members (whether institutional or individual) and their environments. Members require a different type and level of support, and the tension this may create must be arbitrated in a manner suitable to the specific 'social arrangement of the network.' Networks, almost by definition, have a multitude of needs and goals, as they are loosely coupled systems with mixed memberships. Goals of donors, for example, may conflict with those that form the membership of the networks; a compromise must be struck that keeps money flowing while preserving the loyalty and ownership of participants.

**Main Lessons**

- As social arrangements, networks are inherently messy. Their implementation environment is multiple, shifting, and difficult to predict. The critical role of individuals is a determining factor, further characterizing the unpredictability of networks.

- Networks are most effective, "where they: (a) engender mutual agreements among members to enhance the value of collaborating toward shared goals; and (b) provide the support for such collaboration in the face of complex and unpredictable environments" (Ibid.: 29).

- "They are effective where they enable all those members, users and donors, who need to commit to the network to make it work to participate in the ... 'complex assembly job (of) fitting together (their) different interests and priorities' (Ibid.: 39; Fudge and Barrett in Najam, 1995: 13).

- "...responding to authoritative decree, to available resources, to a chance to escape from failing institutions or professional isolation—may be sufficient to initiate participation, but is unlikely to sustain it..... Networks begun as a consequence of pull, therefore—toward realizing a defined goal, filling a recognized gap or simply perceiving a value in coming together—are more likely to persist" (Ibid.: 39).

- "...networks are successful where they are learning organizations. Effective networks act not simply on the basis of optimizing within constraints (Metcalfe in Armstrong, 1995: 27) by attempting to force-fit predicted, linear and regulated programmes of work onto dynamic policy and client communities. Rather, they hone capacities and create mechanisms for the regular feedback and reflected analyses that are needed to deal with the ambiguity of these environments, and to adapt interactively with them" (Ibid.: 39).

- Solid network arrangements are those "most likely to encourage in leaders and members the kinds of risk-taking behaviours research indicates as necessary to implementing the policy, programme and methodological innovations typical of networks." (Ibid.: 40).

- "Adaptation, as distinct from simple adoption or co-opting, implies that both the innovation and the environment change as a result of the interaction. It is this mutuality of adaptation that is perhaps most central to assessing the sustainability of a network: is it able to adjust to, and introduce permanent change within the conditions of knowledge and/or action it is intended to address?" (Ibid.: 40)

## 4.1.6 Linkage between Research, Networks and Policy Setting

Historically, IDRC has always been occupied, to one degree or another, with the idea of influencing policies in the South to effect positive change. In 1999, IDRC began a major study to develop a deeper, more distinct understanding of what is meant by 'influencing policy' in order to improve programming efforts. To meet this need, the Evaluation Unit undertook a strategic study designed to answer three fundamental questions: (1) what constitutes public policy influence in IDRC's experience; (2) to what degrees, and in what ways has IDRC-supported research influenced public policy; and (3) what factors and conditions have facilitated or inhibited the potential of IDRC-supported research to influence public policy?

In addition to a literature review, a conceptual framework was developed to guide the strategic evaluation. A second element of the study consisted of 25 field studies. These studies include more than 60 projects in over 20 countries. Since there is relatively little documentation and literature with respect to policy processes in developing countries, a broad scope was preferred to better understand and report on this area.

There is a vast range of types of policy influence that rests on a continuum between 'direct impact' or research that directly affects legislation, and which are considered to be more broadly defined such as, for example, 'changing the prevailing paradigm' or 'enlightening' policymakers. Research for development is located 'upstream' from any kind of actual development 'impact'. Because a linear process is considered too simplistic in its presentation of policy processes, most policymakers and academics have discarded the notion of research directly influencing policies and policy processes. This renders attribution of results difficult in the best of circumstances, at times presenting an unrealistic challenge.

For the purpose of the study, three forms of influence surface:

- Expanding policy capacities by supporting new research, the development of new fields of research, enhancing researcher capacities to work on problems or issues as distinct from carrying out disciplinary research, as well as enhancing their capacities to communicate knowledge and ideas to diverse audiences.

- Broadening policy horizons by increasing the accessibility and completeness of knowledge through multi-country networks of researchers or through networks that bring together researchers and others in the policy community. It may increase the stock of policy-relevant knowledge; introduce new ways of thinking into the policy arena; or ensure knowledge is available to policymakers in forms that make it possible for them to use it.

- Affecting policy regimes is about the actual use of research in the development of new laws, regulations, or structures. The most important role for research in the policy process comes normally at the earlier stages of drafting research findings in ways they can find their way into the body of knowledge of policymakers, to be part of the decision process when laws, regulations, and policies are undergoing changes. This suggests it will always be the rare occasion when research can claim a direct instance of policy change.

*Key Findings*

The role of networks in policy changes has always been recognized as central. They are the institutional mechanism that supports North-South and South-South cooperation, linking people and institutions in order to advance and utilize knowledge. In this way, researchers have been able to build skills by working with other researchers with common problems. Many research communities in the South are small, fragmented and significantly under-funded. Networks are thus useful and viable mechanisms that enable researchers to carry out their research as well as provide them with funding opportunities, information sharing and mutual learning, technical support, and training. Since networks are also a manifestation of 'transnational knowledge' these cases also provide examples of the challenges of capturing evidence of any research uptake.

The preliminary analysis of transnational cases confirms the hypothesis that networks are strong mechanisms for influencing policy and provided evidence that is consistent with earlier findings, and further substantiating that they are an effective means for influencing public policies.

## Capacity Building

Capacity building is not just about building the capacity of researchers to do research. It is also about building the capacity to carry out policy-relevant research and to communicate the findings effectively to policy and decision-makers. This can be achieved through career advancements, the credibility/reputation of the research and/or researcher(s), and through networking. As policymakers recognized the quality of the research, they became more accepting of the findings and could see how to use the information for developing new policies.

## Ownership

The notion of ownership is closely linked to capacity building. IDRC supports programs and projects that build the capacity of researchers and policymakers to use their own research/researchers. This encourages the uptake of research within, and therefore influences policy from within. If the developing countries are really to be 'in the driver's seat,' they have to have the capacity to analyze the often difficult economic issues they face. Local researchers, combining the knowledge of local conditions—including knowledge of local, political, and social structures (with the learning derived from global experiences) provide the best prospects for deriving policies that both engender broad-based support and are effective.

## Persistence

Many projects in this study are long-term commitments. IDRC supported two successful networks over periods of 14 and 15 years, recognizing that building capacity to research takes a long time and that it's not a 'single project effort.' The same holds true for the uptake of research for the purpose of developing policies.

## Intent

As much as possible, the intent to influence policy should be part of the project design, not an add-on at a later stage of the project. Transnational knowledge, and its use, has a cumulative effect and this needs to be explicit. This takes time to develop, and in one case, this took over 14 years. A distinction must be made between supporting researcher capacity to influence policy with research, and advocating a particular position. The latter is not the mandate of the Centre; the former is. The distinction is most clearly drawn around the capacity-building dimensions. What is challenging is that the capacity is built most effectively through practice and engagement where the researchers begin to use the research findings as part of building their understanding of how to use findings. In this there is a fine line.

*Communication and Dissemination*

Findings are consistent with the well-documented difficulties researchers face in terms of their ability to communicate their findings, especially in formats that enable policymakers to easily understand and absorb the information. The informal nature of policy influence is not well understood or accepted by many researchers. Enhancing the use of knowledge is often achieved through informal relationships and through creating windows of opportunity to speak with, and provide ideas to, policymakers.

Review of the cases has clearly articulated the non-linear nature of the influence of research on public policy; it is multi-path, uncertain, and changing over time. Within donors, there is a tendency to 'wait and see' if the research is going to be of sufficient quality and then find the funds needed for communication and dissemination activities. The conservative approach, therefore, is to commit funds only when staff and partners know there is strong potential. As a result, dissemination is often too late. Rather, researchers need to be engaging with the policy community early. New modes of project support need to be explored, which allow the elements of the research to be exposed to the relevant communities on an ongoing basis. This might be as simple as creating multi-year flexible budgets and making communication and dissemination funding available from the first year.

## Part 2
## IDRC and the Dnieper River

### 4.2.1 Introduction

Following the formation of democratic regimes in Former Soviet Union (FSU) countries, OECD members considered extending Official Development Assistance (ODA) credits to the region to help finance the transition from centralized and planned economies to market economies. Within the Development Assistance Committee (DAC) of OECD, however, some members argued that Russia, Ukraine, and many other FSU countries were resource- and technology-rich, thus less in need of highly subsidized grants from aid budgets. Furthermore, if they were allowed to compete for scarce ODA funds, the

*1994-2004*

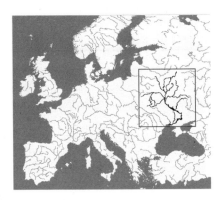

poorer developing countries were bound to receive less aid. Aid would likely be displaced toward FSU countries as they appeared critical to geo-political interests of OECD members. In the end, OECD members decided that some newly created republics such as, for example, Central Asian countries, could be added to the existing list of poor countries and thus eligible to ordinary ODA funds. Others, such as Russia, could benefit from special funds created for the purpose of assisting their transition, by donor countries on a voluntary basis; however, these funds should not be used to measure donors' aid performance. It was generally believed that these countries only needed some blend of subsidies and private capital to 'kick start' the transition.

In 1993, the Government of Canada created a $100 million "Renaissance Fund" for that purpose. The Ministry of Foreign Affairs was charged with implementing this fund. In 1995, however, the Government moved the management of this "Renaissance Fund" to a specially created branch of the Canadian International Development Agency (CIDA). Private entrepreneurs were invited to seek out local partners in FSU countries with whom they could restructure existing industries or enter into new joint ventures. It was believed that Canada had capital, technology, and know-how to offer that could blend with existing CIS industrial and resource capacity.

In keeping with traditional development assistance etiquette, local governments were consulted on priorities for the usage of such funds. The Government of Ukraine at that time insisted upon receiving assistance toward the cleaning up of the Dnieper River. Seven years after the terrible Chernobyl accident, the Ukrainian population was still weary of the safety of this body of water from which 30 million people drew their water. It was said that "mothers fear giving the water from the River to drink to their infant." What to do with this problem required careful consideration and research. For that purpose, the Ministry of Foreign Affairs sought the expertise of IDRC in environment and research. IDRC's founding law constrained it to developing economies from the South, however, the Board of Governors allowed IDRC's staff to work on this program with the strict proviso that all necessary resources for this program, including core administrative costs, come from outside sources.

In 1994, IDRC and the Ministry of Foreign Affairs of Canada initiated a program of activities called Environmental Management Development in Ukraine (EMDU), to be managed through IDRC's newly formed Office for Central and Eastern Europe Initiatives (OCEEI). The suite of activities focused on the Dnieper River Basin, and pursued a multifaceted approach to environmental management capacity building in relevant Ukrainian ministries, research and educational institutions, and non-governmental organizations (NGOs). In 1997 a second phase, financed by CIDA, was approved and it ran until December 2001.

The goal of the program was to support and to strengthen the onoing reform process in Ukrainian institutions for better environmental protection activities, improved economic policies, and increased environmental awareness. The program objectives were to:

- Promote business/investment activities that have a favourable impact on the environment of the Dnieper Basin.

- Improve environmental management in manufacturing, the residential sector, municipalities, and agro-industry.

- Increase the Ukrainian public's environmental awareness through the media and educational institutions.

- Promote measures to improve the provision and optimize the use of drinking water.

- Improve environmental management practices through training.

- Enhance international environmental management of the Dnieper River through cooperation with riparian and other international partners.

The EMDU program encompassed nine related projects broken down into specific activities. These included projects such as: Base Line Studies of the Quality of the River Waters, Water Management Information Systems, Public Outreach activities, Environmental Audits and the Introduction of Clean Production Methods, and a number of others. The contracting party representing Ukraine was the Ministry of Environment, known then as the Ministry for Environmental Protection and Nuclear Safety (MEPNS).

Over a period of seven years, IDRC provided grants to 70 discreet research activities varying in size from CAD$ 10,000 to CAD$ 250,000 for one large undertaking. In total, CAD$ 12 million was spent toward this objective.

## 4.2.2 Learning to Work in Terra Incognita

*Moving Away from the Soviet Era*

"International technical assistance to Ukraine did not really exist before 1991, when Ukraine gained its independence. Receiving grant money, especially receiving it from former foes, was definitely a new concept. At first, some influential officials were even against the idea of receiving any 'paltry dole' from 'capitalistic hands'; the 'self-sufficiency' ideology dominated, with the world changing faster than minds. Many perceived that western donor agencies were coming simply to collect data about the current status of science and to state the problems, but were not there to help resolve these problems. When the first years of independence passed and the economic miracles did not happen, Ukainians realized that structural changes were necessary, and that without western money and know-how economic growth in Ukraine would remain elusive. Industrial countries started to be perceived, not as a source of danger, but as a source of funds and ideas. Fear and pride began to dissipate and Ukraine found itself in free competition with the South for the North's grant money. Yet, in the event, it became obvious that the absorptive capacity for western assistance was low.

- During the Soviet era, numerous research institutes and ministries were accustomed to abundant budget financing. In particular, fundamental research found favour in the state budget. The strategy for receiving financing was to submit a proposal containing a thick folio full of scientific jargon, very detailed background information, and a long list of references. Budgets consisted of only the total project sum, which was intentionally doubled or even tripled. Peer review and systems of checks and balances were not common practices. In effect, the most important factor for budget appropriation was related to an established network of decision-makers, government officials, and civil servants. Therefore, positioning one's institution well in those networks ensured a regular flow of research funds.

- When international technical assistance became available, research institutes began using the same approach that they did in the past to get funds, with many perceiving the assistance as a continuation of budget funding. This was the first stumbling block for Ukrainian scientists and researchers looking for donor aid: the strategy that worked well for the Soviet bureaucratic machine became useless for foreign aid projects. Demands for 'unwarranted details' were often perceived as fault-finding or even espionage. It was feared that by answering such probing questions, scientists might run into problems with authorities. The flexibility shown by some donors, along with their tolerance and understanding, were the main reasons for the acceptance of technical assistance in the first years of Ukraine's independence.

- By the mid 1990s, almost all research institutions in Ukraine had had some exposure to the grant process. They formulated an assembly line approach to proposal preparation: identical proposals were sent to different donors, duplicate reports were submitted as outputs, and old data were used.

- By the late 1990s, proposals fell more in line with donors' demands: years of teaching and learning yielded fruit. Nonetheless, the technical and budgetary content remained poor.

- In the early and mid 1990s only US, Canadian, and UN agencies were working in Ukraine in the environmental field. By the late 1990s, Japan, the Netherlands, Denmark, and Finland also became active. Every donor has its own target areas, expectations, and, most importantly, implementation mechanism. From the perspective of Ukrainian recipients, most of the implementation mechanisms looked alike: to spend as much money as possible in the donor country itself. Some donors applied puzzling 'tied aid' rules that forbid recipients from buying equipment outside the donor's country, while others refused to make use of local consultants, relying solely on western consultants. The main outputs of such assistance were reports that often were not even read by local officials and decision-makers. For this reason, the Verhovna Rada (the Ukrainian Parliament) and the Cabinet of Ministers admonished donor agencies. After much hesitation, international technical assistance was eventually exempted from VAT and import duties by President Kuchma's decree only on June 1, 1999, eight years after Independence. The exemption lasted exactly two months, with the Verhovna Rada overturning it on July 30, stating that the provisions of the proposed decree were insufficiently rigorous as "in many cases international assistance that is not required is given to Ukraine." In particular, the Verhovna Rada wished to ensure that such exemptions would not be turned into loopholes for tax-free commercial imports, nor become a means for western interests to rid themselves of poor quality products and services" (Guilmette and Iskra, 2001: 83-84).

- At first, the high level of secrecy, euphemistically referred to as 'soviet caution' characterized Ukrainian scientists' behaviour. They were reluctant to share essential information among themselves, with their own civil society and, with foreign experts, including lending agencies such as EBRD. "Soviet caution" hindered the implementation of the program. On the one hand, the fact that foreign experts could use information was risky for those who provided such information. In particular, a 1937 law decreed that the information on cities' water systems (vodokanals) was secret for fear of biological attack: otherwise, malevolent foreigners could poison an entire city. One scientist who was part of an IDRC-sponsored research project faced criminal prosecution for violating this law while conducting approved research. In addition, program participants had difficulties getting information from other government organizations. At times, they had to pay for data.

- In Ukraine, decision-makers perceived the lack of concrete and applied scientific research as a major constraint for its utilization. Researchers for their part believed that the under utilization of their research product was related to the inability of the decision-makers to think globally, to define their needs, and to realize the importance of the issue. Disconnection between policy and research was also seen as resulting from lack of coordination among universities, institutes, ministries, and local administrations, except when research institutes were directly subordinated to a particular state body.

Twenty-five years of partnership with the South did not fully prepare IDRC to meet the specific challenges prevailing in CIS countries. Eventually, we had to remind ourselves regularly that a vast majority of Asian, African, and Latin American countries shared many values and patterns of behaviour with us. Most developing country elites were trained in universities of the North, where they became familiar with northern governance systems through years of colonial rule. At independence, Britain, France, the Netherlands, Portugal, and Spain left behind various administrative and legal systems as well as diplomatic traditions that, for the most part, still operate today. In addition, most tenets of a market economy were never as profoundly challenged as they were under Soviet rule. On the other hand, countries under Soviet rule were closed for seven decades and missed out on many of the paradigm shifts that characterized western evolution in the 20th Century. In contrast with many countries in the South, however, education in CIS countries was widespread, and diverse scientific institutions operated within a well-structured system. Technological knowledge and equipment as well as the capacity to produce research equipment were well advanced, unlike the case of developing countries.

### How IDRC Managed the Program

To cope with this unique environment, IDRC had to adapt quickly and tailor its approach to resolving unprecedented problems. It became obvious from the outset that pragmatism should govern our work. As an example, one of IDRC's very first 'research grants' was for the gathering of telephone numbers within the Ministry of Environment Protection and Nuclear Safety and the publishing of a phone directory.

In the South, IDRC provides research grants directly to local institutions by making use of one of its six regional offices to transfer moneys and to provide technical and administrative support locally. It frequently makes use of existing research networks, or creates new ones, to guide the overall research process. In Ukraine different means had to be found. On the one hand, it was impossible for IDRC to provide cash grants to local research institutions or to NGOs. On the other hand, a strong tradition of centralized power and a deep suspicion of anything foreign barred IDRC from interacting directly with local institutions or from creating 'bottom-up' types of networks. The cooperation of the Ministry of Environment became an essential element. The various ministers and deputy ministers who oversaw the Ministry during those seven years were determined to improve the quality of the water in the Dnieper, or as transliterated from Ukrainian, Dnipro, and to make good on Canadian cooperation. Their full collaboration and strong commitment became a key ingredient in what we jointly like to believe became a success story.

## Dealing with Management and Project Selection Issues

A Ukrainian Management Committee (UMC) was created at the outset of this diversified program to provide coordination between various departments and research institutions and with IDRC. In October 1995, the President of UMC, Dr. Shevchuk, raised at the occasion of a private meeting an issue that was creating great strain within UMC. A contract had been let by IDRC with a Canadian firm. His view and that of his Committee was that this contract was costly for work that could be done by a local organization. He was also concerned that program resources had been appropriated by IDRC without the full consent of the Ukrainian Management Committee. In his view, this was reducing its authority and accountability over these funds.

The contract had been let under CAP (Centre Administered Portion) in accordance with IDRC's own rigorous rules. The Terms of Reference corresponded to an activity within the agreed project plan. The selection of the firm followed a tender that fully complied with rules and regulations. In sum, there was nothing inappropriate in the way it had been let. Nevertheless, I felt this issue was of significant importance and I took the decision to grant his wish. From then on and for the following six years, all program activities were first assessed and decided upon by the Ukrainian Management Committee. It was empowered to draft policy, to set priorities, to allocate research resources, to select local partners, to assess proposals, and to review scientific results. In sum, the Committee was providing overall governance to the program. Through this process, the UMC selected implementing agencies. In a number of cases, this involved a Canadian or international firm that would act as partner to a local organization.

It has proven to be an invaluable mechanism that corresponded well with the culture of the region. It provided needed discipline and rigour as well as a forum for discussing problems, raising issues, and debating new ideas. Most of all, it fully involved Ukraine and Ukrainians in every decision, and significantly contributed to stimulating their feeling of ownership and responsibility. It may be argued that the Management Committee was the embryo of a peer review system. The commitment of Ukraine was constant and unfaltering throughout the duration of EMDU, and despite the fact that two elections took place, the head of the Committee remained in place and the Committee continued meeting monthly.

OCEEI staff members were consulted throughout the process. They provided comments, suggested improvements, and did due diligence on every case to ascertain the implementation entity was capable of delivering the output as planned, on time and on budget. Once the UMC had done its part, that is either approved a project, the selection of an implementation organization, or a report, then the OCEEI management team would do its part and confirm funding for the activity, sign a contract with the selected organization or proceed with making final payment. In essence, EMDU operated like a two-keys safety box as found in bank vaults: each party remained fully accountable for its role in the entire process and both had to concur about each decision. Argued differently, it operated according to consensus rules as it is practiced in OECD.

IDRC eventually realized that, during the Soviet era, the military was the only client that effectively took care of transforming a new technology into practical usage and deriving know-how. Highly trained scientists in Ukraine had acquired little experience in those fields, and the search for improved know-how and management became our most pressing task.

### Dealing with Fiscal Issues

The problem of disbursing untaxed funds for local research remained unresolved for some time. Faced with what can only be described as 'predatory' fiscal systems, IDRC had no choice but to help the Ministry of Environment find a durable and practical solution for moving aid resources into the country. For that purpose, the International Dnipro Fund (IDF) was created based on a model initially operating in Poland. This Ukrainian NGO was empowered to collect fines and grants and spend them for the purpose of improving the Dnieper's environment. This became the conduit of IDRC's grants to local research institutions and remained its only mechanism until the EMDU ceased to exist. The Dnipro Fund has expanded its activities to promote environmental audits, and it now functions as a fund-raising organization and has established branches in Belarus and Russia.

## Critical Elements for Success

We believe fully empowering our Ukrainian partners, was central to the project achieving its goals. The funds were perceived as a true, and very scarce, Ukrainian resource whose usage should be maximized at all times. As a consequence the UMC ensured that cumulative savings be put to best use, that projects be carried out without cost overruns, and reports and results be of the best quality possible. When outside experts were budgeted, it was then clear to everyone that no local and/or less costly alternative could be found. Feeling in charge, the UMC never lost sight that these resources were meant to improve the quality of water flowing in the River, thus, when appropriate, government policies were changed.

We strived to introduce cooperative habits between formerly stove-piped institutions. We invested in bringing about confidence and trust where soviet practices had planted mistrust and fear. We gradually introduced modern management practices, such as budgeting and measuring unit costs, and reporting against budgets and against outputs. We introduced information-sharing practices and imbedded those ideas into water management systems. With the concept of information sharing came the related idea of sharing standards and measurements, and of involving the widest possible audience made up of individuals and groups (companies, associations, institutions).

## SECTION 5

## COMPONENTS OF THE EMDU PROGRAM AND IMMEDIATE RESULTS

The major components and major projects of the program were:

## 5.1 Water Pollution Control

In autumn 1994, the *Baseline Water Quality Study* was undertaken to provide reliable information about surface water pollution. Information about the state of the River was obtained and organized, and a network of scientists and managers has been providing data online for the management of the River ever since.

## Water Toxicology

*WaterTox* project (phases 1 and 2) was aimed at demonstrating the validity of a battery of inexpensive and simple, yet effective, bioassays to test water. The *Joint use of Biotests* project allowed the recipients to compare the effectiveness of the WaterTox battery with that of another suite of tests already being used by the Ukrainian Scientific Research Institute of Ecological Problems. Ukraine is now participating in an international network for testing and calibrating water quality using bio-testing methods.

## Information Systems Development

A substantial number of projects were aimed at informational support and creating computer-analytical databases that deal with the chemical composition and the quality of the Dnipro water. A *National Atlas of Ukraine* project led to the development of an Electronic Atlas version, which was widely distributed.

## Demonstration Projects

*Environmental Audits and Environmental Entrepreneurship* projects allowed the introduction of low-cost measures to make production more environmentally friendly at selected Ukrainian enterprises. *Training of Environmental Entrepreneurs* project was aimed at training a leadership group of entrepreneurs. A group of Ukrainian scientists has since formed a consortium to provide such audits nationally.

The *Demonstration Shoreline Project* entailed putting in place a 2-3 kilometre managed shoreline that demonstrated protection measures applicable elsewhere along Dnipro reservoir shorelines. The *Solid Waste and Landfill Remediation* project involved designing and installing a leachate collection system to intercept contaminated ground and surface waters from the disposal site. A *Drinking Water Technology* project provided for the construction and installation of equipment for drinking water treatment. The *Rising Groundwater Protection* project allowed working out economically and ecologically efficient ways of rising groundwater protection. The *Organomineral Fertilizer Production* project introduced technologies for organomineral fertilizer production from sewage sludge and other kinds of waste.

## Public Outreach

The *Raising Public Awareness of Environmental Problems* project disseminated information about the present environmental situation in the basin of the main Ukraine waterway. The *Environmental Television Program and Videos* project helped develop TV materials, and helped promote nature-preserving consciousness within the community. The *Dnipro—the Artery of Life Book* project published an illustrated full-colour book in Ukrainian and English. Civil society has increasingly become involved in the program through outreach activities such as numerous television programs for local stations and a web page.

*Direct Program Outcomes*

In 1997, a National Program for Rehabilitating the Dnieper and Improving Water Quality was drafted by the Ministry of Environment and approved by the Verhovna Rada. Many Ukrainian specialists perceive it as the most important outcome of the EMDU cooperation experience.

To those immediate and direct results, we must add indirect outcomes related to securing other funds from various donors:

- Ukraine's Ministry of Environmental Protection and Nuclear Safety has taken measures to obtain a US$ 7 million grant from the Global Environment Facility (GEF) to define a Strategic Action Plan (SAP) for the rehabilitation of the River Basin and ameliorating its effects on the Black Sea.

- Significant improvements in the provision of public utility services in the city of Zaporizhzhia have led to the approval of a loan by EBRD (US$ 30 million) to upgrade water and sewer systems. In contrast, an adjacent city was refused a similar loan because it has not yet learned to provide utility services in a financially viable manner.

- The Government of Denmark has provided funds (US$ 1.2 million) for environmental audits of industries in the city of Zaporizhzhia

## SECTION 6

### EFFECTS OF THE PROGRAM ON POLICY FORMULATION

The Evaluation Unit of IDRC hired Dr. I. Lyzogub to carry out a review of EMDU's influence on policy formulation in Ukraine. The case study is part of the study referred to in sub-section 2.3. Under the direct supervision of the Evaluation Unit, Dr. Lyzogub interviewed about 50 participants and end-users of the EMDU program. Her judgement on the results attained by EMDU is divided according to five *types of activities* that are essential for connecting research to policy. These were based on the Evaluation Unit literature review. Her findings are summarized below.

## 6.1 Expanding Policy Capacities

Almost all projects (as well as the EMDU program as a whole) were intended to have policy influence from the very beginning. Therefore, including the active participation and involvement of decision-makers was important. The Ukrainian Management Committee did that. The people who managed the program also had the power to use its results in the decision-making process. Furthermore, since UMC members occupied high-level positions in different government and research institutions, they were not in boss/subordinate relationships and were not afraid to openly express their views.

- IDRC's research on policy influence also revealed that 'policy entrepreneurs' are often an essential feature of a successful process. Dr. Shevchuk, who had been a chairperson of the program from its inception in 1994 until its last meeting in February 2001, was such a 'policy entrepreneur.' Throughout the program implementation, Dr. Shevchuk occupied authoritative decision-making positions, yet he maintained his full commitment to this program until the program ended.

- The IDRC approach helped expand policy capacity by relying on local partners and providing them with an opportunity to decide the course of research. Furthermore it fostered the most important ingredients in self-help: self-confidence, trust, and friendship with other partners and between countries.

- The *Baseline Water Quality Study* project allowed the early assessment of the crucial issue concerning radioactivity in the river waters. It helped ease the anxieties of the population and the drafting of sensible policies to deal with this emotionally charged problem. For example, in 1993 a Nationalist Party ran its electoral campaign on the idea of destroying all dams that were erected on the Dnipro during the Stalin era in order to return it to its natural rapid flow. The *Baseline Study* revealed that Chernobyl radioactive fallout had sunk in the bottom of the river. It had been covered by 15 centimetres of silt, thus isolating the riverbed and the direct contamination of its water. The best way to deal with the problem is therefore never to stir up the mud accumulated at the bottom. This would inevitably happen if artificial lakes were destroyed.

- The EMDU program addressed the issue of secrecy by sharing openly all information pertinent to the management of the program. IDRC's willingness to share information seemed 'amazing' to Ukrainians. IDRC also facilitated data exchange and dissemination through various 'information-sharing systems' using Geographic Information Systems (GIS) that appealed to technically minded experts. Perhaps the most successful project aimed at data dissemination was the *National Atlas Project*. The CD-ROM created within this project was widely disseminated among different organizations after the project ended. Finally, two scientific conferences allowed for the publication of all reports and research results.

## Maintaining Scholarly Standards and Providing Bases for Education

In many cases, IDRC provided support to good institutions that would not operate otherwise. Brain drain of highly trained scientists might have been the result. Along with acquiring a higher level of professionalism, researchers had an opportunity to educate others on the basis of the program results. The postgraduate student inflow to the scientific institutions was stimulated by the IDRC-sponsored projects. The program also resulted in publication of various textbooks, and most prominent project results were thus incorporated into the educational process.

## Supporting Recipients to Develop Innovative Ideas

The project also resulted in working out the *Program of Implementation of Organic Fertilizer Production and its Use in Agriculture*. The State Committee on Construction, Architecture, and Housing Policy, Zaporizhzhia Oblast Sanitary Epidemic Station, and Zaporizhzhia Ecological Department approved this program and lobbied in favour of its expansion in the country. The connection between research and policy was enhanced when decision-makers perceived scientists as providing solid and practical ideas.

## Broadening Policy Horizons

Initially, Ukrainian research institutions did not always use internationally recognized research and methodological standards that could meet with peer review research criteria. As for the presentation of data, old USSR indicators were in use to the puzzlement of western scientists who did not know to what these indicators referred. At the beginning, Ukrainian scientists found it difficult to meet the requirements of IDRC. Furthermore, project proposals had to be approved by both committees. Researchers sometimes compiled two different documents that presented the same project using entirely different formats. This led to rethinking the usage of country-specific data presentation systems in favour of internationally recognized standards.

Accessing international standards was an opportunity to enter the international scientific community. Scientists published their findings in Western scientific journals, made presentations at international conferences, and Western colleagues acknowledged their level of professionalism.

Furthermore, it allowed collaboration with new Western partners, such as specialized consultant firms and joint ventures. It should be noted that empirical evidence suggests that joint venturing was the result of a lengthy and circuitous adjustment process and not, as it had been presumed in 1993, the departure point of development, economic growth, and 'transition'.

The program has been heralded by a number of scientists as 'the window for Ukraine to see and experience Western technology and Western ideas.' It led to attitudinal changes, for example, concerning the delivery of municipal services, the relationship with clients and users, as well as the need for synergy among related institutions and multidisciplinary work. This was particularly valuable for a country that was closed and isolated for many decades.

### Stimulating Dialogue between and among Decision-makers and Researchers

IDRC dealt with this problem by the way EMDU was managed, by encouraging joint research, by stressing the importance of relevance and giving preference to applied versus empirical or theoretical research, and by trying to convince decision-makers to use research findings.

As Caplan suggests, increasing the use of research in policymaking could not be achieved by merely increasing interactions between policymakers and researchers. It is important to achieve a 'relevance' of research (see Neilson 2001: 4-7). Within the EMDU program, such relevance was achieved through 'learning the applied side of a science.'

Pilot projects can be seen as the way to convince policymakers of the value of research results. Early in 1995, IDRC was confronted with the strong views of the Minister of Environment who openly criticized IDRC's approach toward Ecological Audits: "give us less recommendations and advice and more equipment."

Reduction of pollution was viewed first as resulting from new equipment or new technology. Equipment was often purchased before a thorough evaluation had been conducted. IDF was charged with improving the Vatutino meat processing plant. Its experts were insisting on using high-energy plasma to treat waste. IDRC refused to fund expensive plasma-based equipment, since its own survey of what was known on this topic indicated that it would be impractical in the context. In the words of one member of the IDRC team, Dr. Babcock, "scientists and managers alike tend to focus on technological fixes to problems, rather than adjusting management practices where practical." The unwillingness of IDRC may serve as an example of *research as argumentation*. In the end IDRC was able to convince the IDF director that plasma technology was not efficient for use at the meat processing plant. *Ecological audits* however, may lead to better results. Soon the ecological audit projects demonstrated vividly the value of managerial and low-cost improvements leading to improved production and pollution reduction.

## 6.2 Program's Impact

*On Legislation*

According to interviewees, the program's major achievement was connected with developments in legislation. The following pieces of legislation arose from IDRC projects or were directly influenced by it:

- *National Program on Ecologic Rehabilitation of Dnipro Basin and Drinking Water Improvement* (was considered at and adopted by Verhovna Rada of Ukraine on February 27, 1997).

- *Drinking Water Law* (was adopted on 10 January 2002).

- Presidential Decree on *National Atlas of Ukraine* (was adopted on 1 August 2001).

- Several norms and regulations were worked out within the IDRC-sponsored projects, in particular, the Methodology of Ecological Estimation of Surface Water Quality (1998), regulations concerning water tariffs, and others.

- Law "On Environment Protection" defines *ecologic audit* development in Ukraine. The latter is also regulated by laws "On Auditing Activities," "On Entrepreneurship Activities," as well as by standards and regulations (Dnipro Ecological Rehabilitation 2001: 85-191). At present, the law "On Auditing Activities" provides legislative bases for ecological audits. The draft law on ecological audit has been developed within the framework of the EMDU program and it is now under Verhovna Rada consideration.

Changes in legislation were not always directly connected to ecology and water resources. The (infamous) law of 1937 concerning the secrecy of water systems was changed at the instigation of EMDU program participants.

*Public Involvement and Public Outreach and Learning Processes*

From the outset, IDRC suggested greater involvement of Ukrainian civil society, increased public participation, and NGO involvement. These ideas ran counter to 70 years of socialism and were difficult to internalize. In the past, government officials flooded thousands of hectares of arable land and hundreds of villages, without consultations, to build a hydroelectric station on the Dnieper. With respect to NGOs, Ukrainian scientists granted them little credit, as they perceived NGOs as lacking professionalism and being driven by emotions and political considerations. They also questioned NGO accountability. Public participation was a highly sensitive issue, one that IDRC could hardly tackle directly or in a confrontational fashion. The following story sheds light on the issue and on the appropriate pedagogy.

For example, the project manager of the Riverbank Stabilization project began implementing the project 'soviet style': he brought machinery and diligently started to work. Local authorities and the local population were not informed nor consulted about the changes envisaged to their precious shoreline. Misinformed about the project intentions and on the alert, rumours started to spread within the local population: "Canadians are buying up our land here. Soon, they are going to be building high-rises, and we will never get to the river anymore" they were heard muttering. At some point they interrupted work using pitchforks. The only solution was opening a dialogue between the project manager and local authorities. Had IDRC insisted on a democratic consultative approach as practiced in Canada, it is most unlikely that this project would have led to a valuable learning experience. As a result of this project, Ukrainians (UMC) learned to include public participation and public awareness in project proposals. This was something they learned, not taught to do.

*Positive Aspects of the IDRC Program as Perceived by Recipients*

- There exists an atmosphere of trust, confidence, and real partnership between IDRC and Ukrainian recipients. IDRC's consultants and staff never force their views upon recipients but are open to discussing and exploring all avenues for solving problems.

- All project managers are local Ukrainians and they feel they have a great deal of independence, hiring necessary specialists, choosing appropriate equipment, and approving trips within the project budget. Using IDRC's approach, more money is spent locally and more money reaches Ukrainian scientists and consultants. No other donor agency in Ukraine spends 60% of its funds in the recipient country.

- Many of the projects carried out under EMDU were highly practical with outcomes that will last beyond the end of EMDU and funding from IDRC. Real tangible results can be seen going beyond the usual reports and publications whose utility to locals is questionable.

- A large training component has allowed many Ukrainian specialists to upgrade their skills and qualifications in Canada and other countries.

## Negative Aspects of the IDRC Program as Perceived by Recipients

- What IDRC understood as benign intrusion in practising due diligence and enquiring about administrative and technical issues was regarded as severe probing by recipient institutions. IDRC's approval was expected to be forthright and simple. Sometimes recipients had to revise a proposal four or five times before IDRC approved it. This has led to the senior scientific adviser of IDRC being referred to as "Dr. Niet" (sic).

- Proposal approval, contract preparation, and transfers of funds took too much time. In the current poor economic conditions for many scientists in Ukraine, donor money is the only means of support and delays cause nervousness.

- The list of reports that have to be prepared, along with the final project outputs, is quite long. Many recipients do not see any real purpose and value with the preparation of some of these reports. Moreover, the list tends to grow over time. For instance, results-based management and time sheets for workers on the project were added, joining gender, training, and local contributions reports as a requirement" (Guilmette and Iskra, 2001: 84-85).

## Demand-driven Methodology and Sequencing

As IDRC compared notes with other Western organizations active in the region, the importance of capacity-building methods and approaches became ever more apparent. It is useful to remind the reader that there are four critical aspects for large project delivery: 1) complete ownership by recipient countries; 2) best financial and operational management; 3) highest scientific and technical standards; and 4) collaboration with other partners. It is essential to ensure a good balance among these four complementary goals. However, experience has shown that, in practice, projects are often skewed in favour of one or the other of these goals. Generally, priority is given to ensuring that all procurement and accounting procedures will be meticulously adhered to, and pressure is put on foreign experts and consultants to obtain and demonstrate visible results. As a result:

- There is an over-emphasis on immediate, tangible results such as reports.

- Local ownership and capacity building suffers.

- Long-term sustainability is left in doubt.

In contrast, Ukrainian authorities are now heralding the demand-driven methodology of IDRC as a unique and effective model. Ukrainian partners have expressed a preference for the management methods employed in EMDU, bemoaning the fact that many other aid organizations do not operate in this manner, but rather rely on extensive use of expensive foreign consultants. A few years back, the Ministry of Environment demanded that two donor agencies use the same implementation mechanism that IDRC uses.

In almost all processes designed by humans, sequencing is of the essence. It is true for many chemical and physical processes, for example, and it is also true for development activities. Development problems as unique and new as the reforms undertaken in Ukraine presented a rare sequencing challenge. In part accidentally and in part intentionally, EMDU seems to have adopted the right sequence.

In summary, the sequencing was follows. With empowerment came responsibility; with responsibility came frugality and strategic thinking. Strategic thinking led to building and searching for relevant new knowledge as well as for testing practical ideas. In order to do so, local resources were expanded often through local contributions requiring considerable cooperation and ingenuity. The various activities provided tangible results, results that were perceived pertinent to the specific context of Ukraine. In many instances, the lessons learned revealed new ways to leverage resources, people and to surmount passivity. Combined, these achievements led to self-confidence. The self-confidence and self-respect thus acquired eventually led to audacity; the UMC felt empowered to transform newly acquired knowledge into policy approved by Parliament. It also led to the UMC taking the lead and securing UNDP/GEF funds for the rehabilitation of the River Basin, involving thus Belarus and Russia.

## SECTION 7

## MOVING TOWARD REGIONAL NETWORKS AND MANAGEMENT OF THE GEF PROGRAM

As IDRC's own networks' evaluation has demonstrated (Bernard, 1996: xxxx), local networks often benefit from linking upward into regional and/or international networks.

One obvious extension for cleaning up the main source of water for Ukraine called for involving the two upstream riparian countries of the Dnieper River Basin, Belarus and Russia. This was perceived by IDRC as another opportunity to expand its network management approaches into the region. It might have the complementary or supplementary effect of inducing mentality changes into Ukraine through feedback. Indeed, command and control methods can hardly coexist within an international network made up of sovereign countries. Local experience was limited to former soviet-style international bodies managed under strict Moscow control and resting on the communist party fraternity. The idea of introducing softer and less coercive methods made sense as a means to manage better the River Basin, but also as a means to expand the ideas and concepts that were emerging through EMDU.

---

### Box 2.5

*Global Environment Facility (GEF) 2000-2004 Strategic Action Program for the Dnipro River Basin Belarus, Russia, Ukraine*

The Global Environment Facility (GEF) program, budgeted at US$ 7 million, was designed to develop a suite of measures and their respective implementation mechanisms for the sustainable protection of Europe's third largest river, the Dnieper, and fell under the GEF's International Waters Programme. The GEF Dnieper Programme was intended to contribute to the protection of regional and global international waters. The management capacity, both at the level of the individual riparian countries (Russia, Ukraine, and Belarus) and at the transboundary level, is to be strengthened, while wider global benefits are to accrue to the Dnieper Basin countries, as well as to littoral countries of the Black Sea. The long-term objectives of the project were to remedy the serious environmental effects of pollution and habitat degradation, to ensure sustainable use of resources, and to protect biodiversity in the Dnieper River Basin.

The Dnieper Program was part of the GEF Black Sea Basin Strategic Approach and was a partnership between the United Nations Development Programme (UNDP) and Canada's International Development Research Centre (IDRC), with full involvement of specialized UN and other multilateral and bilateral agencies. The partnership with IDRC facilitated continuity with ongoing projects in the region, brought with it a complementary project laying the groundwork for the GEF Dnieper Program, and provided for greater leverage of donor funds.

**Outline and Objectives**

The long-term objectives of the project are to remedy the serious environmental effects of pollution and habitat degradation, to ensure sustainable use of resources, and to protect biodiversity in the Dnieper River Basin. The project included seven specific objectives:

1. Create a transboundary management regime and coordinating body.
2. Assist countries in the formulation, review, and endorsement process of a Strategic Action Programme (SAP).
3. Improve financial, legal, and operational mechanisms for pollution reduction and sustainable resource use.
4. Formulate National Action Plans by inter-ministerial committees.
5. Improve conservation of biodiversity.
6. Enhance communication among stakeholders and encourage public awareness and involvement in addressing the problems of the Dnieper Basin.
7. Build capacity for SAP implementation.

More information on this project can be found at the following address: *http://www.dnipro-gef.net/*

In the autumn of 1997, I became convinced that OECD offered a proven and tested method for negotiating policy among sovereign nations. This approach is very close to IDRC's practices: it rests on the principle of self-help, peer pressure, and the design of new policy based on the scientific search for facts. The EMDU experiment could therefore be put to good use by expanding its newly tested methods and positive results into Belarus and Russia.

The conviction that OECD could provide a useful model for regional cooperation was the result of the multi-donors' evaluation of 20 years of cooperation within the OECD/Sahel Club that ended in 1997. The Sahel Club was a real-size innovative experiment in international cooperation that was undertaken in 1975. The basis of its method rested on a strikingly different approach to international cooperation and to fund-raising. Its underpinning operative feature was that donors and recipients should work together to define what are the best ways for resolving big problems such as desertification or food deficit leading to famines. They work as a team to identify the key questions and do the research leading to an answer to each of these questions. In this manner, there is a simultaneous buy-in by both the countries and their donor partners for the agreed-upon policies. This breeds mutual confidence— confidence in the  nations. Everything keeps them apart: the size and sophistication of their economies, their physical environments, their traditions, religions and culture, the level of technology and of education. However, the Sahel Club experiment provided a fully tested methodology for conducting dialogue and for reaching consensus among sovereign nations, involving rich countries such as France, Canada, or the United States, and poor countries such as Mali, Niger, or Gambia. It provided a rigorous way for designing policy through a unique blend of scientific research intermingled with dialogue among experts and decision-makers. It provided a useful experience on how to raise funds by involving donors and recipients in a sustained dialogue over difficult subjects such as 'what to do to resolve a difficult environmental problem.' It provided a method for donors to accompany development as opposed to 'do it upon others.' It provided a tested methodology to arrive at an agreed plan of action for an immense task, one that led to long-term commitments as opposed to ad hoc and piecemeal approaches. It helped alleviate the perennial problem related to chicanery and divergent development approaches between donors. Last but not least, it provided a method to breed confidence among seemingly unrelated partners, including partners that enjoy different development levels.

In 1998, IDRC made a formal proposal to Ukraine, Belarus, and Russia, and to the United Nations Development Programme (UNDP) for managing a Global Environment Facility (GEF) financed project aimed at preparing a joint Strategic Action Plan for the rehabilitation of the entire Dnieper River Basin. IDRC introduced for that purpose a model that departed in many ways from traditional technical assistance-driven models. The proposed model rested on four key and interlocking elements:

1. Most of the research and analysis, as well as policy proposals, were to be conducted by local scientists, NGOs, and research institutions, and not by foreign consultants recruited following international tendering processes.

2. All program priorities, related financial allocations, selection of executing agencies, appraisal of results, and final approval of ensuing policies were to be the first accountability of National Management Committees, using a two key formula as tested and developed during EMDU. UNDP would be holding in this instance the second key. For the purpose of administering the regional program, a joint riparian steering committee would be formed with the head of each national committee. This would become the final arbiter of trans-boundary decisions.

3. Donors would be invited from the very beginning to accompany the planning process. They would be invited to discuss and comment 'informally' with the Steering Committee. In addition to seeking their views on how to resolve the problems facing the region, their financial support for additional studies would be actively sought.

4. OECD's highly specific consensus-reaching methodology would be introduced gradually as the project evolved.

Members of the Ukrainian Management Committee supported it, but other partners had mixed views about an approach they had never seen or heard about before. They were sceptical of its potential for resolving policy problems between their nations.

It can be argued that the absence of any existing reference to OECD's model did not help in this regard. In addition, representatives of other donor institutions were generally unaware that OECD's management practices and conventions are strikingly different than the ones with which they are familiar. Because of this, their representatives found it hard to understand and appreciate its intrinsic merits. Nevertheless, some elements of IDRC's proposal were introduced within the management structure of the project. Management committees created by IDRC are salient features of the governance for this project. In addition, very large portions of the project activities and studies have been tasked to local organizations, as opposed to being tendered among international consultants. However, the full range of governance mechanisms and the know-how that are essential to run such a network have yet to be introduced and fully tested in the region.

In our view, it is necessary for donors to design new concepts of development cooperation and invent new instruments for the transfer of assistance so as to become relevant to and responsive to the needs that are now apparent in transition countries. Today, conditions in the NIS region are substantially different from previous situations in either post-war Europe or the developing countries. One would have assumed that an array of new instruments for cooperation and assistance would have been designed to respond to this dramatically new situation. In fact, except for the establishment of the EBRD, which involved little of an innovative quality, little innovation has been attempted to date. The conjunction between the need for new instruments for the transfer of appropriate types of assistance and support for a paradigm shift that must accompany effective reform remained by and large unrecognized among Western donor agencies.

This lacuna, and the imperative for innovation in the development of new and appropriate forms of assistance, seem likely to become increasingly salient issues in the policy dialogue between Western aid donors and the NIS. The challenge is to create a relevant new transfer mechanism with the purpose of bridging an important knowledge gap. We describe these ideas and techniques in the following chapters.

# 3

## OECD's Basic Rules of Conduct

### *A Sociology of its Institutional Culture*

## Introduction

It is not the intent of this paper to give a detailed account of how the OECD functions. Two works have been published in French, from which we have drawn heavily (Bonvin, 1998 and Chavranski 1997). In addition, the OECD web site provides details on the organization's structure. What we have tried to do here is to highlight the main characteristics that explain the fundamental nature of its functioning. As the subtitle of this chapter suggests, it is in effect an essay on the sociology of the organization's institutional culture.

Inevitably, it gives a stylized view of the organization. However, many variations of common practices coexist within the organization and in this way, OECD is rich in its diversity. Even peer reviews are conducted somewhat differently depending on the nature of the subject. Specialists such as, for example, economists and health specialists, have different scientific traditions as well as different means to reach their goals. Such differences eventually work their way into the manner by which this 'network of networks' conducts its business.

## SECTION 1
## FOUNDATIONS OF THE OECD'S INSTITUTIONAL CULTURE

### 1.1 Historical Background

At the end of the Second World War, European countries were physically and morally devastated. Two years later, in 1947, economic recovery had scarcely begun: farm output, for example, was still 25 percent below what it had been in 1939, and governments were still resorting to rationing. The generalized demoralization of Europe and the onset of the Cold War induced in most leaders the fear that "capitalism's days were numbered" (Bonvin, 1998: 6).

## Box 3.1

### The OECD

The fundamental task of OECD is straightforward: to enable its member countries to consult and cooperate to achieve the highest sustainable economic growth, and to improve the economic and social well-being of their people.

OECD offers advice and makes recommendations to its members to help them define their policies. On occasion it also arbitrates in multilateral agreements and establishes legal codes in certain areas of activity.

The organization is a forum for objective, skilled, and independent dialogue, which permits a thorough understanding and true assessment of the problems posed in today's increasingly complex world. The great comparative advantages of OECD are its multidisciplinary approach—a capacity to cover all areas of government activity in a consistent way—and its system of consensus building through peer pressure. Within the different committees the peer pressure system encourages countries to be transparent, to provide explanations and justifications, and to be self-critical where necessary, the practice of self-assessment being the most original characteristic of OECD.

The current member countries are the following (date of accession except for original members): Australia (1971), Austria, Belgium, Canada, Czech Republic (2003), Denmark, Finland (1969), France, Germany, Hungary (2003), Iceland, Ireland, Italy, Japan (1964), Korea (1996), Luxembourg, Mexico (1994), Netherlands, New Zealand (1973), Norway, Poland (1996), Portugal, Slovak Republic (2003), Spain, Sweden, Switzerland, Turkey, United Kingdom, United States. *(http://www.oecd.org)*

Major reforms were obviously called for (see Chapter 1). The protectionist measures that characterized the economic behaviour of all European states had led to drastic declines in trade and led to war. But how should the reform process be addressed? Mistrust was universal and no European government really believed that other states would implement any reforms that might be agreed, without cheating. In effect, governments were facing the 'prisoner's dilemma' (see Box 3.2).

The announcement of the Marshall Plan in June 1947 served as a veritable lifesaver: it provided an input that was rare at that time—hope (Bonvin, 1997: 7). General Marshall's idea of providing financial assistance for European recovery came with some strings attached, however. In exchange for firm, multiyear commitments on the part of donors, participants were expected to cooperate with each other. The reforms were to be introduced over a period of several years, and they would be slow in making their impact felt. The continuity of this financial and technical assistance represented an essential commitment for reassuring the Europeans.

It is important to remember that all the countries of Europe, from the Atlantic to the Urals, were invited to participate in this program. On June 27, 1947, however, at a meeting convened by France and the United Kingdom to discuss the American proposal, Stalin's representative, Vyacheslav Molotov, refused on behalf of the USSR to take any part in a cooperative approach to the economic reconstruction of Europe. Instead, he presented a list of useful imports that might be purchased with the aid of American credits (Griffith, 1997: 34). His refusal also meant that the states that were under Soviet influence would be left out as well (Bonvin, 1998: 7) with the exception of Yugoslavia, which maintained an independent stance toward Moscow and cooperated with western institutions.

What followed was a process of self-selection and taking sides. In the end, the states of Europe split into two opposing ideological camps. On one side were the future members of OECD, most of which shared to a greater or lesser extent the characteristics discussed in the preceding chapters: a democratic political system that respected human rights, and a developed industrial economy that recognized the primacy of the market (Bonvin, 1998: 7). On the other side stood the Socialist states, whose allegiance to Moscow was unquestioned. From a sociological viewpoint, they constituted two separate groups that for the next 40 years would pursue diametrically opposed policies.

The European countries participating in the Marshall Plan met under the aegis of the OEEC (Organisation for European Economic Cooperation); the two donor countries, Canada and the United States, participated as observers. The steady influx of American aid amounts in 2003 dollars amounts to some US$ 80 billion; it helped to reduce the severity of the economic crisis, to overcome shortages, and in this way to assuage political discontent. The much more modest contribution of Canada added a political dimension to this collective effort.

The Marshall Plan has too often been viewed as simply a financial mechanism: in fact, it served first and foremost to instil hope among European leaders and to stabilize the political situation. In this way, it served as a conflict prevention mechanism by helping to establish the social peace that was essential to economic progress.

With the money also came some good ideas. European states now were obliged to work together, to submit all their economic policies to critical review by their neighbours and to provide OEEC with all the information it needed (and not merely the data that they were interested in sharing—a subtle but extremely important distinction). They also undertook to liberalize their economies and to reduce barriers to trade (Bonvin, 1998: 9). A great many ideas thus emerged from the informal debates within the OEEC. Older staff members of OECD recall that it was an American delegate who, at one of the organization's meetings, suggested to the Europeans that they start by working out an agreement on a specific problem: coal and steel. Everyone knows how this modest idea has since snowballed into what is currently known as European Union.

Marshall Plan aid was provided with another important precondition: no country could receive assistance until all countries had reached a consensus on the distribution formula for sharing the American funds (Bonvin, 1998: 13). Besides effectively resolving the perennial problem of aid allocation, this approach marked the first application of the consensus method. Thus the effort to reach consensus and the system of peer reviews were to become two of the pillars of the OECD approach.

In 1959, after activities had ceased under the Marshall Plan, Europe was well on its way to economic recovery and the six-nation European Community was up and running. It was time, perhaps, to do away with OEEC. On the other hand, tensions were appearing within NATO, sparked in particular by France's threat to withdraw its Mediterranean fleet from the NATO high command. Moscow chose this moment to launch an 'economic offensive' in the developing countries. Suddenly, it seemed urgent to do something spectacular, not only to coordinate the efforts of Western countries on behalf of the developing countries, but also to deal with the many commercial disputes that were emerging between Europe and North America.

The idea of transforming and expanding OEEC seemed attractive, but what was to be done with the many decisions by which the European states were by then bound? Would they apply to the new members? Some Europeans saw this as a splendid opportunity to revisit decisions that they found difficult to implement. After hot debate about whether the new organization, OECD, would adopt the commitments taken within OEEC, a compromise was found whereby all acts of OEEC were to be subject to a unanimous vote by members of OECD (Griffith, 1997: 247).

Thus it was that in 1961 the members of OEEC, plus Canada and the United States, undertook to prolong the efforts launched with the Marshall Plan, but this time in order to, "lay the basis for economic relations between the new Europe and the two North American powers that had emerged unscathed from the war. It was crucial, in the end, to establish principles for cooperation and solidarity with the outside world.... Prosperity posed its own problems" (Chavranski, 1997: 8).

It was only after a convoluted process that the legal personality, the conventions adopted within OEEC and the institutional culture of that organization, born in the aftermath of war, were transmitted to OECD and forged the organization that we know today.

Reliance on peer pressure and consensus, and on a coherent set of operational characteristics, then, is explained by the historical and cultural context of the nations of Western Europe that set out to build this organization in association with their two North American partners. There is a degree of cultural homogeneity between these states, based on a shared historical past.

## 1.2 OECD's Basic Rules of Conduct or the Values of the Institution

From the outset, it is important to emphasize the pragmatic character of the OECD negotiation process. The OECD approach to negotiations is designed to lead to an agreement upon policies or policy options and structures that may be implemented by all member countries, since they arise from a consensus-building process. In essence, the OECD process produces outcomes that are seen —by member countries—to be reasonable and acceptable. These policy outputs are generally considered relevant and timely, and can be readily adapted to the specific needs of the concerned member countries. The possibility of adapting policies adopted through consensus is the essence of the very subtle OECD process. If a country adapts a policy in a manner that seems contrary to the spirit of the common policy, the perceived misadaptation will give rise to discussions at the occasion of Peer Review. The process can only be described as intensively iterative; for some it sounds slow and tedious, but it should be argued that it results in resilient and sustainable agreements in the end.

Over the years, OECD members have enlarged the subjects of their analyses. In many cases their concern for reducing trade barriers and creating a level playing field for business transactions has been expanded to include sharing knowledge about 'promising or best practices' on matters that do not involve mutual competition. This is the case for studies on health or education, for example. In such cases the pursuit of consensus and the negotiation process is less critical; sharing 'intelligence' on these matters becomes the real essence of their cooperation.

The success of OECD rests on a 'blueprint' for international and regional cooperation consisting of three elements:

- Espousal of a supra-national policy regime based on respect for human rights, democratic government, and the market economy (see Chapter 2);
- Respecting certain basic rules of conduct (discussed in this chapter);
- Application of certain unique techniques and skills for making and negotiating collective choices (see Chapter 4 and Appendix 1).

The rules for OECD meetings and procedures include agreement on an agenda for achieving practical and defined outcomes. It has a practical, operational mission, which is expected to lead to tangible objectives and to real, demonstrable progress. Its primary product is agreed policy options based on common analysis, but of course allowing for a variety of coherent and consistent responses based on differing national situations. In many instances these will evolve into agreed policies among its members, that will become national policies enforced through subtle yet unequivocal peer pressure methods.

From the beginning, it is probably the position of strength from which the major victorious powers (Canada, the United Kingdom, and the United States) started that explains the predominantly Anglo-Saxon character of the organization. If we observe the functioning of OECD, we find the traits of a juridical system based on jurisprudence or case law, one that evolves by comparison of precedents, by flexible interpretation rather than literal application of statutes and regulations. OECD is thus full of exceptions, gentlemen's agreements, and unwritten conventions that are constantly evolving. In this respect, it follows in the tradition of English law. In its early days, the organization was nicknamed "Whitehall-sur-Seine"! Since then, this original dominant culture has undergone considerable evolution. The success of the organization rests on finding compromises and adaptations to local circumstances. This adaptive characteristic is reflected not only in its overall process, but also in its organizational arrangements and collective behaviour.

We also find the use of recognized scientific methods, in particular the concern to base solutions on research and on objective analysis of the relevant facts. The peer review method comes close to the peer evaluation tradition that is commonly used in scientific research and publishing.

The OECD approach is in fact the product of a mixture of political pragmatism and the search for empirically demonstrated solutions. Countries participating in the organization have gradually become accustomed to seeing their actions dissected by the Secretariat in the presence of their peers. They have gradually come to understand and to appreciate the need for harmonizing their national accounts, and for ensuring that all economic data and analyses are made public and therefore available not only to competing states but, more daring yet, to domestic critics and opposition parties. This has given rise to a degree of steadily expanded transparency across many sectors that were unusual even within democracies. Members have learned as well to appreciate the indirect influence that democratic practices such as peer review can have on improving individual as well as collective welfare.

## Using Game Theory to Better Understand

Moving down the road mapped out by OECD required 'the willing suspension of disbelief.' The theory of games offers some especially useful metaphors for understanding the 'OECD mystery.' The 'prisoner's dilemma' is a classic metaphor in literature of this kind. It helps us to understand the

---

### Box 3.2

#### The Prisoner's Dilemma

"A pair of transients, Al Fresco and Des Jardins, has been arrested for vagrancy. They are suspected of complicity in a robbery, but the evidence is inadequate to convict them. The district attorney interrogates them in separate cells and offers each the following deal. "If you confess and your friend does not, you will be released and your friend will have the book thrown at him. He will get 15 months in jail; and the other way around if he confesses and you do not. If you both confess, both will receive moderately long sentences of 8 months. If neither confesses, you will both be convicted of a minor vagrancy charge and serve 1 month."

| IF | Des confesses | Des does not confess |
|---|---|---|
| Al confesses | Al serves 8 months | Al is free |
| Al does not confess | Al serves 15 months | Al serves 1 month |

What does rationality dictate that our players do? What is the logic of the situation represented in this table?

If Al believes that Des is going to confess, then (reading down the first column) Al sees he has a choice between 8 months in jail (if he confesses) and 15 months in jail (if he does not confess). Confessing is clearly his best strategy. If Al believes Des will not confess, then (reading down the second column) Al sees that his choice is between going free (if he confesses) and 1 month in jail (if he does not confess); again, confessing is best for him. Regardless of what Des does, Al's best action is to confess. Now notice that Des is in exactly the same situation as Al, so Des reaches the same conclusion; Des also rationally confesses. Thus the equilibrium of this game, the outcome of simultaneously rational decisions by both of the players, has both confessing and serving 8 months in jail.

This looks paradoxical. The collective good is better served if neither confess, which results in 1 month's jail for both, a high-level equilibrium. There is a contradiction between what is individually rational and what is collectively rational. Each would be better off if the two could succeed in cooperation. But they cannot. The equilibrium of the prisoners' dilemma game is not efficient. What the prisoner's dilemma shows, in the words of the mathematician Robert Aumann, is that "People who fail to cooperate for their own mutual benefit are not necessarily foolish or irrational; they may be acting perfectly rationally."

(*Source:* McMillan, 1992: 10).

problems facing European states at the end of the war. The second metaphor, less well known, allows us to intellectualize the approach that was adopted for dismantling the trap from which the Europeans seemed unable to escape. The habits induced by the Marshall Plan ran counter to 'received ideas' of the time—because of this, it represented a bold and innovative wager. The metaphor of the 'rational pigs' demonstrates this mechanism.

---

### Box 3.3

#### *The Rational Pigs*

Two pigs, one dominant and the other subordinate, are put in a box. There is a lever at one end of the box which, when pressed, dispenses food at the other end. Thus the pig that presses the lever must run to the other end; by the time it gets there, the other pig has eaten most, but not all, of the food. The dominant pig is able to prevent the subordinate pig from getting any of the food when both are at the food. Assuming the pigs can reason like game theorists, which pig will press the lever?

To solve this game, let us anthropomorphically endow the pigs with deductive capabilities. Consider first the subordinate pig's reasoning. "Suppose I predict that the big pig will press the lever. Then I get a little if I press and more if I don't. If, on the other hand, I predict it will not press, I get less than nothing if I press and none if I don't. Thus regardless of what it does, I am better off not pressing than pressing." Now imagine the dominant pig's thought process. To figure it out, the dominant pig must put itself in the shoes of the subordinate pig. Doing so, it sees, as we saw, that the subordinate pig's best action is unambiguous: don't press. Thus if it presumes that the subordinate pig is rational, it knows it should use its best response to its rival's not pressing: thus it is in its interest to press the lever. Rational behaviour, therefore, indicates a surprising conclusion: the dominant pig presses the lever, and the subordinate pig gets most of the food. Weakness, in this case, is strength. Animal behaviourists have actually conducted experiments of this sort. In most experimental trials, the dominant pig did actually push the lever. The pigs behaved like game theorists.

In contrast to the prisoners' dilemma, the pig's game generates no conflict between individual rationality and collective rationality. This metaphor is illustrative of much of OECD's undertaking and may help some readers understand better the way it works and why it succeeds.

(*Source*: Summarized from McMillan, 1992: 11-14).

---

The 'prisoners' dilemma' is a representation for many diverse business and economic interactions. For example: Two nations trading with each other are driven by rational, national-interest calculations to erect trade barriers when both would be better off if they were eliminated. The rational pig game or metaphor arises in less trivial circumstances. Consider, for example, how, in a sense, General Marshall pressed the lever in 1947 and allowed a flow of resources to 'feed' the European economy. The intent was as generous and enlightened as it was selfish: in the end, the calculation paid off for the benefit of American exports to Europe and for European recovery.

## 1.3 OECD Structure and Functions

OECD's mandate calls for the organization to promote and coordinate policies aimed at achieving the highest sustainable economic growth and employment for member countries and the world, as well as policies to stimulate the expansion of world trade on a multilateral, non-discriminatory basis. The 30 member countries of OECD include all the advanced industrial countries. ·

OECD functions through its governing body, the Council, chaired by the Secretary General, and its network of about 120 Committees and Working Groups, which are issue-related. One deals, for example, with maritime transport, another focuses on competition law and policy, while another was formed to deal with scientific and technological policy. The OECD Secretariat carries out work mandated by the Council and the Committees. The Council approves decisions and recommendations. Generally, decisions of Council require unanimity (consensus). An Executive Committee, chaired by one of the ambassadors to the OECD, provides day-to-day supervision of OECD activities. The Secretary General is responsible for managing the implementation of Council and Executive Committee decisions. Agreed policies are then implemented through the domestic policy apparatus of each individual member country. Overall compliance with these agreements is reviewed and discussed within each Committee. Peer pressure from other member governments provides powerful inducements for implementation of OECD recommendations leading to harmonization.

Representatives from government departments of member countries responsible for the work area designated for the committee attend meetings and, along with specialists from the Secretariat, monitor developments, advance policy ideas, deal with specific problems shared by member countries, and establish standards for the reporting of information and guidelines for carrying out policy. They make recommendations for Council decisions and encourage member countries to harmonize their policies.

As was noted previously, OECD is neither a funding agency nor a program delivery agency. The key to OECD's role in promoting international economic cooperation lies in its continuous review of economic policies and trends in member countries. Draft reports on each member country's economic policies and performance are prepared by the Secretariat for vetting and discussion with its government before being addressed at the Economic Development and Review Committee. At that level, the concerned country is expected to respond to questions prepared by the Secretariat and other members. These review procedures usually lead to frank and open exchanges, often resulting in recommendations for policy changes. OECD also conducts studies of its own intended to enhance the design and to improve the coordination of policies for the management of economic growth, trade expansion, and development cooperation.

One of the principal working committees of OECD is its Economic and Development Review Committee, which examines and monitors economic trends and policies in individual member countries. The Committee thus plays a leading part in the process of multilateral surveillance of economic policies within OECD. Subsequent to each examination, the Committee's country survey and policy conclusions are published. In practice, the economic surveys (and the biannual reviews of the OECD grouping) also present economic forecasts for the year/eighteen months ahead.

Another committee, the Economic Policy Committee, is responsible for the review and surveillance of macroeconomic and structural issues common to member countries, or arising from interactions of national economic trends and policies. Its members are senior officials from economics or finance ministries and/or central banks of member countries.

The Secretariat, with about 1200 staff members, gathers statistical and policy information from member country governments. They process the data, do analyses, forecasts, manage policy reviews, organize meetings, provide translation services, prepare directories and other reference materials, monitor agreements reached by member countries, and publish much of the analyses, forecasts, and statistical information. Member country governments fund the work of the OECD Secretariat. National contributions to OECD's annual budget are determined by the size of each member's economy.

OECD has established mechanisms to help address the challenges of enforcing its international policy regime in the absence of more formal institutionalized systems of global governance. These mechanisms function within the consensus arrangements of OECD, and are managed through OECD itself, mostly without permanent staffing or administrative systems of their own. For example, the mechanism put in place to deal with delinquent borrowers of official loans was the so-called "Paris Club," an ad hoc arrangement of the OECD; this committee is now autonomous. Another mechanism for addressing unfair trade subsidies is the OECD 'consensus arrangement'; here again the consensus is outside of OECD but is related to a committee dealing with export credits. The Development Assistance Committee (DAC) deals with matters concerning aid policy and criteria. This approach to policy enforcement enables OECD to achieve a fair measure of coherence and consistency (if not participatory universality) in the making and application of the international policy regime that governs 'Western' state behaviour in these domains.

## Box 3.4

### *The OECD Regime and the US Federal Reserve Decision on Interest Rates*

On September 29, 1998, the United States Federal Reserve decision to lower its key short-term funds interest rate by 0.25% represented a deliberate and calculated response to a looming global financial crisis. In responding in this way, the American monetary policy authority sought to cushion the threat to US financial confidence and economic performance from the looming global contagion, whilst also helping international financial markets to regain their lost buoyancy. At this juncture, the timing and delicate balance being upheld by US monetary policy had far-reaching significance, not just for the stability of the American financial system and economic well-being, but for the prospects of economic recovery for the rest of the world. Given the parameters of this decision, the US Federal Reserve was acting in effect as central banker to the world.

This monetary policy decision was an extremely delicate and difficult one. The US economy was still robust but global financial conditions were deteriorating dramatically. Capital was fleeing Asia, the Americas, and Russia to safe havens in US dollars. Pleas for corrective action called for a US interest rate cut to provide additional financial liquidity, to heighten overall investor confidence, and to restore capital flows to international markets.

Although the policy-making process of the US Federal Reserve is notably opaque, the decision depended for its timeliness and effectiveness on the reliability and transparency of the economic and financial information upon which the policymakers based their judgments. The requirement for reliable and current information is best indicated by the magnitudes involved (slight changes in interest rates affecting hundreds of billions of dollars in capital flows), and by the delicate balance being maintained between domestic and external policy concerns: countering inflationary pressures, maintaining growth, and restoring capital flow to international markets.

The sources of information used were, of course, American. However, it should be clear that availability of internationally comparable and consistent data on macroeconomic, financial, and trade performance was a tribute to the accomplishments of OECD. By virtue of the OECD's salient role in promoting the integrity, transparency, and standardization of economic information, the US Federal Reserve had access to reliable data on its important international linkages upon which to base its decision.

Through the use of multilateral and peer review processes to achieve high standards and acceptable definitions of financial, monetary, and other economic and social data, OECD helped to create confidence in macroeconomic information among the public and even in the intra-governmental community. Thus, in a complex system like that of the United States, where there exists separation of powers, the Federal Reserve can have confidence that the monetary and other economic information that it obtains transcends and is free from any institutional bias arising from the Administration, Congress, or any other stakeholder. It is the impeccability attached to economic information, reflecting the cooperation culture of OECD, which enabled the Federal Reserve to make highly sensitive monetary management decisions with equanimity.

It is pertinent to call attention to the connectivities involved. The US Federal Reserve's capacity to manage monetary policy effectively is connected to the availability of reliable, transparent, standardized and timely information about the US and global economies. This, in turn, involved connectivity between the American systems for national accounting and the OECD, as a coordinator and reviewer of the information and policy mechanisms of other significant world economies. These connectivities between macroeconomic management and the production of high-quality standardized economic information help create the enabling environment for international flows of capital and other resources that are hallmarks of OECD-supported economic cooperation.

—Martin Rudner

## 1.4 Economics Department

Some of the salient achievements of OECD are exemplified by the work of its Economics Department. The department addresses issues of both a macroeconomic and a structural character, and the interaction between structural and macroeconomic policies and developments. What is unique about its contribution to OECD is the overall economy-wide perspective it brings to every policy issue. Most of the Department's work is eventually published, but its first and primary use is by member governments as represented in a range of committees and working parties. Of particular significance is the Economics Department's input into the work of the Economic Development and Review Committee and the Economic Policy Committee, among others. Here, the department's analysis forms the basis for a process of multilateral monitoring and surveillance.

The department's macroeconomic work is based on continual monitoring of events in member countries, including regular projections of short- and medium-term economic developments. Interactions among individual country policies and developments are of particular concern. The department's focus on structural issues has evolved over time. Currently, its analytical efforts are concentrated on policies affecting, *inter alia*, labour, regulatory reform, corporate governance, income distribution and poverty, and sustainable development and climate change, as well as policies dealing with ageing populations.

In one way or another, the work of this department contributes to policy discussion in committees and working parties and, ultimately, in national capitals. Indeed, many of the participants in committee meetings come for the occasion from national capitals. Committee discussions deal with both the analysis of particular issues or policy areas between countries, and with the country-by-country review of a broad field of policy settings. In typical committee practice, issues are first discussed in a country-by-country setting, with the aim of setting general policy orientations. Then general orientations are considered in the context of individual countries, taking their particularities into account. Finally, once a number of countries have been analyzed and discussed, the lessons learned from country-specific analyses are pulled together and discussed in a multi-country setting. The results of this process can also have an impact on the overall agenda of OECD.

The primary purpose of OECD committee discussions is to help individual governments arrive at decisions appropriate to their own and other countries' conditions. These discussions therefore remain largely confidential. However, four series of publications are produced regularly to communicate conclusions of OECD to a wider audience: various annual reports, 22 journals and magazines, studies, and conference proceedings. OECD now offers over 3500 paperback and 700 electronic publications.

In a distinctively subtle but nevertheless meaningful way, OECD has been at the centre of an iterative and often far-reaching policy discourse. The activities of OECD and its efforts at fostering transparency have helped invigorate the domestic policy discourse on economic and social issues in member countries, contributing to the emergence of an active and articulate civil society. OECD plays a vital role in facilitating the sharing of knowledge and lessons learned and in the formulation of common standards. Furthermore, OECD has provided valuable mechanisms for ensuring overall governance transparency, for rigour in national accounts, for sharing experience in defining many basic governance policies, and for tracking both the implementation of agreed policies and their ongoing adaptation to changing circumstances. Interestingly, OECD is itself at both the sending and receiving ends of this policy discourse. In essence, the OECD annual Peer Reviews in as many as fifteen major sectors, have made data, statistics, and analysis of each country's performance progressively available to civil society, thus reinforcing the abilities of citizens and citizens' groups to voice their views and to influence government policies. In turn, these citizen's groups have demanded more information, analysis, and transparency from their government, thus inciting OECD to probe further into many issues and complex problems.

By virtue of this information-sharing function, OECD has helped inspire increased confidence, connectivity, networks, and standards among its member countries. As a result, public sector initiatives and economic enterprises have become increasingly more efficient at doing what they do best. Moreover, international trade among OECD countries has expanded exponentially, generating employment and wealth among the countries, as well as inducing growth in many developing countries through massive transfers of technology and investments.

As Joseph E. Stiglitz aptly demonstrated, classical economy rests on the premise that information essential to making good economic decisions is more or less equally shared by all actors, and therefore, the market is functioning well; and the 'invisible hand' can play its role. But reality is different: In many cases, information is private and too costly to acquire, thus leading to 'asymmetries of information' between economic actors. This gives rise to a variety of distortions, creating challenges for policymakers who rely only on classical paradigms to guide their action.

Supply, or demand-side economics and many other fads born in classical economic schools, have marked the policies of OECD member's governments over the last forty years. This pendulum-like discourse has also influenced all aid-giving institutions, be they bilateral or multilateral. They more or less echoed the prevalent policy of the day into their programs and most importantly into their 'prescriptions' to aid recipients, generally referred to as 'conditionality'; this elegant euphemism means that aid will be granted if the beneficiary agrees to do certain prescribed things. The beneficiary is, of course, free to refuse the aid thus extended.

Close observation of what happened in reality in the field raised doubt about the wisdom of applying any of those prescriptions. Some development specialists, and I joined their ranks in the early 1980s, noticed that information essential to take good decisions is often so scarce, so distorted or so missing in the essential, that even good prescriptions have little chance of succeeding. For instance, in the early 1980s, at the instigation of World Bank analysts, some countries attempted to move away from state control currency valuation (always distorted, of course) by auctioning daily foreign currency. This seemed a fair and transparent way of handling the problem, however, it soon became obvious that this created bias in favour of rich, well-informed business and weakened even more essential social activities. For instance, hospitals trying to import necessary drugs were seldom capable of winning any bids against commercial activities. "Bidding where there is known to be asymmetries of information will be markedly different from that where such asymmetry does not exist. Those who are uniformed will presume that they will win only if they bid too much ..." (Wilson, 1977: 511-518, in Stiglitz, 2001: 489).

Another example of the way information accrual, policy formulation and economic growth occurs comes from some of the OECD's Sahel Club research carried out when I headed the Club. From 1986 onward, the Club and its Sahelian partner, CILSS, produced ever increasingly precise yearly cereal crop estimates. This was deemed essential to help define food aid requirements. Gradually this new information flow revealed two important policy distortions. In 1989, it soon became obvious that Sahelian Governments as well as donors overestimated food deficit, thus providing greater quantities of food aid. This lead to artificially deflated prices which acted as disincentive to local farmers, thus reducing local production. The contradiction between aid activities targeted at increasing food production and other aid programs providing food aid became obvious. Better information about crops incited Sahelian countries and Donors to sign an agreement governing food aid in 1991. Furthermore, this also led to significant policy changes in most Sahelian countries. A case in point was Mali. Laws had been passed earlier that made it a criminal offence to export cereals. Such a law made sense in time of drought and shortage, but it deprived farmers access to regional export markets. Faced with reality, those laws were changed, thus inducing economic growth. This is another tangible demonstration of the significant role that quality information provided by governments can play in economic growth.

In the meantime, some smart Sahelian traders noticed opportunities along the extensive borders of the region years before governments changed import and export laws. Studies undertaken by the Sahel Club in 1988 through 1990 revealed a strong underground cereal trade that had emerged in the 1980s. The analysis soon made it obvious that West Africa operated as a vast free-trade zone whereby cereals (and presumably other goods) moved across borders in large quantities unimpaired by rules or regulations. Confronted with these facts, donor representatives, experts, and Sahelian officials pondered the significance of this new outcome. Some argued that an underground economy was just another way to attain economic efficiency (balancing supply and demand) when faced with ill-advised government controls and policies. Others argued that it led to human and capital underutilization. It induced a less efficient economy in general, and most importantly, it bred income disparities. Their argument rested in large part on the fact that those that had access to information were generally the same that had resources in the first place: they could bribe officials to access whatever meaningful statistics they could buy. Farmers for their part were seldom given a fair share of profit, as they did not know the real worth of their exportable surplus crop. By not recognizing that information of this nature is a 'public good,' and by not acting decisively to correct this imbalance, governments further compounded 'information asymmetry.' We soon noticed, for instance, that some crafty government officials increased their rent by retaining information longer, thus creating artificial scarcity. In one particular case, some regulations were passed with absolutely no other rationale but to sell the right to circumvent it... Rent seekers are quite smart indeed.

In Stiglitz words, "The most challenging problems for growth lie in economic development. Typically market failures are more prevalent in less developed countries, and these market failures are often associated with information problems... Asymmetries of information give rise to a host of other market failures—such as missing markets, and especially capital markets imperfections, leading to firms that are risk averse and cash constrained." (Stiglitz, 2001: 515, 516).

The way the OECD works has impacted directly in the diversity, quantity, quality, and transparency of information collected and made available by its member governments. This not only created better national accounts, but also expanded the diversity, depth, and range of various census and statistics. It has also led to wider dissemination of the information not only within each nation but also universally. Following Stiglitz' reasoning, by reducing significantly, albeit progressively, 'information asymmetries' has lead into markets that function better as economic operators became increasingly more confident to invest, expand their operations and create employment. Furthermore, it is increasingly being recognized that the arrival of new market information allows a market to expand, not just to operate more efficiently. It is difficult to argue, in my opinion, that this did not have a direct impact on growth.

As explained in Chapter 3, Section 4, the first thing the OECD Secretariat does when tasked with studying a problem is to collect data from each member, and, most importantly, to harmonize it in order to analyze it. This has the obvious result of creating data, statistics, and knowledge that are universally readable. It also results in improving the quality and the transparency of information provided by less diligent members. Through annual Peer Reviews, all OECD members are made to perform at the highest possible level. In other words, a Danish hotel entrepreneur can access and analyze tourist statistics in France with the same certainty his French or German competitor will. He can also benefit from the same analysis and forecast produced by OECD in order to measure his risks and profits. From 1949 onward, the OECD work has progressively reduced 'information asymmetry' allowing economic operators to invest, expand, and create employment with greater confidence and boldness.

## 1.5 OECD's Basic Rules of Conduct

The methodologies deployed by OECD are not well understood, and have rarely been discussed in the professional and scholarly literature.

The success of OECD rests on a 'blueprint' for international and regional cooperation consisting of three elements: (1) promulgation of a supra-national policy regime based on respect for human rights, democratic government, and the market economy; (2) enforcement of certain basic rules of inter-state conduct; and (3) application of certain unique techniques for making and negotiating collective choices among member countries.

The rules for OECD meetings and procedures include agreement on an agenda leading to a practical and defined outcome. This has a practical operational mission that is expected to lead to tangible objectives and real, demonstrable progress. The basic principles of OECD procedures include: (1) respect for ethics; (2) confidence and trust in the other partners; (3) frankness, blended with courtesy; (4) a commitment to respect agreements as they are reached and not to reopen them to obtain advantage at later stages;

and (5) a consensus based on objectivity and common standards (these will be described in more detail later).

Taken together, these principles create a common normative framework for organizational behaviour, and reflect themselves in the style of discourse within OECD and among its members.

In addition, OECD has developed its own know-how on reconciling diverse opinions and consensus building. This is achieved through: (1) iterative peer review; (2) application of common standards; (3) well structured meetings; and (4) transparent processes.

## 1.6 OECD's 'Etiquette' or Unwritten Behavioural Principles

*The Unwritten Rules of the Game*

In the institutional culture of OECD the stress is on informality and on respect for some unwritten rules that, for want of a better term, we may call those of 'decorum and etiquette.' These, in short, are the principal rules, for the most part unwritten, that govern the behaviour of players within the organization. Without this set of complementary rules, the search for consensus would be merely an illusion and peer review would be a sham.

The primary commitments of states (to work together; to submit their economic policies to peer review; to provide all information needed by OECD) have produced what we might call the OECD 'etiquette.' It is summarized below and discussed in more detail later.

*Working Together*

- The dominant ethical code in the organization resembles somewhat that of an old-style English 'gentlemen's club.'

- All decisions are taken on the basis of unanimity, or consensus.

- In committing themselves to work together, member states have never sacrificed their sovereignty, as some did more recently upon joining the European Community. Even when they sign on a specific convention, such as the 'Convention to Fight Bribery,' they do so under no obligation to a majority decision. Furthermore, as there exists no formal enforcement mechanism, one may argue that conduct remains voluntary in all respects.

- The consensus rule, however, is subject to certain exceptions and accommodations in order to make it less constraining.

- Formal decisions are rare: since 1961 there have been perhaps 50 at most (this does not include annual budget resolutions for the functioning of the Secretariat). For the most part, the results of OECD's work are reflected in a range of commitments that are progressively less formal and constraining.

- As the process moves along, many partial agreements are reached: once such a decision is taken, the issue is considered closed and should not be reopened (Bonvin, 1998: 22). This is another rule specific to the OECD, and one that has allowed it to make steady progress over long periods of time. This firmly rooted and thoroughly respected rule allows issues to be ratcheted forward step by step. This method of proceeding is a central feature in the drafting of minutes of meetings. We shall return to the subject in Chapter 4.

- The OECD statutes engage every member to contribute a share of the organization's operating budget, calculated in accordance with a burden-sharing formula based on a country's wealth and size. In addition to the activities that involve the entire membership, members are free to make voluntary contributions to finance activities to which they attach an importance that may not be shared by other members. There are five 'affiliated organs' of the OECD, including the International Energy Agency that have been created and entirely financed by subgroups of members. This is yet another way of getting around the rigid requirement of consensus.

- Respect for consensus is enforced by peer pressure, i.e. a kind of moral and political constraint that can be highly effective but is quite different from that flowing from formal agreements (Bonvin, 1998: 50).

- Working together consistently for four decades has transformed the organization from a negotiating mechanism to achieve 'level playing fields' to rich 'collective learning machinery,' where every member, including its Secretariat, learns from the other. The richness of new knowledge based on comparative analysis and on 'promising practices' is central to allowing member country governments to surmount domestic obstacles, especially interest groups whose resistance is often based on fear and ignorance (see Chapter 6).

*Peer Review*

- It is important here to distinguish between peer pressure, which as noted above helps in reaching consensus, and peer review. This subject will be discussed in detail in Chapter 4. It is important, however, to understand that in peer review, representatives of other member countries serve as a kind of 'jury' to evaluate a country's performance.

- All member countries, without exception, are expected to submit their policies for evaluation and to respond to questions from their peers.

- To forestall any ill feelings or vendettas between officials, various procedures have been adopted. For example, a period of 10 years is allowed to elapse before a country that has evaluated another member is in turn subjected to evaluation by that member (see Table 3.2 and Chapter 4).

- Nothing would change if national administrations were not open and flexible. They must be in a sense 'porous,' so as to absorb comments and modify their habits, their rules and procedures, and even their laws, to take account of OECD's 'informal' recommendations. The latter have no legal force and might indeed be regarded by some as nothing more then interesting declarations of principle.

- This called for discipline and respect for political agreements on the part of the authorities of member states. Protecting the 'honour' of one's government (however quaint this may sound in a modern world which is seemingly governed by interests and geopolitical considerations) is most likely at the core of the behaviour of those bureaucrats who implement and enforce nationally these informal arrangements. Honour is essentially linked with the pursuit of order and stability as it may be achieved through traditions and stable institutions (Berger, p. 89-90). Coming out of the devastation of World War Two, Europeans were in search of order, national dignity, and sought institutional stability. This may explain the relative ease by which agreements reached within OECD (and previously within the OEEC) were adhered to: the 'honour' of the nation was an important feature for the reconstruction of a stable and peaceful Europe.

- Most decisions arrived at by country delegates, no matter what their rank is, seldom require ministerial approval; the OECD *modus operandi* rests on real delegated authority at lower levels of the administration.

- The system will work only if member states, and in particular the principal members, are really willing to seek and eventually to implement a new common approach.

- Respect for power relationships is still one of the unspoken rules within the community. Although all states are equal when it comes to consensus, some are more equal than others. The most important members, led by the United States, will always find it easier to impose their views on the others, and by the same token their opposition will constitute a virtually insurmountable obstacle to any new undertaking. These power relationships may nevertheless shift over time. It is clear, for example, that the predominance once enjoyed by the Americans is now shared with the major European countries (to the extent they can agree among themselves) and with Japan. It is being claimed by some representatives that Peer Reviews are often more direct and frank with smaller countries.

## Providing All the Information Needed by OECD

- The approach to information gathering is highly precise and calculated. Data and studies are made public, and the entire system is reinforced by open publication policy (discussed in detail in Section 5.3).

- On the other hand, the minutes of internal discussions within the Organization, characterized as these are by a great degree of frankness, are considered the property of the members themselves and are not always made public. In fact, "some debates are considered so "frank" and of such strategic importance that they are reserved to a restricted group of members. This is the case, for example, with Working Party No. 3 (Economic issues), in which only 10 members participate [... :] its minutes and records are communicated to other OECD members only on a very restricted basis." (Chavranski, 1997: 63)

- This obligation of frankness implies another rule of etiquette on the part of members: the confidentiality of debates is vigorously protected. No member would think of taking secrets learned during a debate and using them to its negotiating advantage in another forum. Confidence is a precious commodity that takes a long time to build and can be easily destroyed. Without this mutual trust, the entire structure of OECD would collapse like a house of cards.

- OECD does not issue dogma even if a dominant thinking prevails. This explains the tone adopted in all of its work. It would be considered 'poor taste' to make dogmatic pronouncements: these are left to national authors and researchers and to politicians. As a result, the Organization's style of writing is so nuanced and subtle that uninitiated readers may mistake subtlety for vagueness and nuance for indulgence. We shall return to the subject in Chapters 3 and 4.

- Since the Secretariat was expected to serve as a kind of arbitrator *vis-à-vis* national administrations, it was essential to endow the Secretary General with clear and sufficient powers when it comes to staff planning and appointments. (The subject is discussed in greater detail in Section 5.1.)

Taken together, these principles create a common normative framework for organizational behaviour, and are reflected in the style of discourse within OECD and among its members. In the recent past, some NGOs have been included in a number of working groups. This raises an interesting and haunting question: will they accept to observe meticulously those rules created by and for bureaucrats?

## SECTION 2

## A NETWORK DRIVEN BY PEER PRESSURE

By now, it should be clear to the reader that OECD is not a typical international institution whose organizational rules can be analyzed according to traditional descriptive methods. Rather, OECD is clearly a network, or what Pierre Vinde, a former Deputy Secretary General, describes as "a permanent intergovernmental multi-sectoral conference." This is confirmed by the fact that the OECD Secretariat's annual budget is roughly equal to the estimated costs borne by its members to attend meetings in Paris and to keep permanent national delegations in place. It is a little known fact that 40,000 delegates from capitals and national administrations attend various meetings dealing with the work of more than 140 committees and working parties, for a total of 2,829 meeting days (1997 data). Vinde, who first attempted to evaluate these relative costs, has established that there is a ratio of 1 to 1 between members' direct costs and the running of the Secretariat. Such a ratio makes this organization somewhat unique among international bodies. In a report released in December 2002, Vinde reviewed in some detail the relative costs for Sweden. It reveals an interesting pattern worth noting. The Government of Sweden spends around 85 million Kroners (7.75 Kronors = US\$ 1, May-8-2004) per year for its participation in OECD. That figure accounts for a statutory contribution to Part one and two of 14 to 15 million Kroners to which it adds 10 million Kroners as voluntary contribution. This implies that Sweden's own direct cost for participating in this network is about 65 million Kroners, or twice as much as its contribution to the operation of the Secretariat. In other words, the ratio is greater than one to one and presumably Sweden gets 'value for money' from the Secretariat, as it perceives it as the hub of a significant and important network. This may not be the case, however, for a country such as the United States whose contribution represents 25% of the cost of running the Secretariat. In this case the ratio is probably less than one to one. This might partially explain why the US delegation has been arguing for significant cost reductions for the Secretariat, while smaller members, such as Sweden, have agreed to shore up for lost capacity on a voluntary basis.

From an organizational point of view, a network such as OECD differs from an institution in that it is composed of entities that are 'free participant nations', which are never subject to the discipline and authority of a typical hierarchy. They may freely enter into binding agreements and contracts, but they cannot be forced to do so. They may not even be swayed by majority votes. For a concept, an idea or a policy to be agreed to and to be transformed into a general practice, each and every participant in the network must recognize and accept its intrinsic merit. At the very least, it should see it as in its interest to stay with the group or be swayed through other arguments. Occasionally, a majority may decide to proceed and leave a few laggards behind, thereby suspending the consensus rule in hopes that the holdouts will eventually join the consensus; such situations, however, are the exception and are not intended to last very long. The health of a network demands that the entire process be subject to closure.

## 2.1 Peer Pressure

The central element in this methodology for collective choice, arguably, is the use of peer pressure. Peer pressure and its adjunct, peer review or appraisal, serves as an organizational engine to propel participants forward and to ensure progress in procedural terms. This concept will be more widely discussed in Chapter 4, but it is important to distinguish it from peer appraisal as it is known in the scientific world. These two concepts, however, are very close to each other. In a number of cases, the two methods function in tandem.

There are three distinct periods in the negotiation process over collective choices when peer appraisal seems to be most effective: a) When the group concerned establishes a common agenda; b) When the group concerned formulates and adopts a policy choice or policy options; or c) When the group concerned monitors, evaluates, and enforces, again through peer appraisal, these newly adopted policy choices.

*Defining a Common Agenda: Two Contrasting Examples*

In explaining this way of proceeding, it is useful to look at some examples. Following is a deconstruction of two examples of peer pressure, involving analysis of the subsidies that all member states give to their agricultural and industrial sectors. Since the early 1980s, many governments have recognized the need for structural adjustment. The methods—in particular targeted subsidies—that were used to stimulate output, and that did so much to relaunch the European economy, have had a perverse effect: they have engendered new forms of protectionism and this, of course, runs counter to the OECD spirit of cooperation.

In the first example, OECD members managed to overcome their 'visceral' objections, and since 1988 OECD has been publishing a detailed annual report (Agricultural Policies, Markets and Trade: Monitoring and Outlook) on the comparative state of farm subsidies in each member country. By making 'hidden' information available and allowing for objective comparison of country performances, this report has had a steadily growing impact on debate.

By contrast, one major member or another has blocked repeated initiatives at a similar undertaking on industrial subsidies. We shall see below what light these two stories can shed on the concept.

## Agricultural Subsidies

From its earliest days, the European Community has had in place a set of policies for encouraging agricultural output. The initial challenge was to overcome food shortages and restore production to its pre-war levels. Leaders were determined that they should never again be dependent on distant sources of supply, in case the 'cold war' should erupt into open hostilities. Fear of a naval blockade was felt nowhere more strongly than in Finland, where agriculture is protected and subsidized at a very high level.

European farm support is based essentially on shoring up market prices through variable import levies and export subsidies. This is one of the principal mechanisms of the Common Agricultural Policy (CAP). As a result, prices remain high even if output rises. Predominantly industrial countries thus find themselves financing agricultural growth in EC countries that are better suited to farming. Europe is in this respect a protectionist stronghold.

This situation is a constant source of irritation to American and Canadian farm lobbies, as well as those of Australia and New Zealand. During the 1970s and the early 1980s, these countries exerted constant pressure on European nations to abandon its agricultural policy. They saw it as costly and economically distorting, to the detriment of more efficient and competitive producers elsewhere in the world. The Europeans retorted that farm subsidies in the United States amounted to some US$ 60 billion, a figure they considered astronomical and that, they charged, betrayed the real motive of North Americans, which was to increase their market share.

This is an extraordinarily complicated technical issue, since it is difficult to compare the costs and effects of the measures taken by each country and (in the case of federations such as Canada) by every province or state. The Canadian provinces of Quebec and Ontario, for example, control milk prices through 'supply management' schemes. These provinces assign each producer an output quota and impose stiff penalties if that quota is exceeded. This means, in turn, that imports must also be subject to quotas, otherwise the sacrifice demanded of local producers would be in vain. Is this merely an elegant euphemism for subsidizing domestic output, much as the EC does, or is it, as Canadian farmers believe, a remarkable mechanism intended solely to reduce the devastating hazards of *laissez faire*?

It is probable that the debate would still be dragging on were it not for renewed criticism of the CAP within the EC. Complaints were raised that it was costly for consumers and taxpayers alike. Even more important, it came to be seen as providing support to large, efficient producers while doing little to improve incomes for small farmers or to offer effective aid to disadvantaged rural areas (Chavranski, 1997: 92).

In the end, under the impact of peer pressure, OECD members agreed that the Secretariat should shed some light on this discussion. The item was accordingly placed on the organization's agenda. The Secretariat was to play its role in accordance with the method and procedures discussed in Section 4.

After repeated and fruitless attempts to compile comparable statistics, the OECD agriculture directorate had no choice but to innovate and to invent a new operational concept. Basing itself on "incontestable technical foundations"(Chavranski, 1997: 92) , the Secretariat developed a method for calculating producer subsidy equivalents (PSE) and consumer subsidy equivalents (CSE). This calculation includes all monetary transfers that each country offers its farmers and livestock producers, as well as support measures that are the equivalents of subsidies. In 1988, the Secretariat published its first report on this subject.

To nearly universal surprise, this report revealed the full measure of farm support provided by all OECD members. The total figure for farm support of various kinds in OECD countries in 1986 was set at US$ 302 billion, against total output of US$534 billion (based on farm gate prices), or 56.5% of output value. It represented more than 2.3% of total GDP. In some countries, notably Japan, the distortion is even higher (as much as 70%). The analysis showed that every farmer was being subsidized to the tune of US$ 10,000 in the European Union, US$ 16,000 in the United States, and US$ 8,000 in Canada. These practices were obviously causing significant economic distortions not only domestically but also in international trade. Another OECD body, the Club du Sahel, showed that these subsidies were having a depressing impact on developing country producers. Studies by the Club revealed that in the 1980s, Sahelian cattle herders lost their traditional meat market in *Côte d'Ivoire* in favour of subsidized meat exported from the EU.

It was not OECD itself that undertook to negotiate the details of measures to reform these practices. The organization merely recommended to its members that they try their best to do so gradually. But "by highlighting the tremendous burden on taxpayers and consumers, as reflected in the PSE calculations, it had in hand a powerful lever for promoting agricultural policy reform" (Chavranski, 1997: 95). The Secretariat's annual monitoring report has become a key document for objectively assessing progress, while highlighting examples of backsliding and broken promises.

This move had an impact on the Uruguay Round trade negotiations of the late 1980s. At that time, the disagreements dividing the Europeans and the Americans were so deep and so serious (not to mention the suspicions surrounding Japanese protectionism), that GATT negotiations seemed doomed to failure. Indeed, the creation of the World Trade Organization in 1991 may never have come about had it not been for this injection of transparency.

It is also noteworthy that the OECD Secretariat, in inventing the PSE, was providing far more than a statistical indicator: it was in fact laying the basis for a common language among member countries. The PSE now serves as a kind of "Esperanto" for dealing with agricultural support policies.

In short, we have here an example of the complexities and the importance of peer pressure for defining a common agenda and establishing rules for monitoring it. To overcome the impasse, European states that derive fewer advantages from CAP would have had to exert strong pressure on its net beneficiaries. Otherwise, any single member could have blocked progress for a long time on this issue. It is also an example of the central role that information and transparency can play in improving the economy, as discussed in Chapter 2.

Last but not least, it gives us an idea of how difficult it is to demonstrate the value of prevention efforts when those efforts are successful. There has been modest progress since that time, despite heavy pressure from farm lobbies. Subsidies in 2001 represented only 1.3% of GDP, and accounted for only 54% of the total value of agricultural output. These may be modest gains, but the situation could certainly have been a lot worse.

### Industrial Subsidies

On the other hand, things do not always turn out so well in a network. Consider the following history of failure, as recounted by Chavranski (1997: 91):

"In the early 1980s, a few countries, led by the United States, brought pressure within the organization to improve the transparency of industrial subsidies. The objective was, first, to develop an overall view of the importance of subsidies in each member country, with the underlying but not explicit idea that they might eventually be phased out. This was a key chapter in structural adjustment policies. At the time, France objected and the project remained bogged down until it was revised by a compromise in 1987. Since then, there has been considerable progress in the course of peer reviews aimed at drawing international comparisons.

"Paradoxically, the current situation is diametrically opposed to that of the early 1980s. European countries are eager to pursue the project, while the United States and Canada, citing institutional differences between centralized and federal countries, have declared it impossible to provide information on subsidies provided at the state or provincial level - which, according to available data, are far from negligible. For these two countries, the initial results of the exercise were a surprise, and quite different from what they expected, and they are now seeking to rein in the project. In any case, significant methodological difficulties remain, relating in particular to the existence of indirect subsidies through the taxation system that are not easy to pin down.

"Efforts are now confined to analyzing the economic effects of subsidies on the industrial sectors of countries for which adequate information is available. This represents a significant backtracking from the original goal of transparency. This example is fairly typical of the behaviour of certain member countries, and of their capacity to shift their stance when the results of an exercise they supported turn out to be different from what they expected."[2]

Here is what game theory has to say on this subject:

"Cooperation is not the only equilibrium of the repeated game. Suppose one of the firms doggedly charges a low price, regardless of what its rival does. Then the best the rival can do is charge that low price too. [In essence, that is what continues to happen concerning subsidies to industry among OECD member nations.] Game theory does not predict that cooperation occurs in a repeated game; it says only that the repetition makes cooperation possible. Many outcomes are consistent with all the players behaving rationally, and it is possible to be trapped in a low-level equilibrium. Cooperation is just one of the outcomes of a repeated game. The conclusion is therefore regrettably indeterminate." To the related question, "Does it pay to be trustworthy?" the

---

2. It should be noted that this particular issue is now under the responsibility of the World Trade Organization. Using a different approach may result in changing this particular practice, which in essence, contradicts all fundamental rules of fair trade among nations.

answer is "maybe" (McMillan, 1992: 30). This is the reality in any network, including OECD. Therefore, the remarkable feature that should be highlighted is the fact that it has worked consistently for so many important occasions. The fact that at times it does not work should be taken as a natural variation.

## SECTION 3
## CONSENSUAL DISCIPLINE AND DYNAMIC TENSION

### 3.1 Maintaining Balance

Dynamic tension is what creates equilibrium and balance in a network. Forces must at all times be kept in balance, as one cannot count on hierarchy to compensate occasional or permanent loss in balance.

One could argue that within each OECD country, government institutions are kept healthy by constantly being confronted with permanent tension created by conflicting interests and interest groups, as we have seen in the previous example. Agricultural policymakers, for example, are confronted with pressures from farmers, food processors and related industries, and consumer and other interest groups (including their own bureaucracy). This tension balances itself out more or less (sometimes less) over a long time period, so that legislation and adopted practice remain more or less fair to each segment of society. This tension is also reflected within OECD itself. Each country delegate is moved and prompted to adopt positions that, over time, are bound to reflect conflicting national interests.

Changes in the equilibrium, however, are to be expected. They are often the result of strong political forces, and there is nothing anyone in the OECD Secretariat can or should do about this. For example, the Thatcher and Reagan eras, in conjunction with the end of the Cold War, brought about a shift away from many Welfare State creeds and ideas. This push by two conservative leaders opened a general quest for structural adjustments among most if not all OECD members in the 1980s and 1990s. One must recognize that the fulcrum has moved somewhat to the right. It is nevertheless the function of OECD to challenge political fads where it can, and try to illuminate the issues with evidence and nuance.

A long 'rivalry' went on, for example, between those advocating a strict economic approach in the public sector, and those who sought a broader view, balancing policy effectiveness with budgetary efficiency. Classical economists, believing in the virtue of the 'invisible hand', and of the effectiveness of market competition to keep costs down, argued that the private sector was more efficient at delivering services than heavy bureaucracies. They persuaded OECD members to privatize many government-owned organizations and to seek ways to reduce further the overall cost of government. In some cases, governments even privatized natural monopolies, such as municipal water systems, for example, thus losing the leverage of competition to maintain discipline and keep prices down. In addition, as private corporations are bound to maximize profits and not redistribution, social problems could be expected to emerge following privatization. To continue on the same example, municipalities had traditionally found ways and means to give access to water even to impoverished citizens. Obviously, private companies could not be expected to do the same, but targeted fiscal transfers could compensate. However, opponents argued that targeting a segment of population is laden with problems and heavy costs, and therefore not always feasible. Secondly, many sectors in which the government was present were involving externalities (energy) or concerned public goods (water), in which case the government can be more efficient as it internalizes the externalities. Furthermore market imperfections and the results of market failures have a tendency to constantly affect the same segment of society more than the others. In other words, the single-minded pursuit of 'budgetary efficiency' needed to be balanced by social, political, and other considerations.

To rally a majority vote, it is necessary to convince only half of the participants plus one, and this in essence is less of a tedious task than convincing everyone, as required under the consensus rule. In addition, in a situation requiring consensus, any less-concerned participating country can wait until all the others have committed themselves and then demand an enormous 'price' to cast its vote with them. If a game is played only once, then the consensus rule gives enormous power to the last one in. But this tactic is unlikely to work in a repeated game. "Once a game is played many times by the same players it acquires a past and a future. Retaliations are in order and, in fact, constitute the principal means to instil corporate discipline" (McMillan, 1992: 29).

Even this factor, however, becomes less and less important as time goes by and the same players regularly interact. After a number of iterations, a collective behaviour will have been developed and a shared language arrived at. An agreed and generally unwritten form of self-imposed discipline arises. Obvious misbehaviour is simply chastised by the others and in the worst case the offending member may be ostracized. Eventually, when one player refuses to join a consensus, a clear message is being given to the group: it has no choice but to listen carefully to the arguments and build a consensus that takes them into consideration. "In the search for consensus, then, everyone is obliged to make concessions and a compromise will finally emerge, after all the essential concerns (to the extent they are mutually compatible) have been taken into consideration" (Chavranski, 1997: 43).

## 3.2 Mechanisms for Softening the Rigours of Consensus

Occasions will arise when concessions and compromises will not suffice. The full consensus rule must then be bent. This is one of the ways by which a network moves ahead and refuses to be held hostage to the slowest, or to what is called the "rule of the lowest common denominator." OECD has harboured a number of mechanisms to foster flexibility and to encourage its members to adopt in all circumstances a proactive attitude, to move as far as it can go to promote reforms and to seek, jointly and individually, the best means to arrive at it. There are four ways of softening the demands and the obstacles inherent in the consensus rule.

*Rule of Exception to the Consensus*

In all cases, the meeting chair will allow the discussion to continue (perhaps over several months) until there are no further formal objections. A member may then simply sit silent so as not to prevent a consensus from being reached. This approach is sometimes less binding than a formal vote. On the other hand, a member may formally abstain. In this case, the 'decision' (or the 'recommendation') will not apply to that member, a situation that differs from the rules of the European Union, where a majority vote (in certain fields) is equally binding on all members (Bonvin, 1998: 50).

*Downgrading the Degree of Formality of Commitments*

OECD has the power to take 'decisions' that, by virtue of the OECD Charter, are binding on all members. Although the Charter does not provide for any sanction mechanism, these decisions engage the political honour of states, and for this reason they are always taken seriously. States are expected to take all the steps necessary to ensure that obligations assumed in this way are effectively respected. Experience has shown that they do respect such commitments. As a result, every article of a 'decision' will be examined and debated in the finest detail. Consensus in such cases is usually a long time in coming. It is therefore a fairly rare form of commitment. Bonvin counts at most 40 decisions since the founding of the organization. Two of the best known and most important concern the 1961 Codes of Liberalization of Capital Movements and of Current Invisible Operations. These codes have had a major impact on the development of economies, by supporting and reinforcing the process of economic opening, as Chavranski has so elegantly and persuasively shown.

OECD is more likely to produce recommendations, which are easier to negotiate and are, moreover, generally followed by the members. They come into force as soon as the Council adopts them, and they are not dependent on any time-consuming and obstacle-strewn ratification process. They are applied in a flexible manner that allows member states to apply them gradually. Peer reviews exert sustained pressure to ensure that this happens.

The Council may also issue declarations, the legal import of which is poorly defined but which, as with everything OECD does, will in the end have considerable moral force. In 1997, 130 declarations were in force. This reflects the fact that the Council can take supplementary decisions on the application of the declarations and can decide later how they are to be applied. Each new stage therefore serves to refine and reinforce the initial consensus.

Finally, OECD members may agree on arrangements or what are more generally known as *"actes innommés*/gentlemen's agreements." These do not carry signatures but are 'officialized' by the Council, which takes note of them and records them in its minutes (Bonvin, 1998: 53 and Chavranski, 1997: 57). There will even be occasions where the Council decides not to take note of an *acte innommé*, if it involves a particularly delicate political issue. In this way, discussions within the 'arrangement' may gradually lead to a consensus that is more precise and operational. The 'arrangement' with which aid specialists are most familiar is that regarding the use of export credits. In fact it eventually came to be known as the 'Consensus.' Its aim was to prevent governments from using tied bilateral aid as a disguised subsidy for their exports, contrary to the spirit and rules of agreements concluded among OECD members (see Section 3.3, Chapter 1).

This simple terminology reveals the flexibility and the subtlety that guide the actions of the organization and that allow it to progress step-by-step as far as possible.

*Nomenclature of the Committees*

The Council is the supreme authority of the organization. Every country has a representative on the Council, with the rank and status of Ambassador, who heads the country's delegation to the organization. It is the Council that takes every important decision, that creates the committees, and that adopts the annual budget.

In most cases, every national delegation will have a number of counsellors with specialized functions, whose mandate is to follow the work of the committees (subsidiary bodies created by the Council) and to prepare reports that will be routed to each of the ministries concerned. In total, national delegations had nearly 600 such diplomats in 1997. In the committees, delegates not only discuss new ideas but also examine progress in certain fields such as economic policy, international trade, science and technology, development assistance, or financial markets.

The structure of committees and working parties is another indicator of the organization's great flexibility. A number of working parties have been established, following the course of events. A consensus had to be struck every time, because every committee requires the mobilization of the Secretariat capacity, and in many cases it implies the creation of a new unit within the Secretariat and consequent costs for member country delegations.

In addition to the Committees, the following entities coexist within the Organization, as established by Vinde in his 1998 internal report:

- Working party: a subsidiary body of a committee. Some working parties operate by electronic communications, without actual meetings, and are referred to as electronic working parties.

- Working group (or possibly, a subgroup): subsidiary body of a working party.

- Task force: an open-ended subsidiary body set up by a Committee or a Working party with a specific and time-bound mandate.

- Workshop: a meeting convened by a subsidiary body for a one-time discussion of a particular topic. Occasionally the terms seminars, ad hoc meeting, special session are used for the same purpose.

- Conference: identical to a workshop but with broader participation and usually at a higher level.

- Forum: a subsidiary body meeting on a regular basis linked to an OECD Committee with participation of non-member countries, other international organizations, and the private sector, particularly, but not exclusively, in connection with the outreach program.

- Expert group: a group with limited participation set up by a Committee or a Working party to study a specific issue, and composed of participants chosen for their particular expertise.

- Steering group: in certain cases there is the need to create a subsidiary body with limited participation to supervise and guide certain activities/ projects on behalf of a Committee, a Working party, or a Working group.

- In addition to all these groups, every year sees an "OECD Ministerial": it is, in essence, a Council meeting held at the ministerial level rather than at the Ambassador level. It brings together ministers of finance and of foreign affairs and trade from all member countries. This ministerial conference discusses the major issues affecting the economies of member states and of the world in general. When deemed necessary, any Committee may be held at the ministerial level.

*Initiatives Financed on a Voluntary Basis*

The annual operating budget of the organization is based on the planned activities and work of the committees (as well as the other subsidiary working groups identified above). Every participating country is expected to pay a quota that is determined by a complex burden-sharing formula The Organization's expenses are shared among its members in accordance with a formula based on gross domestic product during the most recently available three-year period. This principle is subject to three modifications: the smallest countries (Iceland and Luxembourg) may not pay less than 0.10% of the total budget each, while the largest country, the United States, will never pay more than 25%. The size of every other member's contribution is thus calculated from the remainder (74.8% of the total) (Chavranski, 1997: 69). This common budget is discussed and approved by the Council, and it is known as "Part One" of the OECD budget.

Over the years, OECD has expanded its field of action and has agreed to play host to a number of entities that are financed by a limited number of members. As some see it, this plethora of agencies sows disorder and fosters the impression that OECD is a bloated bureaucracy. They argue that the organization would do better to focus on what they see as its principal mandate. Here again, the organization regularly makes efforts to simplify its administration and reduce its costs. It is not our purpose to defend one view or another concerning the existence of the committees or agencies, including those known as "Part Two." It must be admitted, however, that this method has three important advantages.

The first and most obvious advantage is to accommodate the desires of some members without requiring the search for an undoubtedly elusive consensus. The entities created in this way with the support of certain member countries are covered under "Part Two," as opposed to "Part One," i.e. the part of the Secretariat's operating budget to which all members contribute. This is the case, for example, with the International Energy Agency (IEA). The IEA was created in the early 1970s, in the wake of the first oil shock. OECD member countries felt the need for a watching post to analyze changes in oil supply and demand as an aid to refining their energy policies. France preferred to go it alone. Thus, what would otherwise have become a Committee of the

Organization, financed annually under "Part One" of the budget, became one of the entities under Part Two of the organization's budget. It should be noted that eventually France saw to its advantage to join the IEA as a full member.

Second, the great diversity of these activities serves to involve members ever more deeply in common undertakings by allowing them to support the collective effort voluntarily, just as volunteer associations involve citizens in their community. They may provide financial support or 'in-kind' contributions toward those specific goals they believe to be critical. In the recent past, many countries have chosen to increase their voluntary contributions. It is reflected in the fact that following a series of personnel reductions, OECD still employs as many people as it did before downsizing, due to increased voluntary contributions.

*The OECD Family: A System of Concentric Circles*

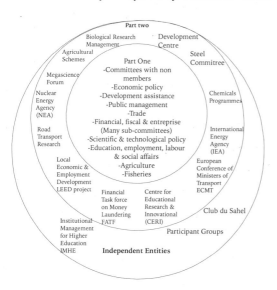

Third, we may note that these activities allow the organization to expand the scope of its moral authority into new communities, which in turn will benefit from the rigour, the methodology, and the reputation of OECD. For example, the library of documents published by the Club du Sahel includes many African authors who otherwise could scarcely have hoped to see their work distributed in European and North American capitals.

A large measure of flexibility blended with rigour becomes the true asset of this modern construct. Possibly as a result of reduced outside political pressures, combined with relative economic affluence, the consensus-based decision-making process has become increasingly unwieldy. OECD has been searching for an alternative for some years with no consensus. In the meantime, pragmatic ways are found to work around each specific obstacle.

To help understand what otherwise appears to be an extremely complex operation, OECD could be seen as a system of concentric circles (see chart). In the centre are the core activities of OECD financed by "Part One." In this core, we find all the main 'Committees' and 'Working Parties'.

There is then a second circle of activities that are closely linked to the core and generally complement it. This second circle is financed in "Part Two" of the budget. Part-two entities also contribute to meeting the general overhead expenses of the organization.

A third circle is constituted by international organizations or intergovernmental activities that for reasons of convenience have chosen to use OECD administrative rules and services, but which have an autonomous status. IMHE is recorded in 'Part Two' activities, other independent entities do not appear in the OECD budget documents.

Many participants, and a fair number of observers, find this architecture needlessly complex. It has been the subject of many internal studies and discussions in order to simplify its application and to reduce its costs. Yet rationalization implies abandoning activities that will be dear to one delegation or another, and consensus will always be elusive. Whatever the arguments pro and con a specific program feature may be, one might suggest that this plethora of arrangements and accommodations reflects, in a sense, the very nature of the organization, and as such is essential to its success.

In fact, these various forms of committees and entities as well as the various forms of commitments, act as a series of 'little tools,' the differences among which are subtle and often difficult to perceive. Their use, however, in the hands of skilled negotiators make it possible to continue flushing out small points of consensus that would otherwise have remained hidden. The sum total of all these efforts and all these partial successes helps to instil harmony and peace within the group. In a universe that is constantly changing, this array of tools would seem to be an essential factor for adaptation. Yet we must recognize that the nomenclature of entities subsidiary to the Council is rather obscure and seems at times to lack consistency. It should be emphasized however, that member countries can always do things that matter to them somewhere within OECD, something they often can't do elsewhere.

## SECTION 4

## POLICY PROCESS, BLENDING NEGOTIATIONS AND RESEARCH

The OECD policy process is itself designed to be progressive, iterative, and empirical: it follows the progress of its members, at times leading, pushing, pulling, or tugging, always moving from common knowledge to new facts, and eventually to new policies. It also makes use of state-of-the-art synthesis of knowledge on a contentious topic. It sponsors in-house or hands-off research to shed new light on a growing topic, and moves the agenda progressively in a seesaw fashion using various techniques.

The entire process can be broken down into six distinct steps or elements:

1. Agreement on a common problem to be assessed and eventually resolved.
2. Establishment of an information base for making comparisons.
3. Analysis of findings and the drawing up of conclusions.
4. Forecasts and scenarios.
5. The preparation and adoption of recommendations.
6. Evaluation through peer reviews.

Not all activities of the Organization comprise all those six elements. Many activities considered very useful by country members include only some of those. For example, between 1961 and 2001, the Secretariat only collected and compared data concerning health. Furthermore, in recent years an increased proportion of the work focuses on exchanging information and sharing experience with the view of identifying 'promising practices' or what many still refer to as 'best practices.'

Each Committee is composed of member states and chaired by the representative of one of them; it is responsible for overseeing the entire process. However, it is clearly understood that the work of a technical and scientific kind (phases 2, 3, 4 and the drafting of recommendations) is primarily the responsibility of the Secretariat. The Committee will take the lead, however, in defining the agenda, adopting recommendations, and reviewing the performance of other members.

The entire process remains at all times rigorous, subtle and, in keeping with tradition, eminently flexible.

### 4.1 Defining a Common Agenda through 'Preliminary Inquiry'

The process begins with a 'preliminary inquiry' designed to ensure that the dialogue among partners is actually feasible and viable, and that it can reach the intended goals. In essence, it is deemed feasible if all partners agree to put it on the agenda, and it is not feasible if a consensus cannot be reached. This may sound like somewhat circular logic, but it works.

Defining the question remains a most difficult task, one that may require much iteration, and may raise many questions. What is to be emphasized? What is excluded from the field of research? Are we working from the basis of a broad question with many related sub-issues, possibly concerning many fields and departments? Should we start with a very limited and operational question, and elaborate it as we move along? Is it a field that is already well studied by other international organizations? Will further research on the question then be redundant or complementary? How strong and how well entrenched are national vested interest groups?

All these questions are obviously linked to national interests and to specific lobby groups, which, at least in some cases, are likely to win or lose depending on the definition adopted by OECD.

Once the parties have agreed on the topic, applying the 'OECD process' then involves the four steps of a more scientific nature, which fall clearly under the responsibility of the Secretariat: a) establishing a database; b) analyzing findings; c) forecasts and scenarios; and d) preparing recommendations (Bonvin, 1998: 56). This typology is typical of scientific research—but as it applies to the resolution of national and international political problems, the research approach taken may differ from the methods of the academic world. Its focus is often broader and multidisciplinary. In OECD parlance, this is referred to as 'horizontal.'

The Secretariat reports to the committee upon completing each of these steps. The ensuing discussions will allow member countries to commit themselves progressively and more deeply to the path of reform.

## 4.2 Establishing Reliable and Comparable Databases

Once members have identified a common problem, the Secretariat is charged with constructing a reliable database of statistics on the subject. The Secretariat must not only compile the data supplied by member states, but must also "make these data mutually compatible in order to facilitate international comparisons over a long period. To do this, it must develop standards and classifications" (Chavranski, 1997: 19).

This groundwork can itself produce results that are sometimes surprising. They may bring to light facts of which governments were previously unaware. They may also reveal discrepancies when the variables stray particularly far from the mean. The publication of reliable and transparent statistical data helps national and international investors as well as economic operators in general to take decisions. This means that capital will move more freely and effectively, thanks to the confidence and certainty generated. For example, reliable statistics on tourist movements are needed for investments in new hotels to materialize (this is fully discussed in Chapter 2).

Finally, these studies may give rise to new concepts and new ways of understanding and describing reality: a sort of *Esperanto* for governance. As described earlier, (see example Agricultural Subsidies) the Secretariat had to invent new indicators, the PSE and the CSE, in order to compare different forms of farm subsidies. A second example of innovation can be seen in the development of Purchasing Power Parity (PPP, see Box 3.5), which has become an essential concept for comparing economies while correcting for distortions induced by exchange rates.

## 4.3 Analyzing the Data

Based on the data it has collected, the Secretariat conducts the necessary studies. There are many kinds of studies that may be appropriate to specific circumstances, ranging from the preparation of synthetic summaries, through inter-country comparisons, to original research. These studies are similar to academic research—after all, OECD analysts generally have the same academic training as university researchers, but they must first and foremost answer all the questions posed by the decision-makers. The scope of their analysis may therefore go beyond the normal bounds of a scientific research project.

The conclusions and recommendations will then have to be fed into the process specific to the OECD committee, which remains the final client for all this work. The organization may also use the analysis "to criticize national policies, in particular on the basis of comparisons with the policies and outcomes of other member countries..." (Chavranski, 1997: 21). This approach in fact constitutes an unprecedented social innovation.

## 4.4 Forecasting

As an aid to decision-making and policy formulation, the Secretariat is often expected to extend its analysis over time in order to show member states the foreseeable consequences of current policies or of modifications to them. This is common practice for economic assessments.

This forecasting work has become the hallmark of the organization. It makes it possible indirectly "to test the quality of studies and analysis on the

## Box 3.5

### What are Price Purchasing Parities?

"The first major study of PPPs was undertaken under the auspices of the OEEC in the early 1950s when Milton Gilbert and Irving B. Kravis produced their pioneering report on An International Comparison of National Products and the Purchasing Power of Currencies, (OEEC, 1954). In the 1960s and 1970s the main focus of this work shifted to the Statistical Offices of the United Nations and the European Communities. However, in 1982 OECD became convinced of the need to calculate a new benchmark set of PPPs for its member countries, partly because of the large movements in the exchange rates between the currencies of some of its Member countries in the 1980s. Exchange rates are liable to change much more rapidly, and in greater amounts, than purchasing power parities whose movements tend to be gradual and small. Nominal figures based on exchange rates do not provide the information that many users seek to obtain concerning real differences in productivity or living standards" (Hill,1989, p. 2-3).

In their simplest form, PPPs are relative prices that show the ratio of prices in national currencies for the same good or service in different countries. A well-known example of a one-product comparison is The Economist's Big Mac Currency index, presented by that newspaper as 'burgernomics,' whereby 'the Big Mac PPP' is the exchange rate that would mean hamburgers cost the same in America as abroad. The OECD-Eurostat PPPs, however, are calculated not only for individual products but also for product groups and for each of the various levels of aggregation up to and including GDP. The purpose is similar to obtain currency conversion rates that eliminate the differences in price levels between countries, and to permit volume comparisons.

A great challenge with such comparisons is that volumes or prices have to be compared across economies that may be very different. Goods and services that are characteristic in one country may be uncharacteristic in another one, and yet common ground has to be found to make meaningful comparisons. Regular benchmark surveys help keep product lists up to date so as to maximize comparability.

Deviations between PPPs and income based on exchange rates can be considerable, as can be seen in Table 1 below. For example, Russia's income per capita is only 6% of the OECD average when calculated by the exchange rate method, but it rises to 26% using the PPP method. The conventional exchange rate method generally tends to overstate living standards in rich countries and to understate them in poor countries" (Chavranski,1997, p. 21).

The calculations of PPPs are described in the OECD publication: *Purchasing Power Parities and Real Expenditures.*

basis of which these forecasts are made. Their credibility depends on the discrepancies between the figures forecast in the past and the figures actually observed" (Bonvin, 1998: 60). Thus, before discussing the recommendations or debating changes in habits and laws, countries must first become familiar with the comparative data so that they can understand and discuss the analysis and ultimately assess the impact of the various scenarios.

## Tabel 3.1

### PPP and International Comparisons of GDP

| Selected Countries | Per Capita of GDP OECD Members' Average = 100 | |
| --- | --- | --- |
| | Indices based on PPPs | Indices based on Exchange Rates |
| Canada (G-7) | 117 | 94 |
| France (G-7) | 102 | 106 |
| Germany (G-7) | 109 | 114 |
| Hungary (new member) | 51 | 21 |
| Italy (G-7) | 106 | 91 |
| Japan (G-7) | 110 | 158 |
| Mexico (new member) | 37 | 22 |
| Poland (new member) | 40 | 18 |
| Switzerland | 127 | 161 |
| United Kingdom (G-7) | 103 | 109 |
| United States (G-7) | 149 | 150 |
| Russian Federation (G-8) | 26 | 6 |
| Ukraine | 16 | 3 |

Source: OECD, 2002.

## 4.5 Recommendations

Unlike the previous steps, preparing recommendations is in reality more of an art than a science. It involves applying know-how to the results of a 'sober' analysis of the observed facts, while constantly avoiding dogmatic approaches and putting forward proposals that will lead to real improvements, with due regard to the existing political situation and the absorptive capacity of each state. These recommendations are discussed in detail by member countries, although they may give only cursory attention to the preceding documents. Primarily, this reflects the fact that monitoring will be based on the recommendation, and so it is important for countries to make commitments that they can respect, since their evaluation will depend on it.

Throughout the process, then, there is a subtle play between the pressure that countries exert on each other to move the issue forward and reach consensus, and the prospect of peer review, the final stage of the entire process, since it is that review that will determine whether each member has respected the consensus.

## 4.6 Peer Review

Peer review is the keystone for this architecture, which is at once fragile and robust. It is a highly structured process, and its rules are never left to chance, given the delicate nature of its task, which is to enlist commitment from the governments of sovereign states.

It is worth recalling that this procedure was imposed on states that were just emerging from a long period of unceasing warfare. We must appreciate how much tact and diplomacy was needed to bring about such a change in values and behaviour. At the same time, we need to grasp the scope of the challenges that had to be overcome and that must never be underestimated, although they are today taken for granted, as is economic prosperity. On this point, analysts who have looked closely at OECD are unanimous in recognizing that the experience of more than four decades shows "by all accounts that the pressure exerted by one or several states is the principal driving force behind the organization's thinking and action, despite the fact that there is no mechanism, even in the case of decisions, for penalizing violations of solemn obligations" (Chavranski, 1997: 32). All of these intersecting methods serve to reinforce the idea that indirect but sustained effort is worth more than a single spectacular act.

Peer review has been taken farthest in the all-important economic committee, which remains the point of reference on this subject. The method can also be applied for evaluating social, health, or environmental policies. Regardless of the subject, the basic rules remain the same. The process of peer review will be examined in detail in Appendix 1, but the first process of peer review in OECD is well described by Bonvin and Morrisson (1998) and is reproduced below.

*The First Example of Peer Review:*
*The Examination of Economic Situations*

"The Committee for the Examination of Economic Situations and Development Problems was created in 1961, to examine annually the economic situation of each country, based on the principle that every member is required to keep the organization informed of any significant change in its economic policy.

"The working method of this committee and of the Secretariat servicing it is worthy of attention, because it reflects what makes OECD's work special.

"A draft report is prepared by the Secretariat on the basis of missions to the country concerned. Information (statistics, trends) is compiled using detailed questionnaires. OECD experts also hold meetings with senior economic policy officials. For several years, a structural dimension (pension system, labour markets) has been added to the studies and the national officials responsible for these questions are also asked to contribute. The draft report is then sent to the national authorities, several weeks before the committee meeting.

"The committee session lasts a full day (Chavranski and other participants have expressed the opinion that this is clearly too short to discuss fully such complex and rich reports) and the delegation of the country under examination consists of senior officials of the departments and agencies concerned. It presents its viewpoint and notes the aspects on which it may disagree with the draft report. For any examination, two countries will be named as examiners and will pose a series of questions. The representatives of other countries may then intervene. The examination is divided into different chapters. The committee chair plays an important role, which is to draw out a consensus, in particular on the conclusions. This process is characterized by what we may call 'mutual pressure' or 'peer pressure.' In fact, every country faces pressure from other countries to ensure that the direction of its national policies will converge with those of its own. An examining country, which may be tempted to take radical positions, must never forget that it too will be examined one day. Moreover, the regular schedule of examinations helps keep countries to their commitments: if the country has undertaken before the committee to move in a certain direction, it will be held accountable at the time of the next examination.

"A definitive report is then prepared between the Secretariat and the country examined, and is sent to the committee for written approval. It will be published in English and French, and often in the language of the country if it is different. This publication generally receives wide media coverage, because it represents an x-ray of the country's economic situation that is as objective as possible." (Bonvin, 1998: 77-78).

Finally, as noted by Thygesen (2002), the OECD peer review process has a number of distinct advantages over the review process of institutions such as the IMF:

- "First, there is more interaction with relevant national policy on the basis of the Secretariat's draft report;

- "Then there is a useful element of having, in a number of cases, such as with the EDRC, two examining countries (which is the closest thing to pure peer pressure that exists in the international system);

- "Furthermore, the subsequent process of revising and approving the report gives some ownership by the country to the final report (though this redrafting does consume a lot of time);

## Table 3.2

*List of Country Peer Reviews in the OECD*

| Subject | Frequency | Review Team | Review Committee |
|---------|-----------|-------------|------------------|
| Macroeconomic & Structural Issues | 12-18 months | Secretariat | EDRC (2 examiner countries) (see annex Chapter 4) |
| Environment Performance | 6 years | Secretariat with consultants and 3 country examiners | Working Party on Environment Performance |
| Aid Policy | 3 years | Secretariat with 2 country examiners | Development Assistance Committee (see annex Chapter 4) |
| Foreign Direct Investment | 11 countries in 3 years | Secretariat | CMIT/CIME and Council Recommendations |
| Competition Policy | 2 countries reviewed per year | Secretariat | CLP |
| Agricultural Policy | One major study per country followed by annual monitoring | Secretariat | Joint Working Party of Agriculture and Trade Committee (2 examiner countries) |
| Education Policy | On request | 3 individual examiners and secretariat | Education Committee |
| Science & Technology Policies | On request | Secretariat and team of 3 to 4 country's individuals | Special session of CSTP in the capital |
| Regional Policies | 1 country selected every year | Secretariat, consultant and (about) 10 members of Working Part | Working Party on Regional Policy |
| **Thematic Reviews** | | | |
| Regulatory Reforms | 1 major study per country | Secretariat | |
| Tertiary Education | 4-6 countries per year | Secretariat & consultant | Education Committee |
| Public Employment per year | 4-6 countries consultant | Secretariat & | ELSAC Services/Labour Market |
| Social Assistance Policy | 5-7 countries per year | Secretariat & consultant | ELSAC |
| Transition from Initial Education to Working Life | 6 countries per year | Secretariat & consultant | Education Committee |
| Early Childhood Education & Care | 6 countries per year | Secretariat & consultant | Education Committee |

*Source*: The information in this table is extracted from Vinde's internal report, 1998.

- "The organisation has also a manageable size (for example, IMF 133, OECD 30) and a limited diversity of membership (which is particularly beneficial in that it is difficult to keep up to date in technical areas);

- "Lastly, there is the continuity (which is typically 3 years for the EDRC) and the experience of the national officials that countries send as representatives (and examiners);

- "On the other hand, the OECD Secretariat has fewer resources to produce country surveys at regular intervals than other institutions using the same process, and this is important, for the determinant of the standing of the institution is the quality of the staff work.

"Beyond their intrinsic interest, the economic analyses produced by the OEEC played a more enduring role. In effect, they accustomed national authorities to providing honest and comparable information on their economies, based on questionnaires prepared by the Secretariat, and then studying and comparing the collected data jointly. This exercise gave them a further occasion to think about their policies and their respective forecasts, and in the end it led to a degree of coordination, as it became increasingly difficult to maintain sharp discrepancies once they were brought to light. The unanimity required for approving the economic reports, although it made the task more difficult, also worked in this direction. This gradually gave rise to habits and indeed disciplines that would be further developed within the OECD" (Chavranski, 1997: 11).

## SECTION 5
## SUPPORTIVE POLICIES

Gravitational forces and counter weights
at play in a gothic cathedral

## Box 3.6

### *Peer Review, a Keystone of the OECD Architecture*

Architects of the Gothic age used the flying buttress to reinforce the walls of cathedrals. This ingenious mechanism made it possible to increase the height of walls, which otherwise would have pulled away and collapsed under the enormous weight of the roof vaulting. If the walls begin to separate, this cancels the pressure holding the vault stones together and preventing collapse. The keystone will no longer be able to play its role. This offers a good analogy for the way the OECD works: Peer Pressure acts in a sense like the stones of the vaulting, each supporting the other. Held together by the stone at the apex of the arch (the peer review), a set of partners can jointly resist the pull of gravity. The pillars, which give shape to this organization, represent the fundamental values of the institution. Finally, the foundations represent the supranational regime based on respect for human rights, democracy, and the market economy. Policies concerning Secretariat personnel and publications constitute the flying buttress in this metaphor.

## 5.1 Personnel Policy

A key factor in the OECD negotiation process is its technique for managing the Secretariat personnel. From the outset there was an agreed convention among OECD members that its secretariat would be sheltered from national interventions. Endowed with 'wise directors', the OECD Secretariat staff was therefore able to play a significant role as intermediaries in negotiations among members, and at times served as respected referees or as brokers of knowledge and of evaluations of national policies.

The Secretariat's operating rules in this complex network are thus an essential instrument of the subtle architecture that characterizes OECD, and keeps the entire system in balance.

The intellectual and moral independence of the Secretariat serves as counterweights to interest-driven pressures from member countries. In order to play its 'honest broker' role, and to provide advice that is as 'scientific' as possible, the Secretary General and staff must be recruited on the basis of their recognized knowledge, moral integrity, and impartiality. They must be protected against recriminations and possible reprisals from member states. Objectivity, professionalism, and the avoidance of conflicts of interest must form the set of values inspiring the rights and duties of the Secretariat. When filling top positions, the Secretary General is generally bound to consult the Council members. In so doing, he must make judgment calls as delegations often argue in favour of candidates from their own country, or from their region. With respect to ongoing personnel activities, such as promotion, and contract renewals, as it is the case for program activities, the organization generally works well and objectively.

The personnel makeup of member country administrations is constantly changing. This poses a significant stumbling block to the proper functioning of the network. New arrivals are generally not aware of how the machine functions: they are likely to assume that it works like other bureaucracies with which they are familiar, and they may be unaware of its most fundamental rules. They can hardly count on older members to give them the induction they need, and this role must fall to the organization's staff. Thus, the stability of Secretariat staff is another essential ingredient for keeping things in balance.

## 5.2 Role of a 'Wise Director'

Professionally, the Secretariat is recognized for its highly qualified staff. Its personnel, in turn, have taken care to uphold standards of excellence in their work and to safeguard the overall professional integrity of the organization. The insulation of the OECD Secretariat from the cross-current of national and international politics gives it a unique professional status and role, analogous in its own context to that of the German Bundesbank in that country's economy. In the 1980s, the OECD Secretariat issued a "Proposed Economic Survey" of the UK that was highly critical of its policies, which infuriated the British Prime Minister. She demanded the Director of the Economic Division, a British citizen at the time, be removed from office. Of course, the Secretary General refused. In the end, some moderate language was found to placate the prime minister's anger, and the Director kept his position.

What role does the Secretariat play in this regard? Each specialized division of the OECD Secretariat in Paris is charged with the task of moving the agenda forward in its own domain. Divisions have developed through trial and error specific traditions and skills that are passed on from director to director and from team to team. In a metaphorical manner, we will then refer to the behaviour of the 'wise director'.

Building a common language is a major task for the secretariat of such a network. Implicit in most of the technical work is the concern for establishing common definitions. This is what is achieved when building a data bank. Disparities in data collection are reduced through the persistent work of OECD analysts. Each concept is scrutinized and eventually harmonized before a meaningful dialogue can take place on how to improve any specific policy. As we pointed out when dealing with the example of subsidies to agriculture, the creation of the PSE was equivalent to the definition of a new *Esperanto* word, one that everybody could use with the certainty of being understood.

But this does not suffice: culture, history, values, habits, and old conventions colour most words used by civil servants, and this can lead to misunderstandings and suspicions. As the example in the box below will reveal, even words as standard as 'preparing detail construction designs' can hide many traps.

## Box 3.7
### *Design and Supervision: Same Words, Different Traditions*

In North America, architects and engineers are generally called upon to design a building and ensure the supervision of the construction company. It is an accepted convention that the architect or, depending on the case, the engineer will remain accountable for every bit of calculation and design. The specifications used to tender all construction tasks are precise and detailed, leaving virtually no place for interpretation. The bidding contractors must comply with the specifications; the engineer must guarantee such compliance to his client. Thus, supervision is thorough and tedious. A representative from the engineering firm will be on site at all times, checking that the quality of the concrete complies with specifications and that it is poured according to norms. If a bridge were to fall, for example, the inquest would first look into the soundness of the design and the thoroughness of supervision. Therefore, engineering costs tend to add up to about 10% of total costs in North America, a higher proportion than in certain countries with different traditions.

In the case of France, for example, the system is based on an entirely different process and state institutions such as Veritas are responsible for the design quality of all public works. The architect or the engineer is mainly in charge of drafting the overall design and putting it to tender. Prospective contractors are expected to do all necessary calculations before they bid. However, the state control firm must also do these calculations and to this end they maintain a large staff of drafters, architects, and engineers. Contractors often simply wait for this work to be done and use the calculations from the state supervisory organization in order to prepare their bid. However, in case of accidents, the inquiry will first look at the work performed by the contractor. Thus, during construction, the architect or the engineer will show up often enough but no more than is necessary to assure him that his design is being properly followed.

It follows that a Canadian engineering firm bidding on an African Development Bank (AfDB) project to supervise the construction of a road in former French West Africa will prepare a budget that is significantly different than that of his competing colleague from France, with the predictable result that it will be evaluated as overly expensive. Canadian firms who had seen their bids rejected over the years in favour of French firms started to lobby Canada's Foreign Ministry against the AfDB, which they wrongly suspected of foul play.

The universe of public administrations reveals countless differences not only in language but also in the whole basis on which things are done (or not done). Each country functions between formal and informal arrangements. In some cases, bureaucrats are allowed to 'tinker with the law,' to adapt it to specific circumstances, while in other countries such things 'are just not done'. This compounds the existing linguistic differences and breeds misunderstandings and suspicions.

To render things even more complicated, bureaucrats in national administrations move around regularly. Often, some key senior figures will change just when a consensus is about to emerge. As those cultural differences generate obstacles to collaboration between national representatives, the 'wise director' spends considerable time in 'pointing the way' to various national representatives so they will know how to influence each other and unblock protracted negotiations. The director's role as a discreet mediator is critical, and second only to authoritative expertise.

In essence, wise directors know they can count on persistent conflicts and contradictions to keep things in balance, and that they can then tip that balance in favour of the most sustainable policy option and enforce consensus on it. In some cases those tensions are such that they can only wait for a new equilibrium to take its effect.

However, there are shifts that may be the product of simple changes in personnel within member countries. A wise director strives constantly to rebuild the equilibrium in order to avoid policy imbalances, which are the result of corporate memory losses rather than substantial movements of the fulcrum. Many techniques are used.

It should be stressed that the success of a Committee rests as well on solid work performed by the Committee's president, who must provide overall leadership, determination, and tact. This will be discussed in Chapter 5.

## 5.3 Publication Policy

Another little known fact about OECD is that, for the past 40 years, it has been one of the largest scientific publishers in Europe. OECD's steadfast policy of publishing the research results used for policymaking has contributed to enforcing those ideas and making a meaningful statement about transparency and accountability.

As a unique forum to discuss, develop, and adjust economic and social policies, the accessibility to OECD work is crucial. The publications and statistics of OECD cover economics as well as social issues, macroeconomics, trade, education, development, science, and innovation. OECD aims at providing easy access to its research reports, conventions, working papers, country surveys, and statistics. There are over 4,000 publications in print, more than 25 statistical databases on CD-ROM and almost all can be accessed on-line.

The OECD on-line library, *Source OECD*, is also of great value. In 2001, approximately 2,000 institutions had subscribed to this library, which includes

OECD books covering 20 subjects, from Agriculture and Food to Transport, and the 24 OECD periodicals. In 2001, the American Library Association recognized this library as a "Notable Government Document" and "an invaluable resource for academic and research libraries." In addition, OECD statistics, which are collected by in-house analysts, committees, and working parties, and by national statistical agencies, are mostly available to the public through electronic and paper publications and through the Statistics Portal.

By publishing its findings, including data and statistics, OECD helps government decision-makers to adopt new measures. According to Chavranski (1997), with its diverse publications and analyses, OECD has a comparative advantage over such institutions as the World Bank and the IMF. Experts, media, and even public opinion make use of these research results thus granting to OECD a real weight in national debate (comments offered by Chavranski in his letter dated September 16, 2002).

In fact, the best-known work of the OECD may be its regular reports on the economies of its member countries. Each of the annual reviews includes an analysis of developments in the country as well as special reports and statistics. These reviews constitute valuable reference tools for governments but also for businesses, academics, and NGOs that can use these reviews in their dialogue with the government. In addition, OECD harmonizes, validates, and presents its statistics in a comparative form. Ministries and policymakers in member country governments utilize OECD statistics; academics, researchers and planners, but also journalists, NGOs, business associations and trade unions, use them and in this way they generate effective collective debate.

Through its diverse publications, OECD provides the results of numerous debates and negotiations. Some argue that the negotiation phase and the discussions leading to the achievement of an agreement should be made available to the public. On the contrary, we have argued that the debate itself should be kept private; some confidentiality has to remain. As we have mentioned in Section 1.2, part of the etiquette of OECD is that the confidentiality of debates is vigorously protected in order to build mutual trust. Finally, some may find the language used in most OECD work a bit too toned down. This may be true in some cases, but the major issues are still identified and discussed and can lead to stimulating debates in the public sphere.

## Table 3.3

### *Key OECD Publications*

| Number of publications | 4,000 | |
| --- | --- | --- |
| | • Books (including 1,000 e-books) | |
| | • 24 periodicals | |
| | • 25 statistical databases on CD-ROM | |
| Books-subjects | Agriculture and food development | Industry, services and trade |
| | Education and skills | National accounts and historical statistics |
| | Emerging economies | |
| | Employment | Nuclear energy |
| | Energy environment and sustainable development | Science and information technology |
| | Finance and investment/ insurance pensions | Social issues/migration/health statistics, sources, and methods |
| | General economics and future studies | Taxation |
| | | Territorial economy |
| | Governance | Transition economies |
| | | Transport |
| Statistics–subjects | Agriculture and fisheries | National accounts |
| | Demography and population development | Price and purchasing power parities |
| | Education and training | Public management |
| | Energy | Nuclear energy |
| | Environment | Science, technology and patents |
| | Finance | |
| | Health | Short-term economics Statistics |
| | Industry and services | Social and welfare statistics |
| | Information and communication technology | Statistical methodology |
| | | Territorial statistics |
| | International trade | Transport |
| | Labour | Non-member economies |
| | Leading indicators and tendency surveys | |

| Number of Key OECD documents available (selection): | |
| --- | --- |
| Best Practices | 75 |
| Case Studies | 298 |
| Country Surveys/Review/Guides (including Economic Surveys) | 573 |
| Guidelines | 192 |
| Policy Briefs | 151 |

*Source:* OECD 2002

## SECTION 6
## ADAPTING THE OECD METHODOLOGY TO A NEW
## CULTURAL ENVIRONMENT

From a very small group of countries, OECD has now expanded to 33 members. Other countries are 'graduating' into the select group of successful industrial economies, and may wish to join this elite club eventually. This raises a challenging question: Can OECD retain its edge and continue using the methodology that has made it successful with a much larger group? Already, some delegates and members of the Secretariat are expressing concern about OECD's absorptive capacity that they feel is stretched to its limits. The temptation is great for larger countries to create a restricted sub-group within the OECD membership. As we have just seen, the OECD method rests heavily on human relations, on bureaucrats learning together, understanding each other, and gradually learning to trust each other. This process is costly and labour intensive and the difficulties related to creating a homogeneous institutional culture are diminished if the group starts with a shared past and a common cultural background.

Should OECD members encourage the creation of regional regrouping that might be inspired by its methods? Can it be exported elsewhere? Those are challenging questions for OECD members to address.

In any case, so little has been written about the organization that very few specialists have thus far reflected on these matters, especially the complexity of transferring this unique method to another set of countries. We offer a few thoughts about the inherent difficulties related to such a challenge.

To begin with, the OEEC example clearly demonstrated the need for some intellectual and moral bases that have to be established in order to define the work to be done. It should be stressed that perhaps the best way to start is to define a broad set of rules, implicit and explicit, through which members' governments should function effectively on a continental or regional basis. It is impossible to conceive of a peer review process that is not grounded in the governance approach in a given region, or at the very least in those countries that wish to be active in the Peer Review process.

It is critical before proceeding with a transfer of techniques to take into consideration two important caveats. In order to achieve a successful adaptation, numerous elements have to be taken into account, including the internal coherence characteristic of any management system as well as the inherent difficulties related to the introduction of new values. The first considers the importance of preserving the intrinsic or essential linkages, to the proper operation of a system and, the second reminds us that it is practically impossible to simultaneously introduce several new values in the behaviour of societies.

## 6.1 Respect for Essential Linkages

Any management system, such as, for example, Peer Review, the manufacturing of cars 'just in time,' or even management by objectives, includes aspects that are essential to the functioning of such a system and which we cannot ignore without endangering the operations of the whole. This is what Berger (1973) calls intrinsic linkages. But for each of these systems, there also exist parts that are not essential to the operations and that can be modified or abandoned without creating problems. These constitute extrinsic linkages. It is vital to distinguish clearly the intrinsic linkages from the extrinsic linkages when there is a transfer of technology, or when one is trying to introduce a management system conceived in a different culture (Berger, 1973: 27). Berger introduces the concept of componentiality, i.e. "a strategic element in the cognitive style [...or, said otherwise]. The apprehension of reality in terms of components is essential to the reproductibility of the production process...From this follows the interdependence of components and their sequences." Reproducing a given process (technological or bureaucratic) and reaching same or similar results is possible because the components are "continuously interdependent in a rational, controllable and predictable way." Therefore, to successfully transfer a package of interdependent components such as Peer Review requires careful analysis of the components and their interdependence. If this was technological, it is doubtful that it could be transferred without much preliminary research, testing, and adaptation. However, Berger later argues that bureaucratic systems have "a greater degree of variability than is possible in the technological production. ...In political bureaucracy there is less pressure from the logic of technology and therefore more of a chance for the peculiar "genius" of bureaucracy to unfold" (Berger, 1973: 42). This is possibly the challenge that confronts any new importers of this method.

For example, if we want to operate an airline, not only must the pilots learn to fly but we must also ensure that they manage time in a very precise manner. An airplane is neither a truck nor a horse that we can stop whenever we feel like it. If the pilots do not calculate the flight time correctly, taking into account winds and the weight of the cargo, airplanes may crash. One must also ensure that preventive maintenance of all the airplanes is performed. It would be out of the question to just take off, saying to ourselves: "If it breaks, we'll stop by the side of the road until the tow-truck comes to get us." We can therefore say that time management and preventive maintenance constitute intrinsic 'linkages'. These practices form a coherent whole and are absolutely essential to the operation of an airline.

Conversely, the presence of flight attendants on airplanes is not an essential linkage for the proper operations of an airline. We could replace them with stewards or supervisors or, worse case scenario, we could even ask the more experienced passengers to help the novices. This is therefore an 'extrinsic linkage' that could be adapted, modified, or even ignored.

Too often, unfortunately, those who attempt to transplant new ideas into a different environment are unaware or even forget to highlight these important distinctions. The new users, poorly informed, change things willy-nilly and often without realizing that some of them are essential. The OECD Basic Rules of Conduct as they are defined in Section 1.2 are composed of a set of rules, which, for the most part, are clearly essential linkages that must be taken into account when introducing Peer Review into a new political, economic, and social context. A few rules, however, could be simply modified. One would assume, for example, that the 'Part Two' approach to introduce flexibility in the organization might be replaced by other more suitable methods.

## 6.2 Introduction of New Values

Experience has shown, in a very convincing manner, that 'values' are still the hardest thing to import and to modify. We can learn new techniques or acquire new knowledge, but it is notoriously difficult to adopt a behaviour that is based on values that are foreign to one's society. Societies' fundamental values evolve gradually, and the introduction of new values is always faced by traditional reflexive reactions. The problem of modernization is not to get people to work (there is widespread evidence that people in just about every area of the world have the capacity to work systematically and well, to be trained in modern methods of work and to acquire high degrees of technological skills), but to get them to work in a particular way. This involves the imposition not only of external patterns of activity but, equally important, of specific structures of consciousness. Until identification with the latter has taken place in the consciousness of the individual, the external patterns are perceived as alien and essentially meaningless. As long as the new patterns are not internalized (that is, integrated within the individual's subjective structure of consciousness), they 'sit on' the individual in a loose and superficial manner. Adherence in one context can only imperfectly be transferred to another context (Berger, 1973: 124-125).

Those who are going to use methods specific to Western cultures must, therefore, demonstrate both insight and ingenuity. In fact, to properly adapt a management system, which, as we have seen, is always imprinted with cultural perspectives, we must generally find some means that can support these new behaviours with the 'importing' society's own values. Indeed, we must understand our own traditions thoroughly to be able to integrate their related values with those coming from abroad. It is also often necessary to tinker a bit to find bridges that will make it possible to undertake such transitions. Thus, it is out of the question for a foreigner to adapt the structures from his society to a society whose operating rules the foreigner only partly and superficially understands. Such a task would, therefore, fall onto the shoulders of the managers of those who are, in a sense, importers of technology. It is the importer who must define the essential adaptations.

OECD's institutional culture corresponds to a value system that, as we have explained, is linked to the Anglo-Saxon mentality. It is a flexible architecture within which decisions and informal relationships end up carrying a lot of weight and, even sometimes, more weight than formal declarations. There are many conventions that are unspoken, but that does not mean that they are not followed to the letter. To the three founding values—respect for democracy, human rights, and the benefits of the market economy—are naturally grafted the other values that already existed within Western societies. The following examples seem particularly relevant.

- The Western tradition of so-called "decentralization of power" is not new, but corresponds to old traditions so firmly anchored in custom that we no longer think about it. Therefore, it was completely normal for those who designed OECD's operating rules to insist that mid-level management were, in fact, the clientele targeted by the institution. It is the latter that, within Western public administrations, design, initiate, administer, and write amendments to policies. During my readings, I found this interesting observation made by an Arabic commentator during the Crusades. It is quoted and commented on by Amin Maalouf in his book, *The Crusades Through Arab Eyes* (Malouf, 2002: 301): "among Westerners, the power of monarchies was governed, at the time of the Crusades, by principles that were difficult to transgress. Usamah [Ibn Munquidh] remarked during a visit to the kingdom of Jerusalem, which "when knights render a sentence, it cannot be changed nor annulled by the king".... Their society [that of the Franks, of the Crusaders] has the benefit of being a "distributor of rights." The notion of the citizen does not exist yet, of course, but the feudal "infidels" the knights, the clergy, the universities, the common people and even the peasants all have established rights. In the Arab East, the procedure for tribunals is more rational, but there is no limit to the arbitrary power of the prince."

• We could say as much regarding the respect we, in the West, give to the linkage between science and government. The Renaissance[3] saw the rise of the notion of the separation between scientific knowledge on one hand, and spirituality and the Revelation, on the other, and then between the religious powers and the civil ones. Afterwards, all these notions became interwoven and gave birth to the idea that the art of governing could be studied 'scientifically' like any other subject. This conviction, firmly anchored in custom, inspired the founders of OECD, who designed a model based on the notion that governments can examine themselves 'objectively.' In addition, they can help each other to do so with a professionally neutral and objective secretariat that would not hesitate to criticize their behaviour, with no risk of reprisals or censure.

• Finally, the peer review system presupposes that the members are what some sociologists define as 'tolerant of conflict' in order to accept having their behaviour criticized and, in turn, to be able to criticize that of other members. Here, the terms 'conflict' and 'conflict tolerant' refer to divergences of opinion, to conflicts between interest groups and, more generally, the acceptance of open and equal debates where each person can express his or her views without concern about power differentials or hierarchical differentials. Violent conflicts are the unfortunate result of poorly managed conflicts. Violent conflicts characterize 'conflict avoiders' as much as they do those who are 'conflict tolerant'.

If it were not for this deep capacity to accept conflict and to engage in debating in an egalitarian manner, this method could easily be adulterated. In fact, we should be concerned that individuals start avoiding saying the slightest disagreeable thing for fear of starting a debate, bothering or injuring someone who, some day, could do the same to them. The result is then a weakened and essentially useless evaluation system. It is evident that no society could survive

---

3. Out of concern for history, we must remember that these great ideas often found their origins in the great Greek philosophers, particularly Aristotle and Plato. After passing through Arab philosophers, these ideas returned to Western Europe in the 15th Century and started what was then called the Renaissance. At the political level, Machiavelli was the first witness to the new thinking regarding 'good governance' while he was writing The Prince, which is still considered as the first treatise on Power. But historians will put forth the argument that it is really during the Reformation that the concept of the separation of Church and State was established and translated into reality

for very long without the possibility of criticism at all levels, because it is criticism that triggers the search for innovation and the pursuit of new behaviour and new values. Cross-cultural studies reveal that there exist, in most cases, traditional mechanisms that play this' role while still respecting the solidly Imbedded taste for etiquette and courtesy. These could be the inspiration for the method used to adapt peer review to a new environment and to different reflexes.

## SECTION 7
## SUMMARY AND CONCLUSIONS

*"What good is melody?*
*What good is music?*
*It don't mean a thing*
*If it ain't got that swing"*
Music by Duke Ellington,
lyrics by Irving Mills, 1932

In short, the peer review system should not be considered in isolation, nor should it be viewed as a universal panacea that will guarantee good economic and political governance for countries that are badly managed. It requires a very strong national motivation, inspired most likely by the general recognition that without reform the country's future is at risk. We may say that it is a strong remedy that requires firm commitments both on the part of those who want to reform their management and those who want to help them. This symmetry of commitments between partners is analogous to what we find between patient and doctor: without mutual trust, without stability, it is vain to expect much from this method. It represents a long-term effort and a gradual and collective learning process. The financial effort, the discipline, and the political steadfastness required of each member state to sustain this approach are considerable.

With time, and especially with the sustained economic growth of its members, OECD has grown and has come to make use of all the powers granted it by its charter, which today makes it a costly, complex, and multifaceted model, possibly too big and too complex, some representatives may argue. But, in any case, it did not start out this way. Europeans, with the help of their 'American cousins,' began with only the bare bones of an organization. They devoted all their attention to solving a few very concrete problems, such as lowering tariff barriers, something that seemed to them, a priority, both important and possible. This initial success bolstered their confidence and emboldened them to tackle increasingly complex and difficult tasks. This is surely a reasonable path that could be imitated by other countries.

The essential features to bear in mind are the following. First, everyone must start with a strong motivation on which a commitment can be built. This commitment breaks down into three aspects that are interrelated and must always be present: a commitment to work together, a commitment to submit economic policies to peer review, and a commitment to provide all the information that the organization needs. It is important to understand thoroughly and, when necessary, to adapt all the complementary mechanisms supporting the delicate architecture of peer review, which we have lumped under the heading 'the rules of the game'. This method will not be appropriate in all circumstances, and it will be important to assess its feasibility in great detail before proceeding.

Chavranski, for example, considers that "the Asia-Pacific Economic Community (APEC), which only recently made its appearance and is now growing in power, has been presented (or conceived) as a possible alternative to the OECD, and perhaps even as a way of isolating a Europe that is running out of steam. The great economic, social, and political disparities of APEC members, and the persistent tensions between China and the United States, make this a highly unlikely scenario" (Chavranski, 1997: 14). Furthermore, careful consideration should be given by any other group of countries wishing to make use of the peer review method to adapt the OECD methodology to local cultures and traditions, as well as to specific conditions and governance systems.

We believe, however, that many of the techniques essential to the functioning of OECD could be exported, and could perhaps in time lay the basis for a specific institutional culture in which peer review could be introduced. In short, before we place the keystone at the top of the arch, we must first build solid walls on which each of the stones in that arch will rest. And we must also have good masons and skilled architects.

# 4

## OECD Techniques for Managing the Iterative Policy Process within a Multicultural Environment

Management systems, such as at OECD, or in the automobile industry, function well not only because they rest on solid foundations and structures, but equally because they are supported by trusted techniques, tools, and skills. These components are essential to maintain the integrity of the system. This chapter provides practical and concrete examples and techniques related to managing an iterative process, making use of a combination of meetings, research, and other essential elements for policy development. This chapter follows a simple logic. First, the unstated goal of OECD is to foster common and harmonized policy changes among its members. The word policy is well used within government circles but seldom defined. We will first define this concept. Second, arriving at agreed-upon policies must be achieved among significantly different cultures: we discuss how this additional complexity can be understood and surmounted. Third, the OECD process rests on a series of techniques that include roles, especially that of the chair, a precise syntax for documents, and how to manage meetings.

### SECTION 1

### THE POLICY PROCESS

#### 1.1 What is a 'Policy'?

The most common use of the word policy refers to a course of action or intended course of action conceived as deliberately adopted, after a review of possible alternatives, and pursued, or intended to be pursued. This definition, however, does not explain the process through which a course of action will be conceived. In a modern democracy, the process has become as important as the goal, or to paraphrase Marshall McLuhan, "the process is the policy." The definition above applies equally to a course of action defined under dictatorship, or under any democratically elected government that generally has to go through intricate and open public consultations before committing the state to a course of action. In this sense, the so-called most common usage does not have the merit of universality.

Furthermore, the word 'policy' does not translate in many languages, including French and Russian. It may be translated as 'politics' or 'politiques', which often leads to serious confusion.

For our purposes, public policy is defined as: "A decision, a direction or a position to be preferred in the pursuit of one or more public objectives of the government. To arrive at such a preferred course of action almost always implies a set of processes involving the participation of a great number of concerned actors. These could include other governments, international organizations, and other government levels, representatives of civil society including citizens, users, clients, and stakeholders, scientists, and legislators who will discuss the various alternatives and input into the choice to be made."

In my view, this better reflects the way policy drafting is understood today in democratically governed societies. This policy development process, however, was not always the way things were done. The process has evolved over the years. In the early days of democracy prior to the Second World War, the executive defined policy (in the case of Britain and Canada, by Cabinet). It was eventually submitted to legislature if and when it was necessary to adopt or amend a law to implement the preferred course of action. This was often more or less a form of rubber-stamping, especially when the governing party had an absolute majority and applied strict party discipline. It was the golden age of mandarin-dominated policymaking, where a few senior politicians and civil servants decided on most national policies. This was the case at the foundation of OECD.

In the 1950s, and in some cases late into the 1960s, most OECD governments evolved toward increasingly involved citizen participation. Parliamentarians, including so-called backbenchers, have been involved in policy debates through various forms of specialized committees, where they heard and discussed arguments raised by interest and lobby groups, experts and researchers, and non-governmental organizations (NGOs). Recently we have seen the birth of 'policy communities' or groupings of various interest groups coming together under a broad single interest. The media may become part of such 'policy communities' and might express support for one viewpoint or another. Governments have learned that passing a law does not suffice to deal with an issue, but an instrument must be created to implement a policy and to adapt its enforcement over time and changing circumstances. In Canada, for example, the CRTC (Canadian Radio-television and Telecommunications Commission) is an independent agency responsible for regulating Canada's broadcasting and telecommunications systems. Since 1932, the Government of Canada has been regulating and controlling broadcasting through such an instrument; over time its mandate was regularly updated to take into account technological progress. Another Canadian example can be found in Canada's Banking Law that becomes null and void at the end of each decade, thus creating an obligation to review regularly every aspect of this most important train of law, and to adapt it to changing circumstances.

It has now become general practice for governments to take polls on a regular basis and modify its stand depending on the results. Because of this, large and important events may exert significant influence on the adoption (or not) of any given policy. For example, the dramatic death of Diana, Princess of Wales, had a significant impact on pushing forward a cause she supported, the limitation of land mines. On the other hand, the terrorist attacks of 11 September 2001 have caused many shifts in policy, often in contradictory directions, in the United States and in many other OECD countries.

It should become clear how much any significant policy is widely debated and goes through an intricate set of processes before it becomes a preferred course of action.

## 1.2 OECD Influence in National Policy Drafting

In the circumstances discussed above, public servants continue to play a key role in drafting policy. They prepare briefings for elected officials, thus having an opportunity to make use of information generated in international organizations such as OECD. While conducting research for this text, I consulted Barry Carin about this. Mr. Carin had been Assistant Deputy Minister responsible for Policy in the predecessor to HRDC—the Canada Employment and Immigration Commission in the Federal Government before retiring. He vividly recalled that at one time he and his team of specialists needed to find persuasive arguments in favour of a new policy they were submitting to Cabinet. In order to sustain his argumentation, he used his discretionary research funds to sponsor a 'best practice' survey by OECD, thus generating additional and compelling arguments.

Every year, 40,000 senior officials from national administrations attend 3,000 meetings, covering close to 200 subjects, at OECD headquarters in Paris. Senior officials are regularly called upon to appear at parliamentary committees to testify about such things as best practices, scientific evidence, legal and practical constraints and, most importantly, about existing commitments and international covenants, such as those reached within OECD. This would include Peer Reviews, whereby a country's performance in a given field is assessed and commented upon by the other members of OECD. Undoubtedly this practice has a direct influence on domestic policy formulation. Senior public servants are also involved in preparing documentation and summarizing argumentation for Cabinet decisions. In this manner, OECD findings, international agreements and covenants, formal or informal, are generally taken into consideration before any decision is made. It exerts a strong influence on any national policy choice. In addition, those experts who appear at parliamentary committees often cite research results published by OECD; research results may even be quoted (with or without attribution) by the media. Academics, who have studied the way policy is drafted, tend to rely on published sources and data. Because governments rarely explain the way in which they use OECD findings, it remains a mystery. It should therefore come as no surprise that an important section of the policy drafting 'iceberg' remains hidden and underestimated.

OECD has developed over the years a long-term iterative process that blends discussions and analysis. This methodology has been used with a real measure of success, and is at the root of the economic and social progress experienced by member countries over the last 40 years. It is action oriented, not research driven. It blends research with negotiations, and moves the agenda forward incrementally in a ratchet fashion. The policy development process follows various steps and iterations as demonstrated in the Box 4.1.

This process is iterative and often protracted, irregular, and erratic, and almost always case specific. So many factors are at play at any moment that it is difficult to predict in advance or to generalize about questions such as: Who will exercise the greatest influence in the final decision? Will a policy be decided upon based on scientific evidence, demagogic bias, or commercial or partisan interests? Can a policy sail through discreetly or even secretly, or will it raise intense public interest? Will OECD discussions be fully taken into consideration?

## Box 4.1

### *The OECD Iterative Process*

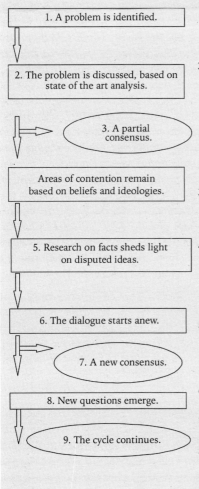

1. A dialogue begins a continuous process. It first identifies a question or a problem. It may lead to the creation of an 'ad hoc discussion group,' for example.

2. A thorough analysis is based on the most up-to-date information and state-of-the-art technology and methods. The Secretariat will proceed to: a) gather data from members, b) harmonize it, c) analyze it, and d) prepare a state-of-the-art synthesis. Based on this, it prepares 'recommendations'. This analysis leads into the next round of discussions.

3. A consensus emerges on some issues... once agreed upon, this consensus will not change.

4. Areas of contention also emerge, however, usually based on beliefs and ideologies. These often conceal commercial or even bureaucrats' vested interests.

5. A search for new and relevant facts ensues, shedding new light on those divergences. This phase may involve innovative research.

6. This leads to a renewed dialogue.

7. Another consensus is developed.

8. More in-depth questions are likely to emerge.

9. The process continues, inducing regular changes in norms, behaviour, and policies.

SECTION 2

## ARRIVING AT POLICY CONSENSUS WITHIN
## A CROSS-CULTURAL ENVIRONMENT

Cultural and political differences are never to be taken lightly in an international network such as OECD (see also Chapter 4, Section 6). Increasing economic integration within the EU, as well as globalization, have given rise in the 1990s to a body of literature concerning management and cultural diversity. Obviously, managers are becoming more curious about the problems arising from mismanaging this important feature of human relations; this is a welcome change from the times when managers and negotiators were complacently satisfied in knowing how to do things at home. Country representatives attending international meetings are most often blind to the way other representatives think and build up their line of argumentation. A 'savvy president' and a 'wise director' act proactively to bridge the knowledge gap between nations. The following notes are not intended to substitute for a course on cross-cultural management, but merely to provide examples of tools used by the Secretariat and by those delegates with long experience in the art of international negotiations. We have suggested additional readings for anyone keen to learn more about this subject. When dealing with 'cultures' there is always the implicit danger of oversimplification. Country representatives cannot be reduced to a few simple observations, trends, or anecdotes. To paraphrase an old idiom, "even in Rome, some Romans do not act like Romans." The following text is intended to open one's mind and certainly never to close it.

### 2.1 Development and Culture

Culture is understood differently depending on the perspective of the observer. As this text is action oriented, we suggest using a definition by Boyd and Richerson (1987) (in Homer-Dixon, 2001: 205 from Boyd and Richerson, p.67).

"Culture is information—skills, attitudes, beliefs, values—capable of effecting individuals' behaviour, which they acquire from others by teaching, imitation, and other forms of social learning."

Understanding, or showing true empathy for the cultures and for the historical perspective of various participants, is an essential element for grasping "the logic of the situation. We understand people's actions if we see how those actions are objectively appropriate to the situation, and how the observed actions are consistent with rational behaviour" (McMillan, 1992: 8). Lacking a clear historical perspective of where the country is coming from has often been a failure of the classical economist. Fernand Braudel's historical

## Box 4.2

### *The Case of Former Soviet Union Countries*

Very little has been published on this topic. In the case of Eastern Europe, the notion of drafting public policies through multilayered consultations with civil society and NGOs was not common practice during Soviet times and has yet to be introduced. The few authors who have written about the way things are done now have focused on emerging think tanks. The evaluation is terse: "Ivan Krastev remarks that there are several factors explaining the so-called "influence" of think tanks on policy: it was not the strength of the independent research but the weakness of the other players in the realm of post-communist policymaking that made think tanks influential players. The lack of confidence between the reform governments and the administration that they inherited, the weak policy capacities of the political parties, the unwillingness of the universities and academies of science to commit themselves to policy research, and the underdeveloped business community are the main factors explaining the 'Heritage moment' [or the direct influence on the governmental agenda] of the post-communist think tanks."

The EMDU project has recently been assessed for the purpose of assessing if research led to policy changes. Under the leadership of IDRC's Evaluation Unit, Dr. Irina Lyzogub carried out the various interviews with principals, analyzed the findings, and drafted an overall assessment. The following preliminary conclusions are based on her unpublished report.

Western understanding of the policy process as the one that implies involving the participation of a great number of concerned actors is not always applicable to Ukrainian reality. For many decades, Ukraine was organized as a hierarchical system. "There was little experience of democracy and political rights, which ... were limited to ritual participation in elections..." (Maravall, 1997: 207). The leaders made the policy, and everybody else implemented it.

The opinions of the interviewees, key participants of the EMDU program, differed. However, the current situation in Ukraine in relation to the development of civil society was frequently characterized in the following way: the state policy depends either on the president, or on different regional clan, and oligarchic groups; the political system is characterized as a Presidential Republic (though the interviewees are aware of the fact that it is declared to be Presidential-Parliamentary); people are not ready to acknowledge that their opinion should matter; and public officials and oligarchic groups have little concern for the public good or for what people think. They compete for the spoils of office. Usually, policymakers do not consider public outreach in their undertakings.

"As interviews reveal, changes can be made. These changes require an understanding of their necessity as well as courageous people ready to lobby for these changes ('to fight for their ideas'). These changes require bright personalities, not groups or public organizations. At the same time, interviewees agree with the necessity of wide participation as well as the necessity of informing people."

perspective about the functioning of market economy is a good reminder of the essentially empirical character of the market economy and therefore of the intimate relationship between today's practices and their origins.[4] Both the president of the committee and the 'wise director' play a key role in helping

---

4. See "Afterthoughts on Material Civilization and Capitalism" a translation of his famous 1976 conference at Johns Hopkins University titled in French: "La dynamique du capitalisme" edited by Flammarion in 1985.

various participants understand the logic of the situation that prevails in the various member countries. They help bridge the gap of suspicion that marks relationships between competing nations.

Another important issue is the link between development and culture. Development is governed by ambiguity. It must deal simultaneously with transformation and conservation. No transformation can take place without the destruction of the initial form. For example, a sculptor destroys the stone or the tree to create a new image out of the material. The child must die for an adolescent to take his place and eventually he must in turn die for the adult to take over. However, while this happens, the personality of the individual retains its main characteristics. Some characteristics are acquired genetically while many others are acquired through early socialization and through learning and education. In addition, some characteristics can be changed easily through learning, while reflexes and character remain fairly stable and are most difficult to modify. All these elements give birth to the personality of each individual.

The search for change and stability is ancient and was discussed as early as the 6$^{th}$ Century by Greek philosophers such as Heraclitus. Humans always seek for something that remains the same while it changes. This is also true in the area of development, where some specialists often emphasize the virtue of modernization, of 'changes in mentality', while others expound the importance of retaining tradition and the evil of 'deculturation' (i.e. the loss of one's culture).

Irrevocably, development will always be immersed in ambiguity. Ambiguity implies dynamism; it is entropy. Searching for a world without ambiguity leads to a world governed by rigidities and staleness; it is filling forms rather than thinking things through; it is abiding to rituals rather than making rational use of tested routines.

Thus, the art is balancing change while respecting the personality of a culture. This, to a large extent, has been OECD's unspoken challenge for the past 40 years. The OECD's ability to breed policy changes while empirically adapting such transformations to the specific circumstances and culture of each OECD member, has defined its strength and methodology.

In the following discussion, we propose some tools that the reader may find useful to conduct successful international meetings.

## 2.2 The Balance of Social Systems: Weights, Drifts and Counterweights

Every society has values that it holds dear. These values can be viewed as weights, biases or characteristics. The effect of these values acting over time is to create a drift, forms of deviation, or a tendency within society. In most cases, this drift ultimately leads to a dysfunction of this society, and ultimately potentially to its destruction. A society that has survived over time will have developed culturally specific counterweights. These culturally specific counterweights or values, often linked to legal or quasi-legal requirement, counteract the effect of this drift and provide a mechanism whereby a society maintains its integrity and functionality in a dynamic equilibrium between the drift and the countervailing forces. In other words, each culture breeds its own deviations, and has means to surmount their ill effects.

Social systems survive only if they remain in balance over time. The need for such balance is generally recognized within each society. Just as the American system of 'checks and balances' prevents the excessive domination of one of the three branches of the American political system (legislative, executive, and judicial powers); the mixing of these components assures that the balance remains by preventing one to overtake the system.

By examining social systems of different cultures, this search for balance can be observed. D'Iribarne (1993: 55-61) studied four cases to compare the deep rooting of culture in management.

Most often, management models are created in the US, and occasionally in Europe or Japan. These models are generally very difficult to transfer to other cultures because indigenous values are entrenched and generally 'hidden.' Culture is stubborn, and can only change incrementally over time. International organizations dealing with policies are bound to meet with examples of such intractable indigenous traditions.

*The US 'Honest Contract'*

American models of organization rest on an old premise: contracts between parties, whoever they may be, are contracts between 'equals' and between 'free' entities (people, firms, or institutions).

This 'ideal' leads to the establishment of relationships between clients and suppliers as well as between boss and employee. "Clients are free to establish demands from their suppliers and the boss is free to impose objectives to his employees. [...] However, it is deemed "unfair" to change your mind once a contract has been agreed upon. As well, the boss is bound by the objectives he has fixed for his employees" (Ibid: 55).

This in turn leads to a cybernetics approach to social and business organizations. Cybernetics is the science of communication and control of machines and computers. Its rigid logic helps define clear links of accountability between all parties. Hence the use of boxes, lines of authority, and precise organization charts where accountability is divided among discrete and precise units. Conflicts are arbitrated following these defined lines of authority and predefined communication paths.

This contractual ideal is twinned with a great suspicion of all things 'arbitrary,' and leads to defining performance indicators that are objective and measurable sometimes to great excess in details and procrastination. This form of legalistic procrastination may lead eventually to a company's paralysis, hence a characteristic 'drift'.

Americans are at all times 'risk tolerant.' They thus allow market rules to govern a harsh and intractable system of deselecting the weakest or the unfit. This can act as a counterweight to legalistic procrastination and what would otherwise become most destructive behaviour. Firms and governments that get tangled up in details and procrastination are eventually destroyed by competition and/or by other parties.

*The French 'Logic of Honour'*

The French labour force derives its traditions from very old 'guilds,' or the 'ethic of the profession,' also referred to as 'the mission.'

Individuals are thus bound to rights and duties specific to their professional code of conduct. This allows one to recognize what is a job well done, a solid product, and a good way for doing things.

Such traditions are not sacrificed in the quest to attain solid profits. The pursuit at all cost of the bottom line may clash with the honour of the professional group. It is not therefore considered honourable to be serf of a boss, a client, or a company (D'Iribarne, 1993: 57). However, it is honourable to be devoted to a cause, or to bend the rule to reach a higher goal (provided it is being asked according to form).

A boss is therefore not supposed to oversee work in all its details, as is often the rule in American companies where you might hear: "delegation is good, but control is better." As a result, responsibilities are stratified vertically and horizontally (between different professional groups within the same company).

Faced with a problem, improvising a solution is the 'honourable' thing to do. This behaviour can be described by the French words *bricoller, se débrouiller,* which have no exact translation in English. In essence, it refers to untangling a messy situation through improvisation, inventiveness, often at the price of bending the rules a bit. Getting by or muddling through captures only partially the requirement for inventiveness and responsibility that comes with it.

However, baronies and quarrels between departments staffed with different professional groups may lead to a company's demise or to a government's inefficiency, hence a drift typical of the French management system.

French people have a high tolerance for individualistic behaviour; their own professional duty is a strong motivating factor. In combination with conscientiousness and respect for professional ethics, they find ways and means to surmount dysfunctionalities.

### The Japanese Paternal Loyalty

When Americans search for depersonalizing relationships, Japanese search for long-term associations based on many intangible and unwritten rules, a key one being "loyalty in the context of highly unequal human structures" (D'Iribarne, 1993: 58).

The strong are bound by honour to provide a 'certain respect' for the weak, but they reign high in the hierarchy of the company or of the government. In return, they must show paternal loyalty to all the employees of the firm, at all costs. Employees are in for the long run, and in case of difficulty, they will gather together and discuss a solution that fits with the organization's goals, values, and needs.

Faced with changing economic circumstances, firms find it hard to reduce costs and changes are difficult to come by in light of such tradition of mutual loyalty. When change comes, it is often led by outside pressure, as was the case for the Meiji Restoration that, arguably, was prompted by outside events and pressure by Britain and the US.

However, traditions are very strong, and individual responsibility of the 'Samurai' still very strong. Faced with the consequence of poor judgment, he will fall on his sword, ...leaving the place empty for a successor who may be more progressive.

### The African Business Logic Puzzle

The search for consensus is central to many West African social models; as a consequence they tend to avoid direct and open confrontation and conflicts.

Respect for social rules, for social order is entrenched and often leads to lack of individualistic behaviour. Employees in the organization hesitate to move ahead of their comrades to meet set individual targets: it is always better to stay within the group.

"Intentions represent an overwhelming measure of action, much more than the result (intended or accidental)" (D'Iribarne, 1993: 59). Africans generally tend not to separate personalities and work the way Americans like to do. Confidence rests on a social model organized around an ideal system of 'friendship' and 'kinship' where attitudes are governed by apparent benevolence. Any abnormal situation raises suspicion and creates reactions often difficult to control.

Thus Western organizational systems and models, be they public or private, are generally unfit to function well within the prevalent values and behaviour. Foreign experts' regular demands for 'changes in mentality' always meet with the 'stubbornness of culture.' Management methods that put emphasis on 'results' rather than on 'good will,' or that rest on the obligation to quarrel, such as 'establishing priorities,' are bound to threaten and/or destroy organizations.

On the one hand, in the African tradition, loyalty to 'kin' and 'family' remains stronger than loyalty to abstract constructions such as a firm or a ministry. Faced with a problem the group follows tradition and hierarchy. On the other hand, goods are traditionally tradable and anything considered tradable is allowed to follow market logic. Goods are negotiable and the price will generally abide by the law of supply and demand; in this effect, some analogies can be made with the American open market mentality. In conjunction, these two forces generally allow for catastrophe to be averted.

### 2.3 Bonthous' Four Key Dimensions for Gathering Intelligence

Another example of how to take into consideration cultural factors can be found in Bonthous' (1991: 275-310) analysis of intelligence systems, either for military and strategic purposes or for business organizations. He has compared the way Germany, France, Sweden, Japan, and the United States collect and manage intelligence systems. He looked at the significance of intelligence gathering along four dimensions; he then compared each nation's preference in the use of intelligence, and the process by which it leads to strategic decisions. In other words, how is the cognitive system for each of these five nations structured? How is information used and what sort of information is generally considered essential or unimportant for a decision to be made in each of these five countries? For the wise director and savvy president this is rather important because OECD will need to gather and present information that is deemed pertinent by each member country's administration.

## Box 4.3

### *Bounthous' Key Dimensions[5]*

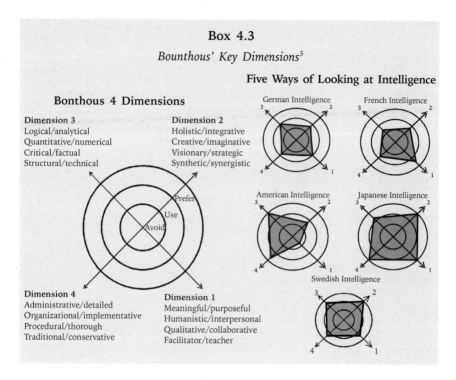

**Five Ways of Looking at Intelligence**

**Bonthous 4 Dimensions**

**Dimension 3**
Logical/analytical
Quantitative/numerical
Critical/factual
Structural/technical

**Dimension 2**
Holistic/integrative
Creative/imaginative
Visionary/strategic
Synthetic/synergistic

**Dimension 4**
Administrative/detailed
Organizational/implementative
Procedural/thorough
Traditional/conservative

**Dimension 1**
Meaningful/purposeful
Humanistic/interpersonal
Qualitative/collaborative
Facilitator/teacher

*Dimension 1* is characterized by meaning and purpose, humanistic and interpersonal skills, the search for qualitative and collaborative behaviour within the group and lastly by facilitating the gathering of information and for teaching its usage among the concerned community.

Bonthous notes that, "in the United States, the traditional association of intelligence with the military and secrecy has prevented the people from perceiving it as an opportunity that benefits everyone: intelligence is perceived instead as part of an underground world, rather manipulative, and bordering on the unethical. In Sweden and Japan by contrast, the benefit of intelligence to society is understood by the majority of people, from farmers to small business owners and big corporations. People, business, and government produce intelligence hand-in-hand."

*Dimension 2* dominant intelligence organizations seek to push their limits further. It is characterized by the search for holistic and integrative information, by supporting creative and imaginative behaviour, allowing for

---

5. Figures reproduced from Bonthous article Figure 2, p.281.

visionary and strategic thinking to take place, and by putting emphasis on synthesis as opposed to listing data and details and synergy within the organization rather than stove-piping divisions and directorates.

Again, Bonthous notes that, "Japan and Sweden have greatly developed this understanding: intelligence is an integral part of the ongoing process of strategizing on the national level and in corporations. Intelligence is not pursued in spurts, or mainly when crises strike…. Intelligence is in every piece of information and not limited to the confidential."

*Dimension 3* is about logical and analytical thinking. It deals primarily with quantitative and numerical data; it is critical and factual, structural and technical.

"The U.S. intelligence reigns supreme in Dimension 3: as a master of logic and reason. Better than anyone, it handles rigorous quantitative assessments and factual or numerical analysis. Problems are solved logically: the complex is reduced to the simple, the unclear to the clear. Sophisticated tools are used to develop generalizations from the specific. Logic and reason rule the U.S. intelligence process. Intuition and 'soft approaches' are discounted: they are perceived as debatable, hard to prove, unreliable. Intelligence processes are formal and quantified.

"The search for knowledge is project-based and problem-oriented, with measurable goals at each step. When the project is over, the thrust of intelligence is reduced. Intelligence professionals have an affinity and capability for undertaking massive projects and tackling tough problems. They function within limited time horizons and seek short-term, measurable results. Projects are completed on time and within budget. Clockwork efficiency prevails. Facts and proof are needed at each step of the way. Performance is measured according to well-quantified criteria. Meeting the bottom line attains satisfaction.

"Creativity is not considered essential: the way to increase performance is to optimize proven analytical models. There is a reluctance to undertake assignments when the output and the return on investment cannot be measured or when there are some elements of vagueness involved. Function and value are precisely quantified and monitored. Concerns for human processes are secondary. The reality is factual, the process mechanistic, and the interaction hierarchical. Authority is preferred to diversity… If this dimension is a master of efficiency, it lags in effectiveness: analytical tools have limited effect on organizational development."

*Dimension 4* reflects the way things are done within the organization: it likes to plan, execute, and implement. Administrative routines and detailed procedures are carried out systematically; it is organizational and implementative, procedural and thorough, traditional and conservative.

"Collecting data, following meticulously defined procedures, combing through data, evaluating, inventorying, and filing data are handled with great rigor. Ambiguity is rejected; intuition and emotions are distrusted. The orientation is mechanical: sequence, procedure and order are favoured... Dimension 4 supports Dimension 3 in its analytical efforts...Dimension 4 professionals have extraordinary capabilities for bringing order out of chaos...[but] unfortunately tends to overlook the big picture."

These four dimensions are complementary. "Dimension 1, reaching into a person's emotional depths, is essential for laying the foundation of a culture of intelligence, for it is based on people rather than on tools and techniques. Dimension 2 allows intelligence reality to grow, and break new ground. Dimension 3 structures this growth, and modelizes it. Dimension 4 brings sequence and order to the whole."

---

### Box 4.4

*Two Types of Intelligence according to Bonthous: The American and The Swedish*

| **American Preferences** | **Swedish Intelligence** |
|---|---|

U.S. inteligelnce reigns supreme in Dimension 3: A master of logic & reason

Dimensions 3 & 4 is very developed. Dimension 1 is ignored and Dimension 2 is merely used.

All 4-dimensions are equally developed

- It handles rigorous quantitative assessments & factual or numerical analysis.
- Facts and proof are needed at each step.
- Concern for human processes are secondary.
- Reality is factual, the process mechanistic, and the interaction hierarchical.
- Clockwork efficiency prevails.

- Integral part of ongoing process of strategizing on the national level and in corporations.
- Not pursued in spurts, or mainly when Crisis strike....Intelligence is in every piece of information and not limited to the confidential.

---

## 2.4 Defining a 'Story Line'

The national approaches to intelligence as described by Bonthous define national 'personality traits' that come into play when delegations from various countries assess documentation associated with a policy issue. When delegates gather around the table to discuss a critical issue, each will scrutinize the proposed documentation according to the variables or dimensions that attract them. The American delegate is bound to look first into the facts and figures and will then check if the analysis is logical and if the paper uses state-of-the-art scientific methodology. The Swedish or Japanese delegates will look into those facts and figures, but they will search for other types of information meaningful for them and for their ministry: for them, a document that deals entirely with facts and figures but overlooks human and qualitative aspects is bound to remain incomplete. The same applies to the French or German delegate.

I vividly recollect an afternoon when we had tabled for discussion a document prepared by a French expert. The document began with a sizable essay on development values; it was eventually followed by inevitable figures describing the performance of every donor to the Sahel region. The American delegate was upset with this presentation, and staring hard into my eyes, he literally tore off the first 50 pages of the report: for him, this was verbiage. Interestingly, French, Canadian, and Dutch delegates were rather eager to spend most of the morning session dealing with the philosophical preamble; of course, all this time, my American delegate was fuming. When his turn to speak arrived, he proceeded to criticize the methodology and the relevance of the whole document. Not all American delegates are that tempestuous, but faced with a document short on facts and abundant on 'qualitative analysis,' they are bound to request a serious revisit of the document and will argue that this does not provide them with a 'story line' they can use in their constituency.

The notion of 'story line' is relevant to the issue of policy adoption. For a new policy to be adopted in any OECD member country, a series of arguments must be presented to various levels of decision-makers and influential parties. In a democracy, it rarely suffices to convince a few delegates; no matter how senior they are, country representatives are merely a link in a long chain of command, and of influence. Having been persuaded about a particular change in policy, they must then go back home and persuade others, and for this they absolutely need to be equipped with the kind of arguments that are acceptable in their culture. For that purpose, I found Bonthous' analysis useful. I kept reminding myself that the work of the Secretariat needed to reflect all intelligence needs of the various delegates, including Sahelian representatives. It also meant that more discussion time was necessary to allow delegates to introduce arguments in their own familiar manner. It is also essential to build redundancies; for example, dividing workload in such a manner as to warrant the hiring of two consultants, one from France and one from the United States, in order to build adequately for each country, the required 'story line'. Ignoring this reality almost always led to stale discussions and lock-up positions.

Little is known of these preferences for Eastern Europe and for Africa. This information deficit makes it very difficult for foreign agencies to make a persuasive and relevant case when advocating any particular policy that they view as more effective for solving problems in either of these regions.

## SECTION 3

## MANAGING THE NEGOTIATION PROCESS

OECD is a network whose members retain their sovereignty at all times. The organization is governed by consensus, so persuading members to act in a certain way requires specific skills, a high level of tact, and strategy. Because it has no formal coercive powers, it must reach 'active consensus' as the outcome of any discussion or negotiation. This implies that all participants not only agree with a recommendation or a decision by the group, but their behaviour has been changed in the process; it is expected that participants will return to their office and 'behave' in a manner different than the way they behaved prior to the meeting, a behaviour that corresponds to the new standards or norms that have been agreed upon. In that sense, the discussion/ negotiation process is closer to a pedagogical one at times, and at other times it is closer to brainstorming and the seeking of new ideas. In a manner analogous to good pedagogy, attention must be given to listening to others; one might further argue that it is equally important to be perceived as listening. It has been observed that most delegates do not mind divergent views, provided they know they have been heard.

Thus, the management of the negotiation and discussion process leaves nothing to chance. The process must be managed in meticulous fashion to surmount the added complexity of ensuring the buy-in by all members. In my opinion, three features are central to this high-quality method:

1. First, participants must understand the way they are meant to play their role for each meeting and within each committee to achieve maximum results. Some of the participants are called upon to play central roles, in particular the chair of each committee or each meeting. In Chapter 3 we

addressed the specific role played by the 'wise director.' In this section we will provide a few suggestions as to the best way a 'savvy president' can best help a committee reach its objectives. We will also discuss how participants can lobby each other to maintain and maximize the use of peer pressure. Finally, we will discuss the use of experts and consultants.

2.  Second, as in theatre, a good play must rest on a solid script and so does a good meeting. For that reason, the drafting of key documents is central to the discussion process. We will discuss the drafting and provide the salient feature for the syntax specific to the annotated agenda, summary records, peer review, and communiqué.

3.  Third, the logistical arrangements of the meeting, the management of time and sequencing of events, will facilitate or hinder the reaching of a consensus depending on the manner in which these elements are structured.

## 3.1 Roles Ascribed to Various Actors

For greater effectiveness, all participants must know in advance what is expected of them and what role they are expected to play. It is also expected that national delegates will prepare their specific national response to the agenda items. They might also choose to contact each other to lobby for their preferred option. This is generally done in Paris between delegations, but may occasionally happen elsewhere.

*The Role of the 'Savvy President'*

A representative from the member countries chairs most committees, subcommittees, and workshops, thus ensuring at all times that the network nature of the organization is fully reflected in its work. A permanent president chairs only two committees: the Development Assistance Committee (DAC) and the Economic and Development Review Committee (EDRC). Otherwise, each group selects its chair in its own way in accordance with unwritten rules, precedents, and habits. As is typical of OECD, these rules may vary depending on the theme or sector. In sum, the selection of a president is considered to be of significant importance by all members, as the president plays a key role in moving the agenda for each of these committees. At the beginning of a task, when things are still informal and uncertain, countries often confer informally outside the meeting, and decide on who will provide the first president.

Because OECD is 'content driven,' members often fix their choice on one of them who seems to rally a consensus based on the person's savvy, knowledge of the subject, leadership, and interest. Being so chosen is considered an honour for the country, and this is even truer for key committees, such as finance; generally the responsible department will facilitate things for the selected president. In some cases, it implies the individual will be left at the post for as long as the person chairs the committee.

Each president develops skills as the committee work progresses. Some start with great intuition, others learn the hard way through trial and error. The following suggestions may help provide general direction. They have no claim to be based on hard scientific evidence, nor are they documented in the published literature. The ideas derive mostly from interviews that were carried out with present and past members of OECD staff. At best, these are lessons learned by those who were close to the action for a number of years.

A 'savvy president' remains calm and composed throughout a meeting, moving the agenda by interjecting probing questions or making statements, demonstrating at all times a clear reasoning and a broad understanding of the issues. The chair must focus on questions that are fundamental to constructing a solution, and spot a fuzzy question, one of those that divert energy into subsidiary issues. The chair ensures that real problems not be obscured by astute smokescreens, and does not let the meeting deteriorate into 'forms, formalities, and rituals,' but keeps the group focussed on the substance of the issue. At the same time, the chair remains alert to susceptibilities and helps his most trusted partner, the 'wise director' in finding true and acceptable language to define a situation or a problem. Every opportunity is used, in the meeting or outside, to push the agenda forward. Lastly, the Chair's personal credibility and intellectual leadership comforts and reassures the group. A solid and timely sense of humour is a recognized asset.

### Two Archetypes: The 'Persistent Diplomat' and the 'Maverick'

The 'persistent diplomat' has chaired many committees with a large measure of success. The person is characterized by a capacity to listen for hours to every delegate, letting them speak late into the night, but won't let go of the objectives of a specific meeting. The Chair literally wears them down by listening patiently and bringing them back to the task at hand.

The 'maverick' is encountered less often, but under certain circumstances, this personality may be the character best suited for the occasion. The maverick must possess a high independence of view, even be financially independent; he rides a group very hard, at times cutting a discussion short to refocus the participants on the real agenda. The maverick 'has an attitude' but also intellectual leadership, and coupled with recognized ethics the maverick is acceptable to trained bureaucrats. The maverick has little chance of success alone, but with a partner and accomplice within the group who can be relied upon to provide timely support, chances of survival are relatively good. This archetype may best be used when the agenda is protracted and requires risk-taking to overcome embedded resistance.

The 'passive diplomat' epitomizes a less efficient type, characterized by not getting involved in the debate, and generally remaining on the fence. This person is content to manage the traffic and ensure that participants speak in turn and respect protocol. If a group is highly proactive, with many committed participants, to which we must add a strong and highly respected 'wise director,' then a committee may wither this person's lack of positive energy. A committee may otherwise lose its dynamism, and eventually a way will be found to secure another president.

*Chairing Efficiency and Effectiveness*

Defining effectiveness and efficiency remains elusive in the OECD context. The difference between the two is subtle but never vague. Each Chair must decide what to strive for and what to sacrifice in the heat of the action at least once per meeting. The difference between reaching the overall goals and bringing a meeting to a close often contradict each other. An efficiently run meeting might leave some participants secretly unsatisfied. Very often, for example, the preoccupations of more important countries overshadow the concerns of smaller states, and in the long run consensus may remain elusive. Small states have means to make themselves essential when the time comes. They either become 'policy delinquents' or geopolitical considerations make them essential and give them occasional leverage. In sum, the 'savvy president' never loses sight of the fact that the fundamental goal of the organization is to foster 'cooperation' among its members. The role of the 'savvy president' is to help bring inclusiveness where the world tends to be fractious.

Searching for consensus should not overshadow other important objectives of the organization:

1. It is a learning organization and what participants learn about themselves, about their neighbours, and about the best way to do things remains an essential and useful outcome of a good meeting. Some even argue that OECD has a 'duty of care' compelling it to understand how each system works, its peculiar dynamics, understanding and demonstrating the relation between the various systems. In sum, for many, learning within OECD is a moral imperative, and never a luxury or dispensable item.

2. It is also a laboratory for new ideas to be tested and implemented: many of its forums act as quasi-brainstorming sessions between states to develop new products and new ways to govern, and to provide services to citizens.

3. A third dimension of the process is the need to set the scene for future Peer Review. The 'savvy president' never forgets that in the end all actions by members will have to be assessed and judged by the other members. Driving an agreement too fast might mean that its implementation will be difficult and member's adherence sluggish. The Peer Review process is a unique function within OECD, and still remains a unique challenge. It is the litmus test of well-negotiated policy, and to a large measure, a performance indicator of the savvy of the chairpersons who conducted the discussions in the preceding stages.

It is often better to call a difficult meeting to a close, short of a consensus, rather than press participants beyond what they are prepared to accept as a group. The 'savvy president' knows when to quit, and to consider learning as the most important outcome of a particular session.

*Committee Structure*

OECD is a complex network, made up of a great number of families. For example, trade representatives from various member countries form a loosely bonded family; likewise for representatives of the ministry of finance or from any other ministry. They also meet in other forums where they are called to discuss issues and ideas that are debated in some OECD committee. They come to know each other well as they meet regularly in scientific seminars, bilateral meetings, and other international organizations (World Bank, International Monetary Fund, World Trade Organization). The world of OECD is a highly connected world. The 'savvy president' is also a member of the same circles, and the wise one knows how and when to push the agenda forward outside of the strict boundaries of the committee. OECD members often confer with each other in large forums and may call upon the Chair to preside over an informal gathering preceding the final session. This may provide an opportunity to move one particular item forward. The next session of the committee may confirm what was agreed to one evening in a hotel lobby. Seen from this angle, one may appreciate better the power of OECD's informality.

OECD has often been used to discuss, to prepare, and harmonize positions in other forums. For example, OECD members used the Exchange Committee to prepare General Agreement on Tariffs and Trade negotiations in the years preceding the formation of the World Trade Organization. The Development Assistance Committee was used in preparation for the Rio, Beijing, and other large international events that were attended by Third World countries. The most secretive Working Party Number Three was used to prepare G-10 meetings in the 1970s, as well as the IMF meeting. It should therefore come as no surprise that some measure of harmonization came to guide members' policies and behaviour.

### Equilibrium Constantly Changes

The high level of connectivity between OECD activities and those of its members means that the work within each committee must adapt to an ever-changing equilibrium. This is both a constraint and a resource for the 'savvy president.' This is one key argument in favour of long-lasting stable presidents as opposed to short-term revolving individuals. Over time, a good Chair personifies and embodies a committee. Combined with flexibility, good judgement, and commitment, the work of the Chair can often result in significant changes in the behaviour of states. This was the case, for example, for the committee to fight against bribery, chaired by a Swiss lawyer, Dr Pieth. In Chapter 6, the unique achievements of this 'ad hoc Committee' will serve to illustrate a success story.

### Managing Time

One essential function of the Chair is to 'manage time'—the 'long time', which can be a period of years needed for a new policy to become accepted practice, and the short time, which is the time of each session and the time in between. This requires an acute sense of timing both at the global level and at the very specific moment within a meeting. As we have explained above, the connected world of OECD changes constantly. The 'savvy president' must adapt to changes in politics, which sometimes facilitate his work, but more often they hinder and slow down progress. At a micro level, the Chair is called to judge when a group is stalled because of fatigue, when a new item should replace the previous one, and when to take charge and flush out a problem.

In many instances, the time allotted to discuss a particular item is too short. For example, the annual review of the economic performance of each member lasts one day each. This may suffice to discuss the performance of Iceland, for example, but is perceived as too short to fully discuss the complexities of the US economy.

### Tricks of the Trade

Faced with a difficult session, the Chair may choose to conclude with carefully considered words rather than belabour a seemingly intractable issue.

It can be brought up again at a more promising opportunity. He then may insist on:

- Determining how much was learned through sharing each other's experience.
- Praising the group for tackling a most difficult problem.
- Encouraging participants to come back next time with means to attack the problem.
- Focussing on methodological obstacles that were surmounted and which can be further used to pursue a difficult dialogue.

Such words carry significant weight when used by someone who is recognized for incisive judgment and for being an expert in the field. Furthermore, for a creative mind, a difficult meeting is often the opportunity to create, to innovate, to spin the group into new areas of thinking, or to invent new tools or search for entirely different approaches to solutions.

The 'savvy president' does not fear the void of silence. He gives time to think. Faced with what is often perceived as 'heavy silence' after the usual introduction, the Chair will choose to wait them out rather than jump into the void by repeating the introduction or voicing personal opinions. This results in de-responsibilizing the group. It is a network of peers and every participant is an owner of the process. One of them will eventually launch discussion. The Chair will not stymie participation, but will make sure everyone has had a chance to speak to an issue before offering a summary that is intended to close a discussion.

Faced with a discussion that is deadlocked, and participants who don't react, the competent Chair will use various tactics:

- Restate his opinions to draw out participation.
- Offer a compromising opinion to influence those who do not have firm views.
- Offer a temporary view: "the sense of the meeting appears to be...."
- Decide to move to the next item on the agenda.

To build the collective memory, the Chair will:

- Offer regular, but short, summaries of what has been accomplished.
- Put forward validation questions such as: "Do you mean that...?, "Does the group feel that...?" or, I sense a consensus building towards... .

SECTION 4
SYNTAX FOR KEY DOCUMENTS

## 4.1 The Annotated Agenda

The negotiation process often proceeds on the basis of an annotated 'agenda', which the OECD has developed into an art form. This agenda mechanism serves as a key instrument for guiding the negotiation into a sustained, goal-oriented dialogue. Not every meeting makes use of this technique. Generally, meetings are part of an ongoing process and thus, their management is considered straightforward. A simple listing of topics to be discussed is enough. But, when a meeting is more delicate, either because the subject matter is new and complex or when partners don't know each other well enough, then a special effort must be made to increase the probability that a meeting will achieve its intended goals.

The OECD method functions like a Matrioshka doll: it's a continuum within a continuum, always moving from the basis of agreed facts toward consensus on common policy. Going back to the six distinct steps of its policy process (see Chapter 3, Section 4), the first step is to agree on a subject. This is the task of the members themselves. Once they have agreed, then the Secretariat takes over the crucial next phases, and applies a rigorous scientific method to move the agenda forward. It always begins with establishing the facts, collecting data, and creating a comparative information base. Analysis and drawing conclusions then follows. Lastly, forecasts and recommendations bring closure to the discussions before peer review can be performed.

Discussions between members on a particular subject take place throughout the entire process, as committee meetings may take place once or even twice a year. For greater effectiveness, meetings should follow OECD's traditional and proven recipe for reaching policy consensus: first moving from agreed upon facts and harmonized data to analysis before proceeding with the more difficult discussions concerning recommendations and decisions.

If a meeting takes place at the very early stage, when little is known about a subject, then the meeting agenda is likely to focus first on what is known, what is the available data, and allow the group to evaluate if the data are of sufficient quality to move ahead. If it is problematic, more effort must be made toward securing a better basis upon which to make a comparative analysis. In essence, the method ensures that a problem is clearly identified before a solution can be discussed. Otherwise, the lack of consensus about the nature of the problem will always slow down or even block the search for a common policy. In sum, each meeting is structured in a manner less conducive to conflicts, and in this way, it maximizes the search for truth and objective knowledge based on facts, rigorous analysis, and contrary discussions, leading to the pursuit of policy consensus and overall cooperation.

A second feature of an effective agenda is to guide the group through the meeting in a most efficient manner. It serves the role of a well-planned and easy-to-follow road map; this maximizes use of time, a scarce resource. Considering the costs of holding international meetings, anything less would be irresponsible.

The following example of what could be seen as a model annotated agenda comes from the General Secretariat, Liaison and Cooperation Unit, and concerns a workshop organized in October 1995 to discuss: "Public sector finances and the evolution of saving and investment balances" (OECD document no SG/DNME"ECO"GEN/A(95)1, 21 September 1995). The stated objective of the meeting was to examine how experience across countries in saving and investment rates relates to the level and structure of public finances and to public policy more generally. In addition to general reports that reflect state-of-the-art knowledge on a given topic, for example, a paper on "Ageing populations, pension system and government budgets: How do they affect savings" and a number of national case studies were tabled for discussion. As this particular workshop was intended for OECD members and so-called dynamic non-members, the case studies dealt with Latin America in general and more specifically Argentina and Brazil, Asia, including Japan, Malaysia, Singapore, Thailand, Chinese Taipei, and finally, the USA. Three topics were scheduled for discussion: First, the role of public policies in the evolution of savings and investments, or more precisely, the role of pension system reforms and the role of other public policies. Then the group addressed "prospect for public finances, saving and investments, more specifically in Latin American and Asian DNMEs." Readers will notice the subtle shift from reviewing cross-country experience, i.e. a factual discussion, to assessing cross-country prospects for fiscal policies. Lastly, the discussion dealt with policy implications.

## Table 4.1

*Annotated Agenda, Example and Comments*

---

The Agenda for each session follows the same format.

First, the aim of the session is explained in succinct terms.

A listing of all the documents that have been produced expressly for that workshop.

Lastly, suggestions are made for discussion.

In three short paragraphs, the general issue at stake and the purpose of the workshop are clearly and succinctly explained.

Notice the moderate and neutral terminology: 'there are concerns...'

Opening Remarks: Recent and prospective developments in national savings and investment, and their determinants, are an important policy concern for both DNM and OECD economies. There are concerns that private investment is being held back in OECD countries by low domestic saving and high real interest rates, and that investment in many non-OECD countries is also too low. Also, the ageing of the population in many OECD countries may imply that a higher level of savings is desirable. These considerations point, among others, to the role of the public sector and perhaps to the desirability of lower fiscal deficits and debt in many countries, in order to release resources to the private sector.

The second paragraph is essentially based on fact, dealing with elements that have previously been recognized as truthful.

In general, dynamic non-member economies in Asia have high growth, low inflation and balanced budgets, and also very high saving and investment rates. By contrast, many Latin American countries have low savings rates and erratic capital inflows, as foreign lenders have been discouraged by macroeconomic instability. As a result, average per capita growth rates have been low in the past 10-15 years. Many OECD countries are in an intermediate position. In many cases, fiscal positions have deteriorated, and national savings rates have fallen, as have growth rates since the 1970s.

Differences in performance, in both OECD and non-OECD member countries are at once put on the table and not obscured.

Given these differences in performance, and the concerns outlined above, the objective of the workshop is to examine how experience across countries on saving and investment rates relates to the level and structure of public finances and, in some cases, to public policy more generally. Case studies will be used to address specific issues—like the role of pension systems. Also, consideration will be given to prospects for public finance, their impact on saving and investment, and the policies required to increase savings in the future.

---

*contd. ...*

*...contd. ...*

The session is intended to allow the participant to 'review cross-country experience.' This is building the consensus about the factual basis.

The use of questions to induce participants to enter into discussion has a number of subtle advantages.

It invites immediate participation. Faced with a statement, a participant may chose to agree passively. But a question avoids that trap.

It is less threatening as it leaves space for thinking and phrasing one's own mind.

Short statements always sound dogmatic as they lose all the nuances that come with a long text. A question avoids that other trap.

It permits one to attack the subject from various angles, even allows for subtle quasi-redundancies and sub-questions. These appeal to differnt characters, thus involving more participation.

Observe also how the various operative verbs stimulate different areas of the brain: critical (i), analytical (ii and iv), or creative (iii)

The group is then progressively moved toward making its own analysis of the body of evidence that comes from the various case studies and drawing agreed conclusions.

Here again, questions prompt discussions in a direct but not threatening fashion.
Notice the use of "To what extent..." In effect, this question is very direct. It suggests a conclusion: Current or planned policy will have an impact for increase saving, but..." to what extent...? The reader may consider the various alternatives that would try to move the agenda using assertions rather than two line questions.

Session one: The role of Public Policies in the evolution of Saving and Investments
....The aim is to review the cross-country experience...
Suggested issues for discussion:

i) *Are there reasons to believe* that pension systems that are privately funded, or fully funded by the state, are associated with higher levels of national savings?

ii) Is pension system reform by itself *likely to result* in higher national savings, or must other measures be taken as well?

iii) *Do other specific public policies exist,* which durably affect private sector saving behaviour, and how certain can one be of their effects?

iv) To what extent *can different saving rates as between countries be explained* by purely economic and demographic factors? Are cultural and institutional factors relevant?

Session two: Prospects for Public Finances, Saving and Investment
The aim of this session is to assess cross-country prospects for fiscal policy, and the behaviour of saving and investment. Against the background of their possible evolution across countries,
Suggested issues for discussion:

i) Case studies on prospects for individual countries:
   — How will Chinese Taipei's fiscal deficit be consolidated?
   — Prospects for national saving/investment balances in Thailand.
   — What are the prospects for a sustained in saving in Argentina?
   — *To what extent* might current or planned policy reforms affect medium-term prospects for national saving and investment balances in OECD countries?

*contd. ...*

...contd. ...

ii) General points:
— To what extent do participants feel that it is reasonable and prudent to rely on inter national capital flows to equilibrate prospective national saving and investment balances in individual countries?
— How urgent is fiscal consolidation in OECD countries? In Latin America? Is it likely that pressure for greater social expenditure (e.g. on health and education) will build up in Asian DNMEs as their in come levels increase?

The last session finally brings things together leading to conclusions.
Notice for example, that an alternative would have been to deal with each subject in sequence and draw conclusions early on, subject by subject.

This way of doing things, however, invests early in building the overall self-confidence and trust of the group; it empowers it at the end to move in a dynamic fashion toward making recommendations based "...on agreed upon evidence."

The group is moved toward generalizations and the sharing of best practices.

The last question is haunting, leaving much space for doubt and for future discussions. It reflects an old penchant within the OECD for progress achieved incrementally over the long term rather than through one-shot spectacular operations.

Notice that the very last question allows for criticism of the OECD members, the hosts; this may be seen as courteous, giving the last word to outside guests.

Third session: Policy Implications
This session will confront the evidence and lessons from the two first sessions with medium-term fiscal and structural reform programs, in order to draw policy conclusions.
Suggested issues for discussion:
i)    *Do participants agree that, given the theoretical and empirical evidence,* the only sure way for governments to affect saving/investment balances is to act directly on public sector balances?
ii)   *Is Chile's experience in raising its national saving rate exportable* to other countries in the region?
iii)  Even if pension reform were to have no net impact on national savings balances, *is it desirable on other grounds?*
iv)   More generally, *what does the experience* of countries over time, or across countries, *suggest* about a) the interaction between spending on welfare programs (as a proportion of GDP) and national saving rates. Is there a negative correlation here?; and b) the effect of a sustained change in welfare spending on national savings balances?
v)    *Are the policy measures envisaged by OECD countries to consolidate their fiscal positions likely to have the desired effect?*

It should be noted that other forms of agenda are also in use within the organization. The annotated agenda is used for more delicate meetings, those where new actors gather or when a subject is particularly difficult. Otherwise, the committee chair may prefer simple and direct agenda that list the subjects and define what type of action is expected from the meeting. Once again, it should be stressed that this text develops a model structure, and is not a meticulous description of all different practices.

## 4.2 The Syntax For Summary Record

The summary record complements the agenda in the OECD negotiation process, which has likewise been refined into an art form. The summary record is intended to focus the attention of the various member delegations on the common agenda and shared goals, even after they return to their home country. The availability of a summary record of OECD negotiations tends to militate against a tendency on the part of returning delegations to toy with narrow nationalist views at the expense of the wider-ranging, supra-national values and goals reflected in OECD.

As in golf, follow-through is critical to ensure the success of the meeting. In many cases, the most salient output of a meeting is the analytical summary record of the meeting or seminar. That is not to say that the meeting itself is not important: the mere fact of gathering competent individuals, selected for the pertinence of their knowledge and for their key position in government, generally is sufficient to justify the cost of most meetings. However, one could argue that the conclusions reached by such a group, once organized in an intelligible fashion, based on a well structured agenda, should become part of common knowledge and be accepted as authoritative.

The summary records must first and foremost reflect fully and in an analytical manner the conclusions reached and the substance of any preceding discussion. Whatever consensus is reached, partial or otherwise, must be immediately identified and added to the knowledge base.

If the meeting is part of a longstanding workshop, then we would accept an 'interpreted consensus': it is the role of the Chair to interpret (generally with the assistance of the Secretariat) what constitutes a legitimate agreement by participants. It is only when a final document implying contractual arrangements have been reached that it may become necessary to define consensus in a more formal fashion.

Consensus is seldom reached on every agenda item: issues that remain controversial, including their supporting arguments, are as such a valid product that will find usage at a subsequent meeting. It is therefore critical to take note of disagreements, and the summary should endeavour to give back to participants the full richness of their divergences and of the argumentation.

Obviously, it is of no use to simply account literally for everything: the discursive nature of debates makes them often unintelligible.

The speed with which the secretariat provides such a summary is key to ensuring the success of a meeting: it is an underestimated and unsuspected asset. A first draft should be provided at least orally, but preferably in writing, before the end of the meeting. A final summary record should reach participants not later than seven working days after the meeting. Beyond these dates, participants will have formed their own individual perception and these will have "gelled" in their mind. Once participants know that the Secretariat will provide these records with diligence, they generally wait for it before writing their own report and communicating its conclusions to colleagues and senior managers. Experience has shown that summary records prepared by each delegation tend to overemphasize the point of view of the delegation and understate or oversimplify the views of other delegations. As a result, these 'national summary records' tend to be somewhat sectarian, and if not balanced by a more even point of view, they will slow down the development of a final consensus.

*Key Characteristics*

A good summary record fully reflects the richness of a meeting. In particular:

- It avoids repetitions and redundancies as much as possible.

- It structures the discussions in a manner that allows a reader to fully understand what was said; for that purpose, interventions may be repositioned where they make more sense.

- It underscores agreements and consensus.

- It does not gloss over dissensions but raises problematic issues frankly and respectfully.

- It lists and provides intelligence to contentious subjects, to questions and new problems that arose during the meeting.

- It clearly highlights commitments and pledges when appropriate.

- It always captures the clear and agreed upon actions to be taken, identifies who is responsible to carry them out, and will often capture those subtle actions and commitments that were implicit.

One must assume all participants to a meeting have something essential they wanted to say and convey. No intervention must be excluded *a priori* from the record as being irrelevant, trivial, or devoid of meaning. Especially when dealing with national delegates, it must be assumed that each intervention, no matter how obscure, was intended and most likely was discussed in advance by the delegation. The summary record must therefore account for all key points raised by participants.

Second, speakers may deliver their key message outside of the agenda items planned for and agreed at the outset. There are many reasons for not following the agenda. It often happens that a delegate will relate everything he has come to say in one stroke, for a variety of reasons. The Secretariat, when drafting the summary record, should not pass judgment on this, but make sure the record remains intelligible. For that purpose, the summary record must reposition all interventions in their proper context.

This having been said, redundancies must be avoided as they clog the text and render it difficult to read and understand. Care must be taken when summarizing to make use of the words of various speakers, and not always use the words from the same one.

The summary record must scrupulously avoid creating tensions, especially by polarizing groups unintentionally. Any forms of 'us-them' language is barred at all times. Often without our noticing, we tend to group things in a binary fashion: "On the one hand, some argued this..., while, on the other hand, others argued the contrary...." In an insidious way, this method breeds tension and may pit one group against another through 'subliminal summarizing' so to speak. It is generally better to recognize subtle nuances and reflect non-binary regrouping. For example: "The group considered various aspects of the question. Some argued that...others considered this...while another group viewed it as key to the resolution of the problem." Regrouping into three or more categories of argumentation will generally reflect the nature of the discussion while ensuring that an accidental cleavage does not compound dissension.

All statements eventually belong to the group once expressed and discussed. In most instances, it is therefore unnecessary and even counterproductive to ascribe positions, opinions, or even factual statements to any particular member. It is better to say: "The group considered various points of view: for some..." When two or more members suggested divergent facts or statistics, one could write: "the discussion revealed divergent views with regard to statistical evidence: for some the growth rate was closer to (say) 5% while others argued that 8% better reflected reality..." It is preferable to raise a problem and often underscore the capacity of the group to properly deal with issues and contradictions.

There are very few meetings where nothing was achieved in terms of partial consensus. Whatever was achieved and agreed upon must be fully recorded, and the manner of reporting these partial agreements must convey finality and bring closure to that portion of the ongoing discussion. In so doing, the summary record must be open to future discussions and, in effect, it generally clarifies the next agenda. It must, as much as possible, highlight the task required to reach the next stage and identify responsibility centres.

By definition, networks such as OECD exist because there are conflicts and divergences of views; these instruments have been expressly created to deal with resolving conflicts evolving from differences in policies, habits, behaviour, ideologies, and beliefs among its participants. The fundamental principle is therefore to differentiate clearly what is shared from what brings about conflicts. One has to think as positively as possible to find all and every little or significant agreement and consensus. This having been done, the remaining divergences must be clearly stated so the group can deal with them at the first opportunity.

The tendency to be politically correct, to gloss over conflicts, to use euphemisms to disguise a difference and turn it into a pseudo-agreement, to replace subtleties with vagueness, are all efficient ways to entrench conflicts and ensure they remain protracted and increasingly more difficult to resolve. Modern psychology recognizes that naming your demons is an essential step in recovery. Denial, or double-talk, moves the group one step away from empowering itself to resolve these conflicts. The summary record plays a key role in that process.

A litmus test for a good summary record is found in the satisfaction of participants. As they read and recognize what they said, they will note with satisfaction that the interventions they often made with timidity or uncertainty have taken on a real value once set into the full context of the meeting. They will often discover how much sense their own intervention made once it is reset correctly into the full discussion context. This is where the intellectual agility and profound knowledge of the subject by those who write summary records become essential components of the process. In Canada, the US, and many other OECD countries, it has often become fashion to ask professional writers to draft these documents. In effect, what is gained in writing ability is offset by the lack of technical knowledge; this knowledge deficit means that very subtle compromises, implicit or even explicit to the discussion, are not perceived and brought to the attention of the group. Here again the ability to foster progress and reduce tension finds its outcome. These abilities are made of a real combination of intelligence, knowledge, and a true measure of humility. The records are meant to underscore the capacity of the participants to resolve problems among themselves.

This brings about a paradox and a quandary. Successful directors make everything sound natural, and in this way, the group generally believes it is solely responsible for achievements. This may lead the group to underestimate its own Secretariat, its role, and its true accomplishment. In a world that is increasingly dominated by media, and which rests on worshipping individual heroes, the 'non-flashy servants' of the group may become the victim of their own true success.

Following is an example of a good summary. It is an extract of the record of proceedings of the N'Djamena meeting of the Sahel Club, which took place January 26-27, 1988 (doc. no. CR(88)58E).

*The Context*

One of the issues being debated at the N'djamena meeting concerned cereal production policies. This was central to survival strategies of farmers in the Sahel region: "Should local cereal producers benefit from protectionist measures? If so, should aid donors assume directly or indirectly, the financial support for such measures." From 1976 to 1988, this subject had given rise to lengthy and passionate debates and many expert reports.

All nine ministers of finance and ministers of rural development representing Sahelian countries, and from high-level delegates from Canada, France, Germany, Switzerland, The Netherlands, United States, World Bank, IMF, EU, and the OECD Secretariat attended the N'djamena meeting.

It can be objectively argued that this issue had divided decision-makers and experts into two broad camps. There were those who believed that protectionist measures were the best way to ensure a good level of domestic production—the so-called Common Agricultural Policy (CAP) as practised within the EU was generally exemplified to justify this stance. The second group included those who argued in favour of an open market that, in their view, would eventually provide the right mix of opportunities and incentives for both Sahelian producers and consumers.

Rice, a staple commodity of the Sahelian diet, was increasingly being imported at below farm-gate price from Thailand and other exporting nations. Various subsidies (ironically including subsidies paid by the Government of the United States) had contributed to deflating world price of many cereals, especially rice. Local rice farmers were facing harsh competition indeed. Senegal had imposed a tax on imported rice; however, Thailand rice came through the Gambian port of Banjul and found its way into the hands of consumers in Dakar through porous and difficult-to-protect borders. With the World Bank increasingly involved in structural adjustments programs, this issue was topical indeed. Nobody wanted to antagonize France or the US, since both were firmly entrenched in opposite camps.

Diplomats would characterize the discussion as frank, a euphemism meaning that parties had expressed divergent views in a forceful and direct manner. I was tasked to summarize discussions. Mrs. Anne de Lattre, who was then director of the Club, however, rejected my summary. She proceeded to rewrite it in a manner more in line with OECD's traditions and subtlety. In the following days, I analyzed meticulously the differences between my version and hers. The lessons I learned that day are discussed below.

## Box 4.5

*Summary Record, Example and Comments*

In a few strokes, the sense of topic and the speakers are introduced.

The meeting discussed a document entitled "A Protected Regional Cereals Market, An Initial Exploration of a New Idea." The discussion was introduced by the Mali Minister of Planning and by Mr. Louis Caudron (France). The document focuses on rice production and demonstrates that cereal imports to the Sahel have increased significantly over the past 10 years, which is a worrisome trend from a number of standpoints.

No matter how small and fugitive, whatever consensus emerged is dutifully recorded.

Participants agreed that agricultural development is a crucial factor for economic progress in the Sahelian countries, and that it is impossible to encourage farmers to increase the quantity and quality of production without providing incentives. However, the participants expressed differing view

The key contentious issues are at once introduced.

points on the role that protectionism could play in the rapid development of Sahelian food crop production, and certain representatives of Sahelian countries wondered how it would be possible to reconcile protectionist and liberalization policies, which are recommended simultaneously

Key contradictions, as stated by participants are immediately revealed, thus marking out the limitations of the current debate.

Argument one is introduced.

Certain participants considered that a protectionist policy would not favour an increase in Sahelian food crop production. Even if it was possible to define the geographic area and the products to be protected, protection might distort the distribution of scarce resources and discourage the commercial competition that would increase producers' incomes and reduce consumer prices. If rice was protected,

Argumentation is stated in the form of rhetorical questions, a more neutral, less aggressive way of reflecting diverging positions while providing the gist of the argumentation.

would there be any attempt to develop production of more profitable crops in irrigated areas? Would there be any attempt to reduce production costs, which is one of the key factors in increased cereals production in the Sahel? Would there not be a tendency to reject other measures, which would be just as effective as protection, such as the readjustment of exchange rates?

This is a compromise position. Notice it is set in between the two arguments, thus underscoring the impression that there exists a spectrum of solutions as opposed to black and white opposite views to be followed by some mushy 'grey' compromise.

Other participants adopted a more reserved stance. They recognized that the trade policies of Sahelian countries would have a major impact on certain large-scale investments that have already been made, but considered it overly ambitious to talk of a protected regional market at the present time. These participants felt that emphasis should rather be placed on harmonizing cereals policies in CILSS Member Countries. An initial phase of the harmonization process could involve identifying and ana-

Possible solutions are immediately highlighted, which turn this intermediary position into something where work can commence as soon as possible.

lyzing the measures taken in each country, and in particular measures aimed at introducing protection or creating incentives, in Mali (PRMC, Office du Niger), Senegal, Burkina Faso, etc. Results of this analysis could be disseminated and comparisons made to see whether the measures that have been taken are complementary. There is also a need to examine the prices of imports—which are generally highly subsidized—to ascertain whether these prices are set at levels that will not discourage local pro duction and that will not promote informal border trade. Several participants considered that it was impossible to justify a protectionist policy by focusing on rice production alone, since rice accounts for only one-tenth of total cereals production in the Sahel. The scope of the studies must be widened to cover Sahelian cereals production as a whole, and the studies must investigate the consequences that protection would have on producers, on different groups of consumers and on public-sector finances. The boundaries of the area to be protected must be defined.

Only then do we read about the antithesis.

A third group of participants considered that, although protection is only one of a number of ways to promote the development of cereals production in the Sahel, it must not be overlooked. First, agriculture will certainly continue to be the basis of the economies of Sahelian countries over the coming decades. Those economies must be modernized, and it is unlikely that modernization can be achieved if the Sahelian agricultural economy is not protected from the major upheavals of world markets and from the influx of agricultural produce subsidized by industrial countries. Second, modernization of water supply and irrigation infrastructures might turn out to be impossible without protectionist measures, even if the selling prices of products grown by irrigated agriculture in Sahelian countries are higher than those of equivalent products from industrial countries or from countries with more modern agricultural sectors. Finally, this group of participants stressed the importance of safeguarding producers' incomes in order to allow them to purchase equipment. Over and above these considerations, it would perhaps be reasonable to oppose the outward orientation and de-linkaging of Sahelian economies and to make optimum use of local resources. Protection will clearly have its price. Consideration must be given to how that price could be shared by consumers, public funds and foreign aid, and to whether it would not be more beneficial to use foreign aid to cover part of the cost of protection rather than perpetuate other forms of aid.

Notice how we are referring to a group of participants, not a faction, nor a group outside of the Group, of the Group, but a legitimate part of the overall argumentation.

Should protection be national or regional? Each government should be responsible for defining its own policies, but the future of Sahelian countries depends on regional cooperation, which will make it possible to make the most of the complementarity that exists. This involves cooperation among Sahelian countries on the one hand, and between inland Sahelian countries and coastal countries on the other.

The legitimacy of a strong debate in the context of a highly complex problem is highlighted. Notice the use of 'the meeting,' not 'the group'; a meeting is one step removed from people and the use of this word suggests detachment and objectivity.

Although the meeting was not overly surprised that a consensus could not be reached on the significance of protection for development of Sahelian cereals production, participants were particularly impressed by the objectivity of the exchange of views on such a complex question.

Tasks to be done are immediately noted, further suggesting both consensus and practicality. Again, it's the meeting that issues commands.

The meeting asked CILSS to identify and analyze cereals policy measures that have beentaken by Member Countries, to disseminate findings and submit conclusions to national authorities in order to clarify exchanges of views and guide decision-makers in their attempts to harmonize cereals policies. The meeting further recommended that the study of the role of protection in the development of cereals policies should be expanded to cover cereals production as a whole, with a view to facilitating the ongoing dialogue between Sahelian leaders and donors on this matter.

Future dialogues and discussions are announced, the agenda set; this suggests continuity rather than discord.

In a few strokes, participants are made to feel they have participated in a meaningful discussion, one which has moved the agenda forward and which will be followed by precise actions and further discussions.

Participants have in hand a succinct review of all key arguments summarized in a manner that only comes with knowledge and long practice. No matter how clumsily the various positions were expressed, they come out adding to the pool of shared knowledge.

Last but not least, all members have in hand a balanced report to draw from when they report back to headquarters; note should be taken that a draft version of this summary was read at the last sitting of the meeting.

Work to be performed before the next meeting is clear and the ongoing dialogue may continue.

In essence, anyone reading this text will come out with the feeling that money spent on gathering people from various countries was a good investment.

## 4.3 The Syntax of the Communiqué[6]

"The communiqué represents the concrete, public outcome of the confidential debates that take place during the annual meeting of the OECD Council at Ministerial Level. At first there was a tendency to let the communiqué run on at great length; in time it came to be thought, however, that a shorter and more incisive text was more likely to capture media

---

6. This section has been translated from Chavranski (1997: 45-48) and is reproduced here with the kind permission of the author.

attention and interest. The current product represents something of a compromise that will vary from year to year. As opposed to what one might think, the communiqué is not an instant product, but the result of a lengthy process of preparation.

The draft communiqué is prepared by the Secretariat and distributed to member states several weeks before the ministerial meeting. Putting this draft together demands a very subtle and balanced approach on the part of senior Secretariat staff, which must assess carefully the current status of the various issues that are being put to ministers and the decisions or quasi-decisions that can reasonably be expected from the meeting. The draft is the subject of interminable negotiations among diplomats and experts from member states. Representatives will suggest the amendments their country would like to see, knowing perfectly well that they will be unacceptable to one or more of the others: they will argue them out first with their colleagues, then within the specialized organs, and finally it will be the turn of the permanent representatives or ambassadors.

The discussions will carry on for many long days, producing a series of successive versions in which differences are gradually eliminated. Little by little, debate will come to focus on a few points of divergence, which will vary from one year to the next, and on which representatives stick to their positions, under instructions from their authorities, or for that matter their head of mission. The end result of this process is an agreed text with alternative wordings in square brackets on a few points (the number of which will vary from year to year), reflecting the differences of opinion that persist at the end of this first phase.

The second phase takes place on the margins of the Council meeting itself. Ministers' personal representatives will huddle together, chaired by the Deputy Secretary General (who is assumed to be both completely neutral as well as thoroughly familiar with the subject matter) in an effort to find wording that will be acceptable to all.

Any remaining differences are put to the ministers themselves, and they will attempt to sort things out during a ministers-only working luncheon hosted by the Secretary-General. At this point, the ministers' senior advisors will be set up in a separate room, where they can follow the discussion with earphones. They will, of course, be anxious to see whether their ministers have had the time to digest the disarming arguments and debating points that their staff will have developed and whispered into their ears on the way to the meeting room or the luncheon. In the entire history of OECD, there has yet to be a case where this process failed to produce a text that could be approved at the final session of the Council. In fact, it can be said to be an absolute requirement that, before the ministers and their entourage get on the plane to return home late on the second day, a compromise version of the communiqué must have been agreed.

By way of illustration, we refer to the nine-page communiqué that resulted from the Ministerial meeting of May 21-22, 1996, a session that was particularly fertile in terms of debate and decisions. That communiqué set out the policy directions and the mandate adopted by ministers for the coming year. It did no more than summarize the issues dealt with during the Council since, as the communiqué notes, ministers based their discussion primarily on three reports, the first on investment, the second competition, and the third on employment and labour standards.

### The Constants ('The Boilerplate')

The text of that communiqué may strike the reader as somewhat puzzling and prone to gobbledygook. Yet its meaning can for the most part be deciphered by comparing it with communiqués from previous years and with the many declarations and statements made by ministers to the press during the Council meeting. This of course presupposes some familiarity with the way the organization works. Comparing these declarations can help us appreciate the intentions of the different parties and, up to a certain point, the meaning that should be given to wording that is sometimes ambiguous or vague on points where agreement was particularly difficult.

It is interesting to note that many of the formulations we found there showed up a few weeks later in the communiqué from the G-7 Summit. The Summit and the OECD Ministerial meetings debate much the same issues, and indeed it would be surprising if the positions taken at the end of May by the 24 (now 30) OECD countries were not reflected by the G-7 a few weeks later, even if the latter gathering takes place at the level of Presidents and Heads of Government. The OECD ministerial Council is therefore increasingly seen as a stage in the process of consideration leading up to the Summit, as a kind of 'trial run' that gives smaller countries not attending the summit a chance to make their views known and to inject ideas into the debate.

The text of the communiqué contains self-evident observations that no one would contradict, statements of principles underlying the policies pursued (or that should be pursued) by governments of all member states and, finally, agreements (or the outline of agreements) that have been reached on specific points that were up for debate. On the negative side, the points where there was no agreement can also be detected—they will either be left out of the text completely, or they will be given wording that can be interpreted in several ways.

The communiqué is clearly too long to comment on in its entirety. We may, however, cite a few examples. Some paragraphs are statements of fact ("the strong fundamentals in many OECD countries strengthen prospects for better economic growth...high budget deficits and public debt remain key problems...unemployment remains unacceptably high...to take advantage of these prospects for improved living conditions and progress, individuals, enterprises and countries must show themselves capable of rapid adjustment and continuous innovation," etc.). Later paragraphs confirm the principles of action on which there is a general consensus ("implementing macroeconomic and structural policies that are mutually reinforcing and that will raise growth potential, increase job creation, maintain inflation at a low level and promote sustainable development, giving priority to combating unemployment, strengthening structural reforms, etc.").

## The Variables ('The Real Meat')

All of the foregoing is no doubt useful and important to remember, if only to banish any idea that these basic principles have been in some way abandoned or modified. But the real importance of the communiqué lies elsewhere. In the first place, there is the consideration of progress reports on issues where negotiations are under way but not yet completed: this was the case in 1996, for example, with the MAI (Multilateral Agreement on Investment), where Ministers undertook to reach an agreement by 1997 that would include "high standards of investment liberalization and protection and effective dispute settlement procedures and aim at achieving a higher level of liberalization" and to "engage in an intensified dialogue with non-member countries, in particular those interested in acceding to the MAI."

This is particularly true for new points that were not at issue in previous years. We can give several examples here. The sharp debate over the US Helms-Burton law, which raises the issue of extraterritorially enforcing the American embargo on Cuba, might have been expected to produce a clear condemnation of unilateralism: in the face of US opposition, however, the final wording was cast in a positive if rather convoluted way: "(Ministers) reaffirm the very high priority they attach to an effective and dynamic multilateral trading system, in particular by ...working to strengthen the confidence in and credibility of the multilateral trading system by avoiding taking trade and investment measures that would be in contradiction with World Trade Organization (WTO) rules and OECD codes." All delegations were able to take comfort in this wording— some, because it showed the question had been explicitly raised and the basic principles had been confirmed, others because their policies had not been specifically challenged.

In 1996 the issue of international air transport was raised for the first time (Paragraph 9, viii). Ministers committed themselves to "further work for liberalizing, in the interests of all, international air transport within bilateral and multilateral frameworks in order to ensure that the aviation sector contributes fully to economic development in OECD countries and in the world more generally."

As well, for the first time in a Ministerial communiqué, explicit reference was made (in a thoroughly torturous paragraph) to the issue of tax deductibility for bribes paid to foreign officials, something that had until that time been limited to internal discussions in which there were significant differences of opinion (Paragraph 9, x).

Although one highlight of the 1996 Ministerial was no doubt the arrival of an official and quite unexpected application for membership from Russia, Ministers carefully limited themselves in the communiqué to supporting further cooperation with that country, without making any reference to the specific request received (Paragraph 15, xxi).

Finally, Ministers called on OECD to address issues relating to the setting of priorities in a manner consistent with available resources (Paragraph 16). The Organization's 1996 budget crisis at least had the merit of provoking some urgent thinking about these issues. It remains to be seen whether the special Council meeting that is to deal with this matter will be able to reach agreement on the steps to be taken.

These examples show that the annual communiqué is to a large extent a reflection (even if this is hardly evident to the casual observer) of the various debates under way at any time within the organization, and of the trends they are taking. Rarely will the communiqué reveal any abrupt shifts of position—that sort of thing simply does not happen within OECD. As some see it, the communiqué is merely a rhetorical exercise intended to persuade public opinion that the Organization is moving forward and is adopting a definite policy in the many areas of its jurisdiction, even if the wording that is so painstakingly created is promptly forgotten. This is surely a pessimistic way of viewing things. For others, every sentence, every phrase, represents a commitment, a benchmark, on the basis of which all member states will be expected gradually to refine and spell out their positions. The reality is likely to fall somewhere between these two views."

## 4.4 The Syntax of Peer Reviews

Peer reviews are at the core of all documents produced by OECD. They must, at all times, embody the high quality of OECD's drafting capacity. Peer reviews represent a dual challenge and thus a most complex balancing act. They must be critical of a country's activity, while fully respecting its culture. One should never lose sight of an important feature of a sovereign nation's capacity to create nuisance issues. Review writers are caught between their professional ethics and practical considerations. Following are some tricks of the trade.

The traditions upon which OECD's respectability is based rest on well-established scientific traditions. Thus, everything starts with the establishment of a solid factual foundation. Facts, however, are elusive because they often depend on the perspective of those who look at them. Over the years, OECD has contributed to the building of rock-solid data-gathering mechanisms and truthful national accounts. Not every fact is captured or described by measurable data (see earlier discussion), however attempts should be made to make full use of data produced by the member country and agreed by it. Any error, misinterpretation, or distortion at this level must be corrected in the early stages of informal discussions with the country.

This also applies to the establishment of the factual basis upon which analysis will be made. A shared interpretation of facts must be agreed upon early and informally. In this regard, a form of scientific humility combined with poise and self-assurance are a must for analysts. Truth is elusive, and must be found through persistent, probing, and courteous discussions, not through intellectual smugness or doctrinaire argumentation. The establishment of facts is likely to become a solid element of the analysis if and when it has been fully agreed upon by all parties. This is more likely to happen when facts are based on data and evidence provided by the country itself.

Once this has been achieved, then and only then can the Secretariat proceed with formulating its own analysis. The analysis has always clearly been the prerogative and the responsibility of the Secretariat. In making the critical analysis of the country's performance, the analyst is confronted with a multitude of choices: what must be underscored without any compromise, and what must be dropped. Each case is specific and there exist no hard and fast rules to govern this careful selection. To help in the selection of issues, I used the following simple structure.

### Table 4.2

*Table of Decision for Difficult Issues*

|  | Issues that are relatively easy to raise with the country | Issues that are difficult to discuss |
|---|---|---|
| Issues that must absolutely be included in the analysis | To treat with usual rigour and courtesy. The argument must be persuasive, not just well put. | To treat with utmost circumspection. Facts must be thoroughly researched using appropriate methodology to arrive at impeccable conclusions. Language must be guarded, prudent, and devoid of any emotional content. Objectivity must be obvious, thus care must be taken in recognizing achievements by the country before entering into criticism. The argument must be judged for its capacity to be persuasive. |
| Issues that are secondary, or embellishments | To treat with the same rigour and courtesy, but always raised. | To consider raising at another opportunity. |

### Box 4.6

*Third-Rail Issues*

In the metro, there are two rails upon which the train rides: one can walk safely on them, but one must beware of the third one, which transports electricity. In an analogous manner, there exist some issues that are most politicized in one country. A third-rail issue is immune to objective discussion and is generally politically touchy. Third-rail issues are most difficult to deal with, yet, they are often most important in the search for economic growth and good governance. What is taboo in one country is generally considered open for discussion in others. For example, Japan does not consider immigration a solution to its depleting and aging work force. Furthermore, it is not interested in entering into debates within OECD about this subject, despite the fact that all other members have more or less adopted such a practice as an element of the solution when faced with a similar problem.

Third-rail issues are different from other difficult issues in the sense that there is no hope of change in the short term. Japan, to continue on the same example, is facing difficult restructuring of its economy, as the 2002 economic survey makes clear. Dealing with weak banks, however, once the pride of Japan can be considered and discussed openly. But third-rail items must be given very special treatment; which is discussed below. The analysis of the way the economic department of OECD has dealt with those provides useful clues as to the manner by which one should write a solid peer review

## Box 4.7
### *Dealing with "Third-Rail" Subjects—A Few Examples*

#### Canada and the Export of Water

In Canada, the idea of selling water in bulk or through diverting large bodies of water is a very sensitive issue, one that politicians seldom discuss. Objectively, economists will argue that exporting water, especially for a country that owns 40% of the world's drinkable water resources, is a perfectly legitimate issue to consider.

In the adjacent paragraph, notice the prudence used by OECD drafters in raising the issue and in constructing a favourable argument for the eventual sale of water.

- At first, a recognized fact leads to a recognized cause (1). Followed by an accepted solution (2).
- This leads to a broader and more encompassing opening, i.e. transferring water rights; notice the careful caveat: provided it does no harm to the ecosystem... This could have been implicit without any, danger, but it was essential to Canadian anxieties (3).
- In other words, there exist overriding non-economic factors at play (4).
- OECD will only raise, in measured and calculated terms, the prospect of exporting water (5).

" [...] (1) *overuse of water, because it is under-priced,* has become a problem is some regions, despite the abundant supply overall. While the government has been endorsing the principle of "economic pricing" of water for some time, provincial and local government, which are responsible for water management, are moving only slowly in this direction [...] To bring about more efficient water use, provincial and territorial (2) *governments should therefore implement the principle of "economic pricing,"* without delay, (3) *while making water rights transferable in problem areas (provided that does no harm to the ecosystem).* This requires substantially increased use of water metering, which is still far from universal, and the elimination of quantity discounts. Such a policy would be consistent with the recent decision to ban bulk water removal, thereby preventing exports, (4) *which reveals a very high implicit social valuation of water.* Nonetheless, (5) *a carefully designed export licensing system might allow Canada to reap some benefits from its abundant aggregate water resources, while at the same time preventing harmful environment effects."*

(Policy Brief: Economic Survey of the United States, 2002, p.3-5, OECD 2002)

#### Switzerland and Banking Secrecy

Swiss people look upon their banking system with great pride, and generally view its rigorous secrecy as a clear asset for the economy. They are extremely reluctant to introduce measures to make it more transparent as a result of foreign pressure. Furthermore, this is a rare occurrence. However, reforms about money laundering or tax evasion require everyone's collaboration.

- Positive aspects are carefully noted before entering into the argument (1).
- And things could be improved further if...regional government interfered less (2).

"Concerning money laundering, (1) *legislation is very strict*; it relies on the control of four supervisory authorities and on self-regulation organizations. Regarding the latter, their effectiveness will have to be assessed. The resources of the agency that oversees the fight against money laundering in the parabanking sector, while having increased, are still limited.

- The *raison d'être* of such interference is fully qualified: in other words, no reader of the Survey could be left in doubt as to the good motivation of Swiss local governments (3).

That said (1) *the good overall performance of Swiss financial institutions could be improved further* (2) *if the management and credit policy of cantonal banks were less subject to local political interference;* (3) *social and regional policy objectives could be achieved* (4) *more transparently by other means, which would allow an assessment of their costs."*

(Policy Brief: Economic Survey of the United States, 2002, p.3-5, OECD 2002)

- In the same sentence, an advantage for local legislators is highlighted: they could achieve the same results more transparently and with a better assessment of the real costs (4).

- Notice again that something that might remain implicit, is made explicit, thus reducing any possible ambiguity as to the real intentions of the OECD; thus further placating the country representative's fears or susceptibility (5).
- That being said, Peers and the Secretariat remain concerned about the effectiveness of changes in Swiss legislation and this concern is dutifully noted (6).

"Another area of concern refers to the preferential treatment of foreign investment. As noted in the previous *Survey*, the fiduciary investments made by Swiss banks on behalf of their clients in foreign jurisdictions where no withholding tax is levied on capital income potentially enables these clients (as well as resident taxpayers) to escape taxation on that income. Although this would not be different if the taxpayers were directly investing in foreign jurisdictions, the Swiss bank secrecy (5) – *provided no tax fraud has been perpetrated* – additionally impedes the countries of residence to properly tax the capital income under consideration. Since the scope of the Swiss withholding tax has been up to now limited to Swiss-sourced income (6), *there is still a concern on how to effectively discourage such tax evasion.* This problem was the subject of OECD Report of the Committee on Fiscal Affairs, published on 12 April 2000, and which was adopted by all members of the Committee. Member countries, including Switzerland, are in process of reviewing their laws and practices and will report back by the end of 2002."

(Policy Brief: Economic Survey of the United States, 2002, p.3-5, OECD 2002)

## The American Health Insurance Issue

A decade ago, President Clinton tasked his wife with finding a more appropriate Health Insurance scheme for Americans. Following a thorough study and a protracted legislative negotiation, the idea of universal health insurance was shelved. Since then, political wisdom dictates that American politicians stay clear of that issue. It has become a third-rail subject. Increasingly, American delegations to OECD have become impatient with the attitude shared among many other OECD countries that consider the US a backward country for not having a universal health system.

Despite American annoyance, OECD considers the issue important enough to devote almost two pages (of a total of seven) to deal with this matter..

[...] (1) *The US health-care system is unique in the OECD area. It is responsive, adapting quickly to changes in consumer preferences. Moreover, most Americans are highly satisfied with the care they receive.* However, (2) *despite spending vastly more than other Member*

- As customary, the good features of the system are fully recognized (1).
- But the downside is quick to come. Notice the cool and clinical language being used (2).
- It rests on fully recognized facts, based on data that the US itself provided. Furthermore, it sustains the following analysis on solid forecast: by 2011, the cost will represent 17% of GDP (3).
- The conclusion is pure mastery of the economic/diplomatic language. Rather than bluntly suggesting the US move toward universal coverage, the drafters emphasized "promoting larger risk pools at the state and local level" (4).

In the end, the respect for facts, combined with respect for susceptibilities through careful usage of the language makes it very difficult for the delegation to object further.

*countries, both per capita and in relation to GDP, its relative performance on various measures of health status is only about average among OECD countries, and there is evidence to suggest that the same clinical outcomes could be achieved using fewer resources. Furthermore, the US system is the only one among the wealthier OECD countries that does not provide universal insurance coverage.* After broad stability relative to national income over most of the 1990s, (3) *health spending has re-accelerated and is projected to rise from 14 per cent of GDP today to 17 per cent in 2011*, just as the ageing of the baby-boom generation gets underway. The expansion of managed care succeeded temporarily in limiting cost increases, both by curbing prices paid to providers and reducing use of inpatient hospital care. With providers now exploiting more effectively their bargaining power with health plans and patients pressing for greater choice of providers and treatments, the managed-care approach seems to have largely exhausted its cost savings potential. As a result, (3) *premiums for private health insurance are again rising at double-digit rates. Public programs are also facing unsustainable cost increases.*

[...] Finally, the problem of cost induced shrinkage in insurance coverage by firms using the small-group market should be addressed by promoting larger risk pools at the state and local level.

(Policy Brief: Economic Survey of the United States, 2002, p.3-5, OECD 2002)

Forecasting is more than just one additional feature of a solid analysis; it plays a dual role. It serves as a test of the analytical ability of the Secretariat staff. It acts as a measure of overall competence in a manner analogous to profit in a private company. It is a form of bottom-line. In the context of third-rail issues, it builds confidence in OECD's ability to see clearly through foggy circumstances. The result is that countries generally seek its advice once they decide to deal with one of these most difficult issues.

In conclusion, it is useful to remind ourselves that the OECD process is multiform, and valid outputs characterize its work. It may be difficult to draft the perfect Peer Review every time, but other outcomes are equally essential. OECD is a learning organization and what participants learn about themselves, about their neighbours, and about the best way to do things remains an essential and useful outcome. It is also a laboratory for new ideas: many of its discussions act as quasi-brainstorming sessions between states to develop new products and new ways to govern and to provide services to citizens. In essence, it may be that a country under review will benefit less than other participants in the discussion. It is a loss for the country, not for OECD.

## SECTION 5
## ORGANIZATION OF MEETINGS: FROM WORKSHOPS AND SEMINARS TO COMMITTEES AND PLENARY

The OECD technique for managing meetings forms another component of its negotiation methodology. The success of meetings in achieving their objectives depends in large measure on precise and detailed preparation and careful attention to organizational procedures for each phase of the negotiation process. Meetings, whatever form they take (workshops and other technical meetings or high level conferences and plenaries) are never improvised. No detail is trivial and left to chance. Full consideration is given to various elements that have a direct or indirect bearing on the meeting's outcome.

### 5.1 Expectations and Results

The most significant result of the seminar will be to change the way participants view or understand a problem. This shared new perception or paradigm shift in fact constitutes a significant product. If such change involves managers and decision-makers, and if they have been fully engaged in the discussion, the new vision that they will take back to their home institution will often be enough to induce major changes in their behaviour, and above all in the policies pursued by their ministries or agencies.

Academics and researchers, for their part, generally consider the emergence of new knowledge as an acceptable final product, provided it involves publication. Decision-makers, on the other hand, will not feel that such an outcome justifies their time commitment, even if it is recognized that this could lead to a great many changes: they prefer activities that will help point the way to future actions, and perhaps even result in an action plan. This difference of perspective as to the outcome of the debate, or as the experts like to call it, the 'output', can lead to significant ambiguities and tensions.

This difference of perspective leads to different ways of addressing problems and pursuing solutions. To put it simply, the world of researchers and academics is dominated by 'the problem,' and they spend most of their life in the 'problem zone.' They will therefore always be very circumspect, cautious, and even sceptical about committing themselves to a solution. Moreover, they will do so only with rigorous regard for research standards. Intuition plays a role in this process, of course, but it will always be subject to verification of any hypotheses. Once a solution is found, researchers will generally disengage themselves and move on to a new problem.

In contrast, managers generally spend their life in the 'solution zone.' They will generally have attended good universities where they will have learned scientific method, but they will be promoted on the basis of their ability to 'make things happen' and their reputation for 'decisiveness.' They must be able to transform a 'solution' into action promptly—for example, by ensuring that legislation is actually adopted and carried out to the letter.

What is defined as 'a problem,' then, rarely involves questioning the solution, and is scarcely an invitation to innovate: rather, managers will turn to an old and tested inventory of practical solutions within which they must choose.

In many cases, the problems that managers deal with are primarily of a scientific nature: for example, the fisheries ministry's division of fishery resources will be made up of scientists, and their debate will focus on scientific subjects. But this is not always the case, and in many ministries managers tend, instead, to be generalists.

This helps us to differentiate the approach of each of the various OECD committees. It is common in a seminar to see administrators fidgeting and becoming impatient when the debate over the analysis of a problem drags on. They are often more disposed to rely on their own experience and intuition to decide what action should be taken, and they are reluctant to question the rules and procedures that guide their actions.

Yet the fact is that if a subject is on the OECD agenda, it is precisely because the old rules and the old ways of doing things have posed problems. What is needed, then, is to rethink the problem, often in terms not previously considered, and to undertake an objective and scientific process to find new approaches. To do this, it is recognized research methods that will offer the best approach, assuming that managers have the appropriate experience and an in-depth understanding of the constraints.

Researchers and decision-makers, then, often work at a rhythm and pace that are totally different, and this can be a major problem when a 'wise director' is trying to put together the agenda and to harmonize debates among representatives of these two broad schools of thought. The wise director will often choose to listen to the two sides separately, and to rely on a support team to make the difficult transition between the issue as defined by the researchers and the solution preferred by the decision-makers. But this is not always possible or even desirable, and so seminars must be held where government representatives and experts can work things out together. Moreover, it is important to manage the agenda and all available resources, including time, in a calculated and harmonized way.

## 5.2 The Agenda as a Management Tool

*A Specific Strategy for the Agenda*

The agenda must always be conceived to achieve the maximum of objectives and to ensure significant forward movement. Moreover, when a meeting is open to many kinds of delegations, it is absolutely critical to prepare a very clear and precise agenda.

The Secretariat will generally have done its work, and a summary of the current state of knowledge on the subject will be made available to all participants well before the meeting. It is important to go beyond what is already known internationally, by supplementing general knowledge with the specific experience of researchers and participants.

Experience shows that any debate will usually involve four distinct moments or points in time. Failure to take account of this rhythm often leads to tensions and reduces the prospect that a consensus will be reached. The agenda for the seminar should be organized to take this into account.

*Moment One*

The first item on the agenda should achieve four complementary objectives:

1. This is the most critical moment for clarifying the issues for debate, and for setting limits to expectations, to avoid discussions based on unreasonable hopes.

2. It must help to 'warm up' the atmosphere and integrate all participants into the group.

3. It must also provide a platform for participants to express their values and to make clear their field of expertise, from which they will later draw conclusions: in this way, a common language can be built.

4. Consequently, the output from this first moment, which must be as positive as possible, makes all participants feel that they belong to the group and ensures a constructive approach to the preparation of a consensus.

It is important, then, to introduce the subject properly and to ensure that the first two or three interventions set the proper tone and direction for the meeting.

At the outcome of this first session, participants should share 'roughly' a common vision of what can and must be done. They should also be agreed as to limits on the actions that might be considered.

## Moment Two

The second item involves reflection. This is inevitably an iterative process, and may be painstaking and torturous. Contradictory ideas will be put forth, either openly or indirectly, and sometimes even surreptitiously. Misunderstandings and divergent opinions will inevitably arise, and the meeting must try to anticipate and deal with them as successfully as possible.

This difficult moment should be followed by a lengthy break. It should be organized so as to facilitate interaction among participants with diverging views. If it is a one-day meeting, the lunch hour will provide an opportunity that must not be missed to facilitate the natural reconciliation of differences.

## Moment Three

This should be considered the most productive moment: it is where a consensus (or at least a partial one) begins to emerge. The discussions must be pursued in the most positive and constructive way possible. It is too late to undertake any new substantive debate, and there will not be enough time left to resolve any conflict that emerges at this moment. For example, no participant should be put on the spot or have his actions questioned.

All the items on the agenda should be managed so that it will be perfectly clear to all what is at stake in this second half of the seminar.

## Moment Four

This is the moment when the meeting's 'productive' output becomes apparent. Here we are looking for concrete and practical elements to demonstrate clearly that the seminar is making progress. If differences of view persist, as is generally the case, the group will simply take note of them: they can then be set aside for subsequent debate.

## 5.3 Time Management

The principal resource that participants in a seminar consume is time. It is important, then, to have a careful measure of the time available before discussion begins.

For each day of the meeting, there will generally be nine hours available. From this total we must subtract the time that will inevitably be taken up by coffee breaks, the time for participants to assemble in the meeting room, and the time needed for lunch.

We have no more than about 6 hours, then, for all participants to express their views. This also includes the time needed for servicing the meeting (introduction, summaries, administrative announcements).

This constitutes an absolute constraint, and one that it is essential to take into account in organizing the seminar. The time resource must be used in the most productive way possible, taking full account of things that are 'inevitable.' We must never forget that we are dealing with groups from different cultures: in their effort to make their thinking intelligible to everyone, it will be difficult to expect them to take shortcuts. This will inevitably have a great impact on the time required.

Following are some important items that must be taken into account when it comes to time management:

- If a number of participants feel that they have been unable to explain or discuss their points of view, especially if they have travelled great distances to attend a meeting, the result will be hostility or disappointment. Experience shows that when participants from different cultures meet together for the first time on an issue that involves values, opinions, new facts, or vital interests, every intervention will last an average of 10 to 13 minutes. When participants are better acquainted with each other, and especially with the subject of the agenda, statements may be kept to 7 to 9 minutes. Finally, when a meeting ends on a subject that is thoroughly under control, where the objective is practical and concrete, we can expect short interventions averaging 2 to 3 minutes.

- As a rule of thumb, every participant will take the floor 1.75 times on a major topic. Before finalizing the agenda and deciding how long the meeting will take, we must therefore estimate the time that is likely to be taken up by confirmed participants.

There are measures that can help reach objectives while reducing tensions, conflicts, and disappointments:

- Documents and the agenda for the meeting should reach participants not less than one week in advance. This documentation will be designed to make clear the object of the discussion while avoiding any ambiguity. The list of invited guests may contain biographical notes if this is perceived as essential for the group. Guests should be arranged alphabetically around the table (in order to facilitate the Chair's work) and each should have a nameplate that is clearly visible from all directions. These measures will reduce the time needed for participants to get to know each other. Participants wishing to speak could up-end their nameplate and leave it there until they have finished their intervention. In this way, everyone can see how many people have requested the floor. Depending on the number, participants will often tailor their interventions accordingly. By exercising such restraint, the group accepts co-responsibility for time management.

- Some participants will have a very precise role that will have been communicated to them in advance and discussed with them before the meeting. This applies, for example, to the Chair, the rapporteurs, the 'topic introducers' the 'practitioners,' the first two speakers, and a 'wild card' (see the section on "roles ascribed to participants" in Section 6). The two coffee breaks, and the midday meal in particular, should be structured so that they can be used to reduce misunderstandings or resolve nascent conflicts.

*Participant Handbook*

Each participant should receive an information package in preparation for the meeting, one week in advance. It should contain:

- A clear and concise statement of the objectives of the seminar.
- Annotated agenda.
- List of participants as well as their biographical notes.
- Basic documentation.

## 5.4 Real Cost of an International Seminar

A lack of cost awareness unfortunately often leads to lax behaviour in preparing and conducting a seminar. What follows is, in our view, the best way to estimate the real cost of an event. We may distinguish three kinds of costs: direct costs, hidden direct costs, and indirect costs. It is the total of these three categories that will provide the true measure of the resources that must be devoted to a meeting, and it is on this basis that we must assess whether the benefits are worth the costs.

*Direct Costs: Normally Covered by the Conference Budget*

- Professional fees, travel costs and per diem for participants and invited guests.
- Rental of the meeting room and equipment.
- Interpretation, secretarial services, photocopying, and communications.
- Reception expenses.

*Hidden Direct Costs (Normally Not Mentioned)*

- Salaries for all participants (delegates and secretariat staff) for each day of the meeting, plus travel time.
- Travel and per diem expenses for every day spent away from the office.

*Hidden Indirect Costs: Generally Ignored*

- Days worked to prepare for the seminar in the Secretariat, in delegations, and in national capitals.

The scenario set out in annex one has been based on rather conservative assumptions that underestimate, in particular, the considerable overhead costs of public administration. We have calculated that a three-day international seminar involving delegates from 30 member countries (or associated countries) of OECD will cost at least US$ 600,000, when all the preparation time needed by each of the delegations is taken into account. The amount directly budgeted is at most US$ 80,000. In other words, the submerged portion of this 'iceberg' is 6.5 times greater than the openly recognized and budgeted cost.

The only conclusion we can draw from such a calculation is that it is important to invest all the time and all the effort needed to ensure maximum output from these consultations. In an international seminar, nothing is too trivial to be neglected or left to chance.

## 5.5 Managing Workshop Meetings: Room Set-up

There are some fundamental principles that contribute to a successful network such as OECD:

- The president of a committee is no more than a first among peers: all participants are equals and should feel as such.

- No participants should be left idle: everyone is present to work toward a common solution, not to receive orders and/or to adopt a passive attitude.

- Participating meaningfully in a group involves more than standing up in turn and expressing one's opinion. It involves eye contact, being aware of body language signals and taking action when appropriate, thereby drawing other partners into the discussion.

- A true consensus is not the result of passive actors who have been lured into not objecting, but the result of a committed group of individuals who have come to design and adopt wilfully a common position.

- Some room and worktable arrangements are conducive to conflicts and passivity, while some arrangements have proven to assist significantly in building up true consensus. Experiments carried out by specialized research institutions have demonstrated the usefulness of paying great attention to the physical set-ups to increase the probability of a successful outcome. It has been observed that most people react to the size of the room and its general allure. They notice, for example, the absence of windows or the colour of the walls and many other details. The seating arrangements have a significant bearing on the outcome of the meeting. For research purposes, an American university randomly selected students and had them discussing the same topic in two identical rooms. The only difference was that in one of the rooms, all the chairs had their front legs shortened by two centimetres. On average, the discussions in that room ended aggressively, significantly more often than in the control room.

*Recommended Styles*

**Round or Octagonal Table**

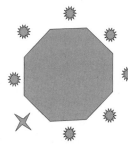

For small groups (6-12 participants), this is clearly the best arrangement. It explicitly suggests a meeting among peers. The round table allows every participant to establish eye contact and the chairperson can see who wishes to talk and who should be drawn into the discussion. This set-up suggests active participation and renders passiveness difficult.

## Rectangular Tables

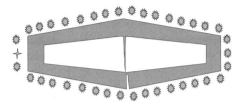

For practical reasons, it is difficult to build or assemble from modules, very large round tables. Square, oval and rectangular tables are therefore the next best alternative for larger groups of 18 to 30 participants. Large square tables have the inconveniences of leaving out certain participants, particularly those seated on each side of the chairperson. Indeed the latter may not be visible to these participants and/or see them. However, nothing is perfect and one has to manage with whatever is practical. One of the preferred alternatives are the rectangular tables that will sit five to eight people maximum at the head table and between 10 and 15 on each side table. If the side tables can be somewhat angled out to form a wide v, or the equivalent of a six-sided table, then we have a most desirable arrangement.

The important features are: establishing eye contact between as many participants as possible, including the chairperson; suggesting equality among participants; inducing active participation; and making it as awkward as possible for anyone to become passive.

## Hole in the Middle

Many people are afraid of emptiness, and the hole in the middle of an arrangement can represent a challenge. Various means are used to fill this hole, for example putting a large flower bouquet in the middle. However, one should note that the optical illusion of emptiness is not that important. The more significant issue remains the distance between people. If participants cannot see each other nor establish eye contact, the group is likely to be less productive. When asked, people will often underestimate the distance between tables where there is a gap and overestimate the distance when a table is full. This suggests that the mind fills in the gap and is awed by a flat surface.

Empirical tests conducted in United States universities have led to the conclusion that a gap does represent a challenge, however, it does induce individuals to communicate more and better rather than less. People seem to want to bridge the gap and reach out across the void. A large but empty flat surface can be intimidating and may induce people to take their distance from those on the 'other side.'

## Two-tier Arrangements

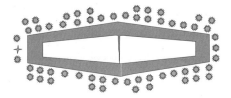

It is difficult to run a workshop or a seminar with more than 20-24 four active participants in one session, including the chairperson. To have an active meeting implies that each participant must speak once at the very least. A long session leaves no more than 180 minutes of working time. This is all the time that is left for interventions, after factoring in necessary pauses and the chairperson's summaries and probing. Each participant will therefore have access to an average of seven and a half minutes of speaking time. This might mean one single intervention from the participant of seven minutes or two of a little over three minutes. Quite obviously anything above 24 participants suggests that only a few people will have access to the only common resource to be shared, which is time.

However, sometimes more individuals attend the seminar or the meeting than can be accommodated. This situation often happens when national delegations are invited and decide to send more delegates than planned for. It is better then to add rows of chairs behind each national delegation, thus turning some individuals into passive spectators, than to enlarge artificially a working table to sit everyone around. Delegations may then rotate between sessions or leave some of their delegates as ringsiders for the full duration of the seminar without impairing the group's capacity to function as a group.

*The Heritage of Soviet Days*

## The T-square

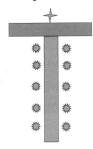

The T-square style is favoured in situations demanding command and control. This set-up is often found in Russia and Ukraine where it garnishes the office of directors and deputy ministers. In this setup, the leader of the meeting sits at the head of the T-square and participants line up on each side. The T-square may be useful for a colonel issuing marching orders to his officers; however, it is the worst manner for conducting a discussion among peers, especially in a network made of representatives of sovereign nations or international organizations. It pervades the group dynamics and impacts on the results of the process in many ways. A true consensus may therefore be elusive.

### The Long Narrow Table

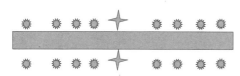

The long narrow table was very much of a Cold War device. This set-up allowed head to head confrontations and negotiations between highly disciplined factions. Sitting face to face in the middle of the long table, head of delegations discussed pre-scripted positions that did not involve participation from the underlings who sat in hierarchical order on each side of their 'leaders.' This set-up has the advantage of sorting out ranks so that generals and captains facing each other may be called upon to resolve discreet issues at their own levels.

As with the T-square table, this set-up is highly counterproductive when trying to create a spirit of collaboration within a network and even worse when the network is composed of various sovereign states. Indeed, the long narrow table will lead to tensions and conflicts if used for that purpose. The participants sitting face-to-face have a tendency to be combative and easily lose sight of all others situated parallel to them. As a result, the group becomes fractious, undisciplined, and cantankerous. Furthermore, in this set-up, the chairpersons are seldom able to manage traffic, as they cannot see who wishes to talk at the other end of the table. No less important, they hardly can stimulate and draw into the discussions those that have opted out and remain silent and uninvolved.

### The Classroom

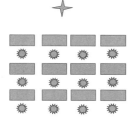

This set-up is meant to focus everyone's attention on the "teacher" and no one else, and it has the calculated effect of shutting out as much as possible any interaction between the students. It is, in effect, a favourite for situations demanding command and control. One should notice how difficult it is to participate in group discussions in this kind of set-up. This set-up leads to passive groups in the best of circumstances and, since it works against active participation, is seldom conducive to problem solving.

## Opera House and Podium

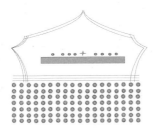

This set-up is another soviet heritage. The opera house is a set-up whereby a large group of people are seated in an arrangement similar to an opera house, with a long and imposing table, positioned above the audience. This set-up is worse than the classroom arrangement to induce dialogue and generally stifles participation. It requires so much boldness to dare ask a question or voice an opinion, that generally the participants hear only opinions and concerns expressed by either extremists or by disgruntled individuals who believe they should also be sitting on the podium. No consensus is to be expected from such a set-up. Any pretence to having reached a consensus in such a situation must be systematically questioned as a most unlikely and exceptional outcome.

# Annex One

## Cost Simulation for a Three-day Seminar Held at OECD Headquarters (US$)

| | Budget | Total |
|---|---|---|
| *Typical Direct Costs* | | |
| Experts and Consultants[7] | $35,000 plus $6500 | |
| Invited Guests[8] | $3750 plus $6000 | |
| Logistic Expenses[9] | $9600 plus $10,000 | |
| Unexpected Reception Expenses[10] | $4500 plus $4000 | |
| | | $79,300 |
| *Hidden Direct Costs* | | |
| Salaries of Delegates[11] | $135,000 | |
| Salaries for Days of Travel[12] | $73,500 | |
| Travel Expenses[12] | $51,000 | $259,500 |
| Hidden Indirect Costs | | |
| Days Worked in Capitals and in Delegations[14] | $225,000 | |
| Days Worked in the Secretariat[15] | $40,000 | |
| | | $265,000 |
| *Grand Total* | | *$603,800* |

7. Two experts, at a rate of $700, will have worked 20 days to prepare the working document, to which we must add five days devoted to participating in the meeting, or $35,000. In addition to their round-trip air ticket e.g. $2000 for a trans-Atlantic trip), we must add five days per diem at $250 ($6500).

8. Three guests from a remote region: five days of per diem ($250 × 3 × 5 = $3700) and travel expenses ($2000 × 3 = $6000)

9. Four interpreters for three days ($800 × 4 × 3 = $9600), secretarial and miscellaneous expenses, including room rental ($10,000).

10. A cocktail for all participants, their ambassadors, and a selection of key personnel, or 90 individuals × $50 = $4500.

11. The cost figure of $1000 per day for senior officials from OECD member countries seemed to us a fairly conservative estimate. It takes into account departmental overhead and the fact that those involved in policymaking are always at a fairly senior level. Hence, 1.5 delegates for 30 delegations × three days × $1000 = $135,000.

12. We may distinguish three zones: those who live in Paris (1 × 1.5 × 0), those who live in nearby countries and come by train or airplane on the morning of the meeting, and who will travel for a total of no more than half a day (6 × 1.5 × 25 days × $1000 = $4500), and finally all those who will have to devote two days to travel (23 × 1.5 × 2 × $1000 = $69,000), or a total of $73,500.

13. (23 × 1.5 × 5 × $250 = $43,125) plus (6 × 1.5 × 3.5 × $250 = $7875) or $51,000

14. For each major item on the agenda, we estimate that it takes at least 2.5 person-days of work to prepare and harmonize each national position, to prepare briefing notes, etc. A three-day seminar is sure to contain three major items, and so we must calculate 30 × 3 × 2.5 × $1000 = $225,000.

15. It is normal for an officer to devote one month to the meeting, to which we must add 10 days contributed by his colleagues and superiors, or 40 × $1000 = $40,000.

# 5

## Why Does it Work?

Why does OECD work? This remains a perplexing question and many external observers are still sceptical. OECD has challenged a number of preconceived ideas regarding the management of international affairs. The international system has always been based on the sovereignty of nation-states and relations based on national interests. How can the pursuit of collective interest overcome these tendencies? How can we explain the survival and success of OECD?

Traditional responses, particularly the numerous protectionist measures, which we referred to as 'mercantilism,' led to the escalation of conflicts in Europe in the first half of the 20th Century. In addition, armed conflicts became bloodier and more devastating with improvements in the art of war and warfare. More than 74 armed conflicts have been recorded between 1816 and 1965. Of those, the four deadliest occurred in the 20th Century: the two world wars, the Chinese-Japanese war of 1937 and the Korean War. Each has resulted in at least one million deaths. In contrast, the Franco-Prussian conflict of 1870 resulted in 150,000 deaths. (Hobsbawn, p.47).

A new approach was therefore needed to prevent more deadly conflicts. In Chapter 1, we describe a number of instruments that were put forward to deal with the situation. However, the situation in Europe needed to be addressed in a particular way so it would not overtake the fragile balance that was being established.

With the Marshall Plan and the creation of OECE (later OECD), a new alternative was proposed that tried to maintain this equilibrium (see Chapter 3). This institutional creation, which is unique in its approach to interactions between nations, can be regarded as a 'social invention.' It will have filled the inter-state institutional void that Homer-Dixon calls "the ingenuity gap." This new invention created in return technological and scientific innovations as well as social and political ones that, not only have sustained economic growth of OECD member countries, but also contributed to its international expansion. OECD released an explosion of creativity, ingenuity, and diversity. It is an invention to deal with this growing complexity of the world.

SECTION 1

OECD AND COMPLEXITY

Complexity has taken over our world, posing another great challenge to OECD. A number of authors have reflected on this growing complexity. With technology and scientific ongoing progress, human relationships have multiplied and have become more complicated to manage. Communication networks have also exploded; our environment is being bombarded by information that leaves the great majority of us with an overload of information in our work environment as well as in our daily life. Every decision we make concerning, for example, our lifestyle or as consumer has become more complicated as we always seem to need more information and better organization.

Systems put in place by humans to deal harmoniously with all sorts of interactions, as well as with their complexity, also follow this same trend. Political, administrative, and commercial structures are all confronted by the world's growing complexity.

What today is called "globalization" is truly the world's new complexity and is the consequence, direct or less direct, of the explosion of innovation in the technological, scientific, social, and political fields. The words 'complexity' and 'globalization' tend to be the flavour of the day and are used in any possible occasion. Faced with this complexity, individuals as well as societies tend to retract and prefer denial and isolation rather than forcing themselves to face changes and risk committing errors. However, this is not an adequate response to the complexity as it only delays the ultimate deadline where the challenges of complexity will have to be addressed. In order to meet these challenges with wit and delicacy, one has to understand the nature of complicated things, the nature of complexity.

### 1.1 The Nature of Complexity

There are six features that are essential to grasp fully the nature of complexity and complex systems (Homer-Dixon, 2001: 111-115).

1.  "An obvious feature of complex systems is that they are composed of a *multiplicity* of things; they are made up of a large number of entities, components or parts.[...]

2.  "There is a dense web of *causal connections* among the components of complex systems; in other words, their components have so many links to each other that they affect each other in many ways [...] The more

causal connections, in general, the greater the system's complexity. A particularly important result of all this dense connectivity is causal *feedback*, in which a change in one component affects others in a way that eventually loops back to affect the original component. [...] Furthermore, sometimes, components in a highly connected system are *tightly coupled*. This means that a change in one component has rapid, multiple effects on other components.

3. "A third feature of complex systems is the *interdependence* of their components. A good way of measuring interdependence is to divide a system into pieces and then see how the change affects the property and behaviour of the pieces. The larger the part that can be removed from a complex system without affecting the whole system's behaviour, the more resilient the system.

4. "The fourth feature of complex systems is their *openness* to their outside environment: complex systems are not self-contained, but are affected, sometimes profoundly, by outside events. As a result, it is often hard to locate a complex system's boundary – that is where the system ends and the outside world starts. [...]

5. "Complex systems normally show a high degree of *synergy* among their components—a fifth common feature. Synergy means, in everyday language, that the whole is more than the sum of its parts. The combined effect of changes in two or more of a system's components differs from the sum of their individual effects. [...]

6. "Complex systems exhibit *non-linear* behaviour—we can't count on things developing in tidy, straight lines. This means that a system can produce an effect that is not proportional to its size: small changes can produce large effects and large changes can produce small effects."

## 1.2 Complexity, Diversity and Adaptation

Systems may also become more complex through a process B. Arthur (quoted by Homer-Dixon, 2001) calls "growth in co-evolutionary diversity." In a 'coevolationary' system, entities that make up the systems (for example, organizations, corporations) start to compete fiercely. Over time, the system's entities can develop webs of interdependence. With the increase of these interactions, whether they are competitive, cooperative or symbiotic, 'new opportunities' or 'niches' emerge among the entities. This growing complexity of the system, in the form of greater diversity and more intricate webs of interactions, tends to bootstrap itself upward over time. With entities providing niches and niches making possible the creation of new entities, the system can feed upon itself. Diversity within the system can provide the fuel for further diversity.

If systems become more complex and more diverse, they can also improve. On occasion, within the system, a new entity replaces another entity that is more basic or fundamental. This change eliminates the niches linked to that more basic entity. Therefore, "the introduction of radically new, simple systems can sometimes sweep away complex earlier systems that have become encrusted with additions and complications." The system has changed, it has adapted itself, it has simplified.

Diversity and complexity are strongly interrelated. Those societies or groups of companies willing to try to adapt and embark on what can be a rocky ride, are generally rewarded by a creative explosion generally mixed with growth (economic or other, depending on the nature of the entity). Those who will not, or cannot, take on complexity, diversity, and the creation of new entities 'will remain quiescent indefinitely.' In other words, passiveness or withdrawal in front of complexity can result in stagnation or even underdevelopment.

In 1947, the world of European Nations was extraordinarily complicated. In the preceding 30 years, all the achievements of the 19$^{th}$ Century had literally evaporated. The list of catastrophes is impressive. Treaties among Nations signed in the period prior to 1914 led to the First World War; treaties signed in 1918 were incapable of avoiding a subsequent catastrophe. Two great wars, that involved two-thirds of humanity, killed 15 million (1914-1917), and 50 million (1939-1945) individuals and destabilized all previous equilibrium. In addition to losing millions of people, a large portion of the casualties were productive and trained adults. A substantial proportion of fixed capital was also destroyed during 1939-1945 (USSR lost 25%, Germany 13%, Italy 8%, France 7%, and UK 3%) (Hobsbawn, p.77). A major economic recession (1929-1938) of a size unheard of expanded throughout the globe. Fascist or communist regimes replaced most democratic institutions created during the liberal era of the 19th Century. All the empires created in the previous centuries were destabilized and even deconstructed, including Turkey and Russia, leading to a period of decolonization and the creation of a large number of new countries. And the Society of Nations, created in 1918 to avoid international dislocation, had failed miserably.

In essence, it can be argued that Europe was crumbling under a super dose of complexity. It was in dire need of simplification. However, simplification was not enough; the process of a massive amount of information was also needed.

Another way of understanding the way complexity affects behaviour and adaptation may be found in the concept of 'brain size.' For years scientists have argued about the reasons that explain the different sizes of brain among primates—chimpanzees, baboons, and humans having the largest brains of all mammals. What seems to correlate with brain size is group size (Dunbar in Homer Dixon, 2001). If you look at any species of primate (or at every variety of monkey and ape) the larger their neocortex is, the larger the average size of the group they live in. Brains evolve and get bigger in order 'to handle the complexities of larger social groups.'

After the Second World War, it was clear that the number of interactions among nations, or the group size, had expanded to a degree that surpassed the existing brain capacity of the whole. At the time, our collective brain could not handle the complexity of relations within so large and diversified a group. Systems of treaties, as was the usual practice from 'times immemorial,' defeated the security purpose for which they were initially created.

Simplification had therefore to be combined with a collective and larger brain able to handle more complex issues and help the region deal with complicated problems effectively.

## 1.3 The Creation of OECD: An Injection of Simplicity and Intelligence

The creation of OECD (and of course of its particular and distinctive method) was a response to the complexity present at the time. It was a simplified response to the complicated definition of relations among nations; it offered to deal with the growing complexity of the world. With rules as easy to follow as the rules of a game of checkers came the end of secrets, and ambiguous, contradictory agreements. The rule of the game became extremely simple: agree by consensus to a common agenda and rely on peer pressure to make things work.

OECD also provided a second element essential to the emergence of complexity: a mutation in the collective brain size, in other words, the European invented a collective instrument for analyzing complex political and economic problems, thus allowing the collectivity to deal with them. This mutation injected competence and simplicity in relations more numerous and complex.

The first task OECD members were to address (done successfully) was the reduction of obstacles to financial transactions. This issue was taken on after it had been established that it was a central issue, but also that the tasks in this area would be feasible and would not encounter major opposition. But methods that had been previously applied were of no use in this case; a new approach had to be taken.

The OECD method has allowed its members to deal with an enormous amount of information. This method not only simplifies overall comprehension and discussion of information by harmonizing and analyzing, but also manages to find solutions that could be practicable and applicable by all. Since there was no need to subscribe to a formal agreement (always difficult to reach), the transition (each at its own pace) could be made from a simple and easily applicable solution to a more complex set of solutions. Since the 1960s, the mobility of a number of things has become less complicated: for example, capital and technology can move more freely. This simplification has led to innovation, creativity, diversity, as well as new entities (most notably the EU)...and a new complexity.

What is most striking when one examines and tries to understand the OECD method is the extraordinary simplicity of the whole mechanism. Let us remind ourselves that we are faced with an advanced form of collective intelligence. For the community (or 'entity') to accede to this intelligence, or rather to initiate its operation, a few simple rules have to be understood and followed. If conventions are respected, this will work; otherwise intelligence will not develop.

## SECTION 2

## EXAMPLES OF WHAT WORKS AND WHAT DOESN'T

To fully understand the effect of complexity on policy-making but also the use of the OECD method to deal with it, let us now look at three examples of complex issues that the OECD deals with or tried to deal with.

The first example examines how OECD handled the health issue. This issue is particularly interesting because health systems are complex systems. If examined closely, these systems even reveal the six features of complexity. The OECD faced with the complexity of health systems developed both a 'simplified' and 'intelligent' solution, the Health Project. It exemplifies the current evolution of OECD, whereby it is often becoming more important to collectively understand a problem than to arrive at a negotiated consensus. Countries are not in competition with each other with respect to Health Services Delivery. But they can work together to learn how to improve the way they deal with this issue and benefit from each other's experience. It is a clear example of the power of intelligence that we reviewed in the preceding pages.

The subsequent two examples, the Bribery Convention and the Multilateral Agreement on Investment (MAI), illustrate the way OECD's method was used to deal with complicated issues. The first example shows how the method can lead to success; the second, how it also may be overstretched.

## 2.1 OECD and Health: Facing Complexity

Health systems are of crucial importance to OECD member nation economies. In fact, in order to flourish as citizens, workers, and consumers, individuals need to be in good health. This helps to explain why OECD countries devote an average of 8-10% of their GDP to healthcare (see Table 5.1). Until recently the scale of health policy work at OECD had been relatively small and fragmented across several directorates. However, in the last few years, the OECD involvement in the health issue has increased in direct response to the greater attention given to the costs and impacts of ageing and healthcare financing.

### Table 5.1

*Total Expenditure on Health, 1980-1998*

| Country (selection) | Health Spending as a Per Cent of GDP | |
| --- | --- | --- |
| | *1980* | *1998* |
| Canada | 7.2 | 9.5 |
| France | 7.4 | 9.6 |
| Germany | 8.8 | 10.6 |
| Hungary (new member) | 7.8 (1992) | 6.8 |
| Japan | 6.5 | 7.6 |
| Poland (new member) | 5.3 (1990) | 6.4 |
| Switzerland | 6.9 | 10.4 |
| United Kingdom | 5.7 | 6.7 |
| United States | 8.9 | 13.6 |
| Ukraine* | 3 | 2.96 |
| Russia** | 4.1 | 4.56 |

*Note:* * Human Development Index.
       ** World Bank, Table 25: Total Expenditure on Health, 1980-1998.
*Source:* OECD (2002).

OECD countries have agreed for many years on the importance of collecting data on the health systems to compare (or benchmark) their growth and performance. In response, OECD has built up the leading international data-set on health system activity, inputs, and expenditure. In 2000, the Secretariat of OECD proposed a three-year program, the Health Project, to complement measurement of the performance of health systems with a series of policy studies to investigate the causes of variations in performance across systems, and to identify evidence-based policies to improve performance. It covers four main areas: performance measurement and improvement, explaining variation in performance, essential ameliorative care, and overall system assessment. To launch this project, Canada, as a voluntary contribution, hosted a conference that brought together the main players (policymakers, medical staff, health economists, and civil societies) to contribute to an international dialogue on health issues. The three-day conference in November 2001 was entitled "Measuring Up: Improving Health Systems Performance in OECD Countries."

The Secretary-General of OECD declared that, "the OECD Health Project is one of the most important undertaken by the organization in recent years [...] our aim is a very practical one: to help public policymakers meet the health challenges of the 21st Century" (Johnston in the OECD Observer). The 'Health Project' was put forward as a simplified approach to a complex issue. In fact, health systems are truly complex systems: Homer-Dixon's six features of complexity can be found in different aspects of the health system.

*Multiplicity: Multiple Health Systems, Multiple Policy Challenges*

One of the first signs of the complexity of healthcare is the existence of different types of health systems in the OECD area. These systems can be based on private or social health insurance, private or public provisions, although actual health systems are often a mixture.

However, whatever the type of health system, one major preoccupation in all OECD countries remains: to improve the performance of the healthcare system.[16] Most OECD member states seem to face multiple policy challenges in assuring and improving the performance of their system. These challenges include the demand for healthcare that has been rising exponentially because of new medical techniques, ageing of populations, and increasing public expectations.

Several main topics can be found on the health policy agenda that are now currently being examined in the perspective of performance and improvement. There are concerns about the efficiency of the health system and containing costs, as well as improving health status (life expectancy, mortality, general health), since there are still some strong variations among OECD countries in this area (Table 5.2). The responsiveness of the system as well as the improvement of safety or reduction of medical errors also raises concerns in many countries. Finally, although average levels of health have risen in OECD

---

16. See, "Performance Measurements and Improvements in OECD Health Systems: Overview of Issues and Challenges", Working Party on Social Policy, OECD, 3 October 2001.

## Table 5.2

### *Health Status-Life Expectancy*

| Country (selection) | Life Expectancy at Birth, 1998 (except Canada, 1997 data) | |
|---|---|---|
| | Female | Male |
| Canada | 81.4 | 75.8 |
| France | 82.2 | 74.6 |
| Germany | 80.5 | 74.5 |
| Hungary (new member) | 75.2 | 66.1 |
| Japan | 84 | 77.2 |
| Poland | 77.3 | 68.9 |
| Switzerland | 82.5 | 76.5 |
| United Kingdom | 79.7 | 74.8 |
| United States | 79.4 | 73.9 |
| Ukraine* | 73 | 62 |
| Russia* | 75 | 66 |

*Note:*   * Human Development Index.
*Source:* OECD (2001).

countries, concerns remain as to whether inequalities in health can be reduced.

The most difficult part of improving health system performance is to put policies into action. In this area, there is also complexity: multiple actors are involved in the process. In general, successful action will involve changing the behaviour of the actors in the health system. However, the aims of the four key sets of actors (consumers, professional providers, managers, and governors) may not be the same aims of those trying to influence them.

### *Causal Connection and Feedback in the Health System*

One of the actions taken by some OECD countries to improve the performance of their health systems was to address the problem of length of waiting times for elective surgery. For example, in recent years, to reduce the waiting time the British Government launched a number of initiatives in this area targeted at managers and providers. At first glance, these initiatives met with success. However, a survey of surgeons conducted by the National Audit Office revealed that surgeons would often reshuffle waiting lists so that no patient would wait for a long period. In effect, the average waiting time remained the same as before. This is a clear example of feedback in a complex system.

## Interdependence in Health Systems

A complex system can also be defined by the interdependence of its components. In health systems, when appropriate information and appropriate incentives are not aligned, progress toward performance improvements may be disappointing. For example, in France, regulatory practice guidelines were introduced to improve health outcomes, to avoid dangerous medical practices and to contain costs. However, physicians considered that reducing cost was the only objective and were against these guidelines. The main principle behind the guidelines was not promoted well enough to get the support of the physicians and the public.

This example, as well as the British initiatives in the area of elective surgery, shows that it is hard to change the characteristic behaviour or 'signature' of health systems, and also that elements of the complexity of health systems always emerge when actions are introduced.

## Health Systems are Open and Affected by Outside Events

Policy challenges in the healthcare area are clearly influenced by the outside environment. For example, new discoveries in other scientific fields can lead to the development of new medical techniques. Although these techniques are welcomed, they are often more expensive than the ones they replace. The ageing population has also a direct effect on health systems. Older citizens need more healthcare: the over-65 group accounts for 40-50% of healthcare spending.

The openness of health systems has been taken into account in the OECD 'Health Project'; the project involves contributors from various OECD directorates, including *inter alia*, social and health policy, economics, insurance-related issues and technology, science and industry.

## Synergy

A complex system normally shows a degree of synergy among its components. Logically, a health system will only perform well if both clinical decision-makers and managers and governors are working effectively toward the same end.

## Non-linear Behaviour

Finally, health systems also present non-linear behaviour. If we take the example of an epidemic, we can see that the treatment of a single patient, who suffers from an infectious disease, especially if this disease is deadly, can have a major effect on health systems. Depending on the response of the system and the treatment of the patient, the whole system could be lightly or severely affected. The recent SARS events in Toronto serve as a good illustration of this phenomenon.

## Fuzzy Tradeoffs

Many of the difficult issues that arise in the health field concern tradeoffs. They are clearly not linear and health policies are constantly challenged by the inherent complexity of the entire system as we have just demonstrated. In particular, causal connections and feedback render tradeoffs fuzzy in the best of circumstances. Furthermore, the endless changes that characterize health compound the difficulty. Like other industrial sectors, technology is constantly changing, but, as witnessed by the appearance of AIDS and SARS, new problems arise as soon as one is solved.

## 2.2 The Bribery Convention, an Unambiguous Success Story

In 1977, the US congress voted the Foreign Corrupt Practices Act, a law that made it illegal for American business to pay bribes to officials in the context of international tenders. This act had the immediate effect of putting American companies at a disadvantage when competing against other industrial country firms that were in a position to meet local demands for bribes. The US Government tried to persuade the United Nations to adopt similar regulations and to restore in this fashion American industry competitiveness, but was unsuccessful.

By 1988, the American Congress was prepared to abrogate this law, but President Reagan found it hard to go against the position of one of his predecessors. It was then decided to confront European countries with it: if they turn it down, then the US would be fully justified to abandon its "holier-than-thou" stand.

In 1989, a modest attempt was made by OECD to placate American pressure. An ad hoc Working Group was tasked with dealing with the issue. Many OECD delegates, however, were highly sceptical: " We have laws in each OECD country safeguarding the integrity of our own public administrations; why should we try to export our rigor and discipline to non-members? Should they not be the ones passing laws in their own country to improve transparency and integrity? What if we (OECD members) all refrain from paying bribes and thus allow jobs and markets to be taken over by Newly Industrialized Countries?"

In keeping with OECD traditional methodology, the first task of the Working Group was to gather comparative data about each member's national legislation, and to clarify all related concepts dealing with offence of corruption committed wholly or partially abroad. In addition, many large and wise texts were drafted, dealing essentially with the feasibility of reaching a consensus on this issue. Also keeping with OECD tradition was the decision to seek a 'soft law' instrument, i.e. a recommendation inviting member states to confront bribery with dissuasive actions outside of criminal law, to remove any provisions that might facilitate bribery. [...]

In 1994, OECD Council adopted at ministerial level a first recommendation to that effect. A new mandate was approved for the Working Party: it charged the Group with examining how member countries intended to follow the recommendation, studying critical areas for feasible further initiatives, and formulating criminal law principles to combat corruption. Properly named, The Convention on Combating Bribery of Foreign Public Officials in International Business Transactions, it was signed in December 1997. It entered into force one year later after Japan, Germany, the United States, United Kingdom, and Canada, as well as a few other countries ratified it. By June 2000, 21 signatory countries had deposited their ratifications (Sacerdoti, p. 41).

It soon appeared that differences in the structure of national criminal codes rendered the adoption of a classical international convention impossible. The innovative concept of 'functional equivalence' helped resolve this conundrum: "Differences would not matter and would be admitted, provided they led to equivalent results, namely effective prosecution and sanctions. The Group moved ahead, formulated eight "Agreed Common Elements of Criminal Law and Related Measures". By May 1997, it was agreed to act on a Recommendation on Combating Bribery and to search for a Convention that was eventually agreed upon in 1997.

It is now in force and the numbers of Peer Reviews that have been initiated testify to OECD monitoring its implementation.

*Why Did it Succeed?*

From the outset, (and still today) Professor Mark Pieth of Basel chaired the Working Group. He corresponds to the Maverick Chair profile described in Chapter 4. It could be argued that his character fitted the task. A complex blend of vested interests, fears and scepticism even cynicism pervaded all debates. Combating bribery is a high moral issue with enormous financial and economic consequences. It is also one where the honour of a country is at stake. By 1990, the costs of bribes were mounting, but neither firm nor country wanted to be the first (and maybe the only one after the US) to forfeit business.

In commenting on his way of chairing the Committee, Professor Pieth admits he is not always polite; he may rough-handle delegates who procrastinate or get lost under politically correct language; he makes regular and often blunt 'suggestions from the Chair' and puts things squarely on the table. As a Swiss, he feels his nationality scares few delegates, but this gives him freedom from etiquette. Giorgi Sacerdoti, an Italian Professor of Law, equally invested with the passion and mission to 'make a difference' and improve international codes of behaviour, has supported him strategically. Together they have moved the agenda forward significantly. Much remains to be done, however, as it is not yet a Standing Committee. Its work cannot benefit from the full forces of a well-endowed unit within the OECD Secretariat that could document bribery cases and draft in-depth Peer Reviews. The request for the establishment of such a unit does not rally consensus; one member still objects. Nevertheless, immense progress has been achieved in the relatively short time of less than 15 years.

Tactically, the key to success was twofold. A common language was soon arrived at allowing members to get into the real task of searching for a common solution. The construction of 'functional equivalence' is similar to the concept of agricultural subsidies indices, ESP, and ESC. Once a form of Esperanto has been drafted, participants are free to seek practical solutions and may find it harder to pretend otherwise. OECD had resolved a similar problem a few years earlier concerning money laundering. The techniques and, most importantly, the sequencing used to agree on measures to combat money laundering were copied in order to move this agenda forward. In particular, breaking down a large problem into smaller discreet issues, and resolving them one at a time, proved to be an essential way to deal with a protracted and complex problem such as this one.

Second, the environment changed. In France, Germany, Italy, and UK, many scandals erupted to the consternation of governments and became the focus of public attention. In addition, the failure of Eastern Europe to control exportation of its internal corruption added pressure on everyone. By 1994, the International Chamber of Commerce and other NGOs such as Transparency International started pushing toward improvements. By then, the passive resistance that had characterized the complacent attitude of a number of delegates changed for the better. Everyone realized it was time to act, and if all acted in unison, then chances were that such an initiative could succeed.

The American Government, sensing this, decided to mount 'peer pressure' against all resistance. This will serve as a good example of how this typical OECD policy instrument can be put to work. Off the record interviews with former colleagues revealed for example that the US Secretary of State at the time, Madeleine Albright, sent strong instructions to all American Ambassadors in OECD countries, inciting them to raise this issue in forceful terms at every opportunity and at the highest levels. Under-Secretary for

Economic, Business and Agricultural Affairs, Allan Larson, even wrote an article in the prestigious German magazine "Der Spiegel" suggesting his German counterpart was condoning corruption.

In essence, this is a remarkable example of an OECD achievement. Its success rests essentially on all the methods described in Chapters 3, 4 and 5: the use of peer pressure, the dedicated pursuit of consensus, and the usage of a variety of tools and skills. Together these methods allow a complex objective to be reached gradually in a ratchet-like fashion.

When asked about a significant anecdote concerning his 14-year experience as Chair of the Working Party, Professor Pieth recalled the following haunting and enlightening story. "A few years back, I was invited to deliver a speech at the prestigious IFRI[17] breakfast. A man approached me afterward and said: "I am number two at Dassau and as such I am an arms salesman. You will become a hero because you have pushed down the commission we have to pay from 25% to 11%"...! This enigmatic statement can be interpreted various ways. Taking into consideration that the arms sales represent on average about US$30 billion, it follows that the amount of hidden money in the hands of corrupt officials may have been reduced from US$7.5 billion to 3.3. This is a significant achievement. One may feel cynical, however, and focus on the remaining 11%."

Either way one looks at it, the Bribery Convention is a clear example of how OECD can influence policy in its member states and even beyond its membership. We have already described similar achievements concerning agricultural subsidies (see Chapter 3) and the improvement of national accounts (see Chapter 2). Many other such stories endow the history of the Organization.

### 2.3 The Multilateral Agreement on Investment (MAI), A bridge too far...

In May 1995, according to a report presented to OECD Council meeting at Ministerial Level: "The time [was] ripe to negotiate a multilateral agreement on investment (MAI) in the OECD [...] an agreement [was] needed to respond to the dramatic growth and transformation of foreign direct investment (FDI) which has been spurred by widespread liberalization and increasing competition for investment capital."[18] Work on the multilateral agreement on investment had been conducted in OECD since 1991, by the Committee on

---

17. IFRI gathers top executives from French industries once a month for a breakfast discussion with a well-informed and often-prestigious guest.

18. see DAFFE/CMIT(95)13/FINAL, 5 May 1995

International Investment and Multinational Enterprises (CIME) and by the Committee on Capital Movements and Invisible Transactions (CMIT). In 1994, five working groups composed of independent governmental experts were set up to explore the issues to be dealt with in this agreement, and undertook technical and analytical work. A year later the Council agreed to start negotiations in OECD of a Multilateral Agreement on Investment (MAI).

Negotiations began in September 1995. All OECD member countries at that time, plus the Commission of the European Communities, took part in them. Argentina, Brazil, Chile, Hong Kong, and China also participated as observers, and this from an early stage. Estonia, Latvia, Lithuania, and the Slovak Republic later joined as observers. The MAI proposal was built around three main pillars: investment liberalization obligations (including the codification of existing liberalization measures and new disciplines or 'special topics'), investment protection, and dispute settlement.[19]

Rapid progress was made in the area of investment protection. There was broad agreement that the MAI should provide comprehensive coverage through a broad definition of investors and investments. The Negotiation Group first worked toward the objective of reaching an agreement by spring 1997. However, in 1997 the Negotiation Group recognized that more work was needed to realize the set goals. In addition, civil society had become concerned by the negotiations and many NGOs denounced the 'secrecy' surrounding them.

In the beginning of 1998, an agreement was reached on a number of essential elements. They included a broad asset-based definition of investment covering foreign direct investment with MAI disciplines to apply to all economic sectors, and at all levels of government. The group also agreed to non-discriminatory treatment of investors and investments, and to certain elements of a dispute settlement mechanism for state-state and investor-state disputes.[20] Agreements on main political issues remained to be found. A broad, though not unanimous, support had emerged concerning labour and environmental issues. In fact, some of the strongest concerns expressed about the MAI had been raised by environmental NGOs.

Discussions were also needed to determine the treatment of intellectual property and of exceptions with respect to national security and public order. In addition, no agreement could be reached regarding measures taken in the context of a regional economic integration organization and in the areas of culture, subsidies, health, social services, and aboriginal and minorities issues.

---

19. see DAFFE/MAI/(95)1, 17 August 1995.

20. see DAFFE/MAI(98)9/Final.

Finally, the importance of an effective dispute settlement mechanism also remained a central issue and generated many discussions; a number of delegations still had strong concerns particularly in the area of investor-state dispute settlement.

Even though there had been progress, negotiations could not be concluded by April 1998 as scheduled. In May 1998, negotiations were suspended for six months, for "a period of assessment and further consultation between the negotiating parties with interested parts of their societies [... and of] active public discussions on the issues at stake in the negotiations".[21] In October 1998, France officially pulled out of the negotiations; many countries followed and withdrew their support. Negotiations ceased in December 1998.

*Why Did it Fail?*

Interviews with OECD officers reveal two complementary reasons that might explain this failure. First and foremost, the desire to reach a 'binding treaty with a dispute settlement mechanism' while retaining a very high standard, created undue pressure on participants. As we explained earlier, reaching a high standard consensus is already an arduous task. It is rendered possible because states know they will be allowed the necessary time and adaptations to reach these new standards; peer reviews and peer pressure will gradually push each of them toward the collective goal; member states will not be penalized as they move along. However, the introduction of a dispute mechanism that is likely to sanction delinquent states, incites members to agree to less stringent conditions, or to attain the lowest common denominator. This was a unique challenge within OECD and it did not seem to fit with the tools available within this organization.

The obligation to reach a binding agreement on a very complex and contentious subject raised the visibility of the negotiating process at a time when the anti-globalization lobby was emerging as a force to contend with. Ministers attended negotiating sessions, compelled by their press and their electorate to take positions and be seen as fighting hard to protect national vested interests. This further reduced the ability of OECD to deal with these difficult negotiations. The involvement of the media in this complex process generated a problem for OECD by putting the organization at a disadvantage as preferred outcomes are generally based on subdued discussions, on scientific (and subtle) evidence, and patient negotiations between 'happy accomplice' public servants. The Western media, forever in search of news with 'solid

---

21. Ministerial Statement, 28 April 1998.

entertainment value,' tend to trivialize complex issues or polarize debates to make them more lively and interesting to the viewer, or to the reader. In that sense, there is an interesting case to be made about keeping OECD away from the limelight and to retain the mundane and uninteresting character of its negotiation process.

## 2.4 The Club du Sahel: A Unique Experiment

In 1973, over 200,000 people died as a result of severe drought conditions that affected the West African region of the Sahel from Cape Verde to Chad. A massive combined effort by various donors was launched to save starving populations stranded in remote areas of the Sahel.

The Sahelian governments decided to create CILSS (Comité Inter-États de Lutte contre la Sécheresse au Sahel) in December 1973 to try to extend the spontaneous (and somewhat unexpected) emergency assistance into long-term development assistance. The countries concerned included Burkina Faso, Cape Verde, Chad, Gambia, Guinea-Bissau, Mauritania, Mali, Niger and Senegal. Their message was that they wanted help to build the means necessary to avoid any recurrent crisis such as this one, and support to ensure their food security and to fight desertification. As part of this initiative they quickly compiled a wish list of project proposals that, it was hoped, would attract a substantial inflow of aid support.

Aid agencies were profoundly sceptical. As much as they wanted to help, they had doubts about the quality of those projects and about the policies sustaining those programs. Many believed that the food pricing mechanisms were awry, resulting in increased desertification when compounded by uncontrolled cattle breeding. Some experts were so pessimistic that they bluntly recommended against further aid to the region, which could have forced its population to migrate to better-endowed lands further south in Ghana, Côte d'Ivoire, Nigeria, and Guinea. Repeated donor 'pledging sessions' held in 1974 and 1975 led nowhere.

Subsequently, the President of OECD's Development Assistance Committee, Maurice Williams, suggested the creation of a "Club des amis du Sahel" as a friendly donor consortium intent on providing policy advice and support to the region. As it happened, circumstances in the United States became suddenly propitious for aid to Sahelian Africa. For one thing, the transition from the acrimonious Gaullist era opened up a window of opportunity for US cooperation with France in development assistance. For another, an increasingly articulate Black Caucus in the US Congress was demanding enhanced commitments toward African development as their litmus test for a foreign policy they could support politically. They spoke of 'a contract of a generation' (a 20 year span) of development cooperation with Sahelian populations. US aid to the Sahel was now given a special line item in the US budget, with a proviso that disbursement would be strictly conditional on the establishment of a coordination mechanism to ensure the sound management of these aid resources.

The initial response of Sahelian governments was negative. There was concern that the creation of a donor-based coordination mechanism would compromise their ability to determine their own policy agenda over the long term.

The deadlock was broken when Canada suggested the inclusion of Sahelian governments into the proposed coordinating mechanism. The President of CIDA, Paul Gérin-Lajoie, delivered a speech in Dakar in December 1975 in which he said: "this Club is for all concerned parties, yourselves first and foremost as well as for your friends, the various donors. Let's speak in the future about a "Club du Sahel". This rallied the Sahelian countries around the first-ever combined consortium mechanism involving recipients and donors in a cooperative regional development initiative. This consortium mechanism was meant to test a new and different modality for aid coordination and policy discourse. To be sure, OECD was (and is) neither a funding nor a program delivery agency; nevertheless, the bilateral donors invited OECD to make an exception and to take upon itself the management of this exceptional initiative. The 2003 members of the Club are: Austria, Belgium, Canada, Denmark, France, Germany, Italy, Japan, Switzerland, the Netherlands, United States and the United Kingdom.

In May 1977, Ottawa hosted the first conference of the Club du Sahel. The conference witnessed the launching of a large and well-coordinated plan of action, composed of a series of projects to rehabilitate the region and to build its agriculture and environment. Of even greater significance, the Ottawa conference witnessed the first policy dialogue between donors and African governments. In typical OECD tradition, the policy discourse was open, candid, and forthrightly reciprocal: donors insisted on reform and liberalization of agricultural policies, while the Sahelians responded that they needed demonstration of the advantages of this approach with well-documented case studies. The Sahelians also countered that donor government restrictions on aid to support recurrent costs, which at that time was not allowed under existing aid definitions, made it impossible for very poor countries to undertake the massive infrastructure investment needed without some flexibility in this regard.

This dialogue engendered the first research work plan for the Club du Sahel. In two early studies, an American economist, Elliott Berg, submitted a cogent and devastating report on Sahelian food policies, while a Canadian scholar, André Martens, formulated the first conceptual approach to sustainable projects and the means to deal with the problem of recurring costs.

## How Did it Work?

Aid agencies are compelled to follow objectives of their own national policy, which often creates confusion and induces a lack of coordination between them and their partners. This has plagued aid delivery for decades, and various methods have been tried to circumvent this tendency or to reduce its ill effects. In the mid 1970s, the Club du Sahel was formed because donors recognized the immensity and the complexity of the environmental problem that challenged a suffering population spread over seven countries (later enlarged to nine). It was understood that resolving such a problem required sound policies and a general plan of action could be designed, agreed upon, and implemented. As an experiment, donors and recipients asked OECD to manage such a policy coordination process. To achieve the desired synergy among various partners, the Club applied OECD's own specific methods that had proven effective in promoting policy consensus.

After 20 years of operation, the Club du Sahel's effectiveness and *modus operandi* have been thoroughly evaluated. [6] The evaluation clearly demonstrated in real circumstances the value of the OECD model for negotiating policies, and undertaking large, complex, and long-term financial commitments. This unique initiative in international and regional development cooperation is today judged a groundbreaking success. Its proponents make the case that this model could be emulated in other areas where major international challenges require collaboration, sound planning, and the combined efforts of donors and regional governments. In many ways, parallels may be drawn between that particular experience and the rehabilitation of the Dnieper River Basin: they both require massive efforts, sound policies, a well understood plan of action, and remarkable cooperation based on true confidence between many different partners, including the riparian governments, foreign donors, and local institutions and stakeholders. In this, the experience undergone in 1976 to deal with the complex environmental problems of the Sahel using the OECD method provides interesting insights and useful lessons.

Despite the scepticism of many, this cooperative club arrangement stood the test of time. Over the years that followed, the policy dialogue, which itself was based on the OECD method, built up the confidence of donor agencies in the capacity of the Sahelian countries to coordinate and to manage their development agenda. Conversely, the self-esteem of Sahelian Governments grew along with the acquired confidence in their new development partners, western aid agencies. As a consequence, aid volumes grew despite the absence of any geo-strategic or even commercial significance to the Sahelian region. By 1980, more than US$ 1 billion was disbursed annually in the Sahel, growing to more than US$ 2 billion at the end of that decade, astounding pessimists and naysayers.

The consequences for the Sahelian societies themselves were no less astounding. Significant progress was made at a country and regional level to sustain food availability despite tremendous ecological and human challenges. For 15 of the past 20 years the Sahel has received below average rainfall; a major drought struck the region in 1985, to a degree far worse than the devastating drought of 1973. Donors responded with a large-scale and well-coordinated emergency food aid effort and starvation was averted. By 1997, food aid accounted for a small fraction of total food availability. The Sahel is no longer food-dependent on donors, despite a doubling of its population during the past two decades (from 23 to 46 million). Cities have expanded almost ten-fold during this time, and yet these societies have been by and large free from conflict. Critical social and technological changes have taken place, and there are indications of incipient political changes. Environmental policies designed to combat desertification in this region were endorsed for their relevance at the global level by the 1992 UN Conference on the Human Environment. The Sahelian countries have weathered adversity and are now beginning to transform poverty into opportunities.

## SECTION 3
## CONCLUSION

The OECD method has proven to work through a great variety of successes. We have given various examples throughout this text. Hopefully other researchers will look into this matter and find many more success stories. Upon closer analysis, it is not as surprising as it seems. True enough, the OECD model differs significantly from other better-known management methods, as they are common among Multinational Organizations. But it works well and is clearly accountable for a significant number of positive changes in its Members' governance.

Here are a few other characteristics that are worth mentioning as they further explain why this unique network has been achieving results over almost five decades.

- Stove piping is broken. In many instances relations between ministries did not exist before OECD convenes a multisectoral meeting (also referred to as horizontal). This creates cognitive bridges that allow surmounting structural dysfunctionalities in governments. These cognitive bridges function through the use of data gathering, analysis, and through the accumulation of 'best practices/promising practices.'

- It works because it is less dogmatic and more pragmatic than most other models. For instance, OECD economists and specialists constantly refer to 'the standards of the profession,' meaning that they keep abreast of any new development in their respective field of expertise. One might argue that the basic economic outlook resembles that of the World Bank and of the IMF. Economists in Washington and Paris are constantly in touch with each other, and they read the same books. But OECD experts have a difficult day when they try to change governance principles in their constituency. They meet with pugnacious representatives from member states. They are forced to document empirically and practically the wisdom of their point of view before it is generally accepted. Furthermore, each prescription must be tailored to each and every member's traditions, culture, and habits. In Chapter 4, we have explained the manner by which they manage to gradually move the agenda forward while respecting local susceptibilities.

- Last but not least, OECD is a powerhouse for innovations at various levels. A number of powerful ideas were born in its midst. Sometimes these ideas became associated with OECD, but often they were allowed to be born there but were popularized elsewhere. We have alluded to the fact that the idea of tackling the difficult and practical issue of coal and iron was first discussed within OECD. From there, it blossomed and eventually gave birth to the related and extremely powerful idea of a European Community. It is another little known fact that environmental concepts such as "Polluter-Pays-Principle," or the notion of sustainable development, were first discussed within OECD. New methods and tools, such as the concepts of 'purchasing power parity, or agriculture subsidy-equivalent' have allowed discussions and negotiations to move ahead when they were stalled.

- In the end, cost sharing principles are the litmus test and the proof that members believe in it. It is a real measure of their commitment to it. States that want to change and improve must be prepared to pay the price for it. Two measures ensure the strength of a true network: sharing costs and benefits among all members and a real commitment from every actor in the system. This includes member states, the secretariat, committee chairs, and the devoted staff.

# Post Face

## This Leaves a Few Haunting Questions

### The NASA Dilemma

In 1986, the Challenger space shuttle, carrying seven astronauts and commissions worth hundreds of millions of dollars, exploded on take-off. It was shown that the accident was predictable and therefore avoidable. The cause of the tragedy was the O-ring: NASA employees had identified the defect, but no preventive measures had been taken. The authorities decided that the launch should not be delayed. The dilemma seemed insoluble: if NASA delayed the launch to replace the defective joints, everyone would know exactly how much the delay had cost, but it would be impossible to prove how many lives and how much money had been saved because the precaution would have destroyed all proof that there had been cause for worry (Guilmette, 1995, p.65).

In Chapter 1, we highlighted the fundamentally conflicting preventive nature of the cooperation paradigm. Considering the Challenger example, to anticipate an aborted crisis or conflict is a process by which, to the extent that it is successful, will usually obscure the proof of its own success. This metaphor will help us appreciate the inherent difficulty involved in undertaking and maintaining interest in a lengthy, tedious, and costly process that was intended to help prevent conflicts through economic growth and increased trade among nations. To the extent that OECD's work is aimed at preventing new economic and political crises, it will always be difficult to appreciate its full value. Who can say with certainty how many crises, or possibly wars, may have been avoided as a result of its persistent work over the last 55 years? Who can deny that there has been such an impact?

There are a few questions that I wish to share:

- What of the future of OECD? Members are currently confronted with a real challenge as many countries graduate into the group of so-called industrial economies, and are anxious to join the select brotherhood of rich democracies. As we have seen, the governing rules of OECD are numerous, subtle, and demanding. Time is required before a new player can master them and participate meaningfully in the rule of consensus.

In addition, more participants increase the overall complexity of negotiations. Essential eye-to-eye contacts and familiarization with other cultural contexts are an essential component of progress. What is difficult to forecast, because there exists no empirical evidence, is when a group becomes too large to benefit from the OECD way of doing things.

- If that is so, what other scenarios can be envisaged? Should the OECD or its members invest time and resources helping other regions create their own OECD, in a manner analogous to the way the World Bank concept gave rise to other regional development Banks, such as the Asian, the Inter-American, and African banks? One could even envisage that these networks could come together to negotiate intra-network issues of concern for the entire group.

- What is the right time to start up? We have seen that the circumstances that surrounded the creation of OECD were historically special: European countries were in dire need of a new approach to peace and stability, and they knew something drastic had to be done about it. Furthermore, the American Government was at its very best, so to speak. The US has a history of interspersing isolationist cycles with expansionist foreign policy. The Second World War marked an era when the US had self-confidence, felt it could afford to be generous, and acted in a most enlightened manner. Its consistency and determination to assist European countries was a determining factor in the build-up of OECD. Those were exceptional circumstances that cannot be duplicated. Analogous circumstances may exist however.

- Can this experience be tried in a smaller dimension? This is the hypothesis we started with; the resolution of problems related to the clean-up of the Dnieper River Basin, involving three nations and possibly a number of donor and partner organizations, seemed a promising testing ground for such a hypothesis. Maybe other groups of countries will be inspired by the method and use it to pursue common goals.

- What are the most effective development policies? This was the key question that OECE members attempted to address in 1947. This probing interrogation is still at the forefront of debates within the OECD. Much of the Development Assistance Committee's agenda deals with the best way to induce development in poor countries. Maybe the time has come to invest more in spending and more time listening than treated with suspicion by civil servants? This is going to be a most difficult challenge for OECD partners, if and when former Soviet countries become members of the Organization.

In this book, I have tried to demonstrate the nature and extent of commitment on the part of OECD members. It is my belief that OECD is directly accountable for a large quantity of positive changes in its members' governance, enough to have helped sustain growth, distribute wealth within its population, and establish generally sound policies. We hope readers will now take a second look at this extraordinary organization the next time they hear on the news: "OECD foresees a growth rate of 2.3%...."

# Appendix

*Glossary*

| *Term* | *Definition* |
|---|---|
| Active Consensus | Defines the qualitative outcome of a discussion negotiation. The participants not only agree with the recommendations/decisions of the meeting, but also modify the way they view or understand the problem, take this new vision back to their domestic institutions, and start to behave differently upon return to their home country. It is content driven as opposed to formal rights and rituals. |
| Agenda | An annotated well-structured summary, featuring the key points of the discussion, which serves as the indicator or guidelines for all members of the meeting: help them to prepare themselves for the discussion and keep their focus on the main issues in order to achieve the maximum of planned objectives and ensure movement forward. |
| AID, Assistance | The words 'aid' and 'assistance' refer to financial flows that qualify as Official Development Assistance (ODA) or Official Aid (OA). See the definition of ODA. |
| Anglo-Saxon Character | Historically cultivated type of organizational behaviour applied within OECD. It refers to understanding and following the unwritten rules within the organization (the OECD's 'etiquette'), use of the gentlemen's agreements and unwritten conventions, implementation of the primary commitments of States and use of the juridical system traits based on jurisprudence or case law (such as English law). |
| Appropriation | Making use of ideas, concepts, techniques, or technologies that are being transferred to developing countries through technical assistance or capital projects. Also an allocation of money that has been set aside from a budget, especially a government budget, for a particular purpose. |
| Capacity Building (Capacity Development) | The process by which individuals, organizations, institutions, and societies develop abilities (individually and collectively) to perform functions, solve problems, and set and achieve objectives. It is a powerful combination of people, institutions, and practices that permits countries to achieve their development goals. Capacity building is the development of an organization's core skills and capabilities, such as leadership, management, finance and fund raising, programs and evaluation, to build the organization's effectiveness and sustainability. It is the process of assisting an individual or group to identify and address issues and gain insights, knowledge, and experience needed to solve problems and implement change. Capacity building is facilitated through the |

*Contd. ...*

| Term | Definition |
|------|------------|
| | provision of technical support activities, including coaching, training, specific technical assistance, and resource networking. The expression came into vogue in the early 1990s among international development agencies such as the World Bank and UNDP. |
| 'Checks and Balance' Systems | A mechanism used to prevent the infringement of the American political system, which is based on the principle of separation of powers (legislative, executive, and judicial), from excess influence by either of the other branches. |
| 'Chess' Strategy | The objective is to capture, and kill the rival king. The supreme goal is to eliminate the opposing side and to destroy the king and rivals; alliances form an integral part of the game strategy. There is no ambiguity in purpose, values, or ends, which gives the image of the centralized state, of duelling and tournaments. |
| Club of Rome | A global think tank and a centre of innovation and initiative with the mission to act as a global catalyst of change that is free of any political, ideological, or business interest. This powerful NGO brings together scientists, economists, businessmen, international senior civil servants, heads of state and former heads of state, who are convinced that each of us can contribute to the improvement of our societies. Club of Rome seeks solutions to what it calls the 'world problematique'—the complex set of the most crucial problems—political, social, economic, technological, environmental, psychological and cultural—facing humanity. (*http://www.clubofrome.org/*) |
| Comecon (1950–1990) The Council for Mutual Economic Cooperation | The Soviet analogue to the network on international level, which was created for the purpose of regrouping of Eastern and Central European economies under the Soviet regime. Its members included Albania, Czechoslovakia, East Germany (GDR), Hungary, the USSR, Poland and Romania. One of the main aims of the Comecon was to promote, in the context of the western embargo, mutual economic co-operation and arrange trade between the former Communist countries. In practice it benefited the Soviet Union more than the other countries. Oil was traded at an artificially low price but so were the products of the other members. As an economic community its main defect was that there was no market. Investment decisions were made using non-economic criteria. (e.g. Czechoslovakia specialized in streetcars, Hungary in |

*...Contd. ...*

| Term | Definition |
|------|-----------|
| | buses, Poland in trucks. The result tended to be one huge factory, which was always inefficient in comparison to a western factory in the same field.) |
| Common Agricultural Policy (CAP) | CAP was established in the 1960s to secure Europe's food supply and to stabilize prices for the benefit of both producers and consumers. CAP encouraged a constant supply of home-produced food by providing farm price supports. The policy was set up against a backdrop of food shortages and rations following World War II, and had five founding aims: increased productivity, a fair standard of living for farmers, stable markets, regular food supplies, and reasonable prices for consumers. It was based on three principles: a single market in farm products with common prices and free movement of agricultural goods within the community, preference for community members, and shared costs. Although spending on CAP has been reduced in recent years, it still consumes almost half the EU budget and represents one of its biggest policy concerns. With forthcoming accession of countries like Poland and its expanse of poor rural areas, there is a question of how to adapt CAP to the conditions of an enlarged Europe. *(http://www.defra.gov.uk/farm/capreform/)* |
| Communique | An official, concrete public announcement or bulletin, which summarizes the outcome of the confidential debates and the issues dealt with during meetings at the Ministerial level. The text contains self-evident observations, statements of principles underlying the policies pursued by governments, and agreements reached on specific points. It is aimed at the general public. |
| Confidence | A concept defined as the confidence in one's society, self-esteem, openness of mind, tolerance of others and of new ideas, accountability for one's actions, responsibility, confidence in the value of science and technical inventiveness, acceptance of diffusion of one's culture. It is a generic term that refers to a general attitude toward things that seem foreign. |
| Connectivity | Refers to the free flow of ideas and goods (material products, cultural artifacts, books), which occurs as a result of both increased confidence and its driving force. Without connectivity, ideas cannot circulate and do their important job as leavening agents. Electronic networks, such as Internet, radio and television, trade activities may serve as the examples of such infrastructure for the end of the 20$^{th}$ Century. The other important aspect of connectivity is the development of fast and flexible means of transportation through complex communication infrastructure (roads, airports, railroads, ports). |

*Contd. ...*

*...Contd. ...*

| Term | Definition |
|------|------------|
| Consensus | A process of reconciliation of the diverse opinions, values and preferences used in OECD to build a sustainable agreement in the course of negotiations. It requires the agreements of all members for the proposal to be accepted. It is reached through the implementation of iterative peer review and peer pressure techniques, the application of common standards, well-structured meetings, and transparent processes. |
| Cooperative | A new pattern of cooperative international relations Paradigm emerged after the Second World War, involving countries of Western Europe and North America, which resulted in the formation of OECD, EU, and NATO. Characterized by synergetic partnering among the countries, increased international cooperation, heightened levels of confidence and connectivity, free flow of information distributed through the pool of networks, and enhanced quality standards, which yields economies of scope and scale for creativity and boosts economic and technological innovation. |
| Counterweights | Culturally specific values (as opposed to weights), often linked to legal or quasi-legal requirements, which compensate for drifts, thus helping to keep the social system in balance. |
| Culture | Information (skills, values, beliefs, attitudes, and motives) capable of effecting individual behaviour, which they acquire from others by teaching, imitation, and other forms of social learning. Culture, as a body of learned behaviours common to a given human society, acts like a template (i.e. it has predictable form and content), shaping behaviour and consciousness within a human society from generation to generation. |
| Cybernetics | The science of control and communication in the animal and the machine. The word originated in the mid 1900's, and its origin comes from Greek *kubern–t–s* steersman, governor, from *kubernan* to steer (source of English govern). As coined by the U.S. mathematician Norbert Weiner in the 1940s (see Weiner, 1949), and stimulated by the advent of modern computing, the term was intended to draw attention to common processes at work in systems of all types, whether these be mechanical servomechanisms (e.g. a thermostatically controlled central-heating system), biological organisms, or social systems. Here it is used to describe the linear way of communications in the companies' organizational structure. |
| Drift | Any tendency, deviation or form of unbalance typical of the particular system, which occurs as a result of the |

*Contd. ...*

| Term | Definition |
|---|---|
| | repeated interplay between tendencies over the iterative negotiation process. |
| Economy of Scale | Reduction in cost per unit resulting from increased production, realized through operational efficiencies. Economies of scale can be accomplished because as production increases, the cost of producing each additional unit falls. |
| Economy of Scope | The situation that arises when the cost of performing multiple business functions simultaneously proves more efficient than performing each business function independently. |
| Effectiveness | Refers to producing an adequate or desired result, it is more concerned with the impact being made or outcome achieved as a result of the meeting rather than with the correct way of doing things or following all the procedures. |
| Efficiency | Refers to the state of being efficient, the ability to perform and conduct a well-run meeting in compliance with its implicit rules and regulations, ensuring accurate performance of all tasks and procedures, thus forming an action-task oriented group, which may eventually lead to effectiveness. |
| Externalities | Factors that are not included in Gross National Product but which have an effect on human welfare. Pollution is a prime example of an external cost imposed on society: national output may only be maintained by allowing a certain degree of pollution, which detracts from the quality of life. A firm will include the private costs of material, labour, and capital used in producing goods and services but will not count the social costs of pollution involved. On the other hand, positive externalities such as the social benefits conferred by firms in training workers who become available for employment else where, are again not counted in national outputs. |
| Game Strategy | 'Strategic games' analysis (Asian game of GO and European game of CHESS), as a way to exemplify the values, goals, and behavioural patterns that characterize the strategic cultures of those societies. |
| 'Go' Strategy | The strategic behaviour is based on ambiguity, synergetic interplay. The object of the game is to enlarge one's vital space by gaining territory with the use of synergetic strategic outlook. The goal is not to kill or avoid being killed but to live and construct. Projects the image of the state relying on its masses, individuals both showing solidarity and interchangeability. |

*...Contd. ...*

| Term | Definition |
| --- | --- |
| Helms-Burton Law | The Helms-Burton law aimed at toughening the embargo against Cuba by prohibiting foreign companies to invest or purchase property seized after the 1959 revolution in Cuba. US Western allies have strongly opposed the law since it was passed in 1996. Helms-Burton has helped scare away some potential investors, yet while the legislation isn't halting investment, it is putting the brakes on, since companies already there aren't leaving, but new investors are cautious. *(http://www.globalexchange.org/ campaigns/cuba/US-Cuba/HelmsBurton.html)* |
| Hobbes, Thomas (1558-1679) | English philosopher and political theorist best known for his book *Leviathan* (1651), in which he argues that the only way to secure civil society is through universal submission to the absolute authority of a sovereign.The question raised by Hobbes—the Hobbesian "problem of order"—remains a central question in sociology. He held that there was a war of each against all; that self-interest was a universal law of social psychology and that in the natural state, life was solitary, poor, nasty, brutish, and short, a phrase which directs attention to the question of the source of social organization. Hobbes argued for a 'civil order;' one in which the best solution to the problem of order is a social contract which puts all power in a Monarch [or a Leviathan]. |
| Homer-Dixon, Thomas | Thomas Homer-Dixon, is Director of the Centre for the Study of Peace and Conflict at the University of Toronto. He has led several international research projects examining the links between environmental stress and violence in developing countries. In recent years, his research has focused on how societies adapt to complex economic, ecological, and technological change. In 2001, he received the Governor General's Non-Fiction Literary Award for his book *The Ingenuity Gap*, where he uses his ingenuity theory to suggest how we might approach complex problems in our own lives, our thinking, our businesses in today's world. |
| Human Rights | Is a key component of an emergent knowledge-based economy, especially in Western political culture, with respect to political values, multiparty democracy, transparency in government, freedom of expression, accessible communications networks, private property and personal rights, and acceptance of market rules for management of the economy. This leads to the release of human intellectual creativity—the main factor in knowledge-based production. *(http://www.un.org/rights/)* |

*Contd. ...*

*...Contd. ...*

| Term | Definition |
| --- | --- |
| Interpreted Consensus | It is a consensus-like legitimate agreement among participants, identified by the Chair with the assistance of the Secretariat, and drawn from the meeting that is a part of a more prolonged workshop. |
| Iterative Process | A renewed dialogue, repeated progressive process of policy review among OECD members, aimed at production of reasonable, sustainable agreements, such as relevant and timely policy outputs, which can be readily adapted to the specific needs of the member countries. |
| Krastev, Ivan | Ivan Krastev received his MA in Philosophy from the University of Sofia in 1990. In 1994-1996 he was a Lecturer at the New Bulgarian University. His doctoral thesis on "Presidential Constitutional Politics in Eastern Europe" is to be defended. He was a Fellow at the Wissenschaftskolleg, Berlin in 1999-2000; a Woodrow Wilson Policy Fellow at Woodrow Wilson Center for International Scholars, Washington in 1998; and a Fellow at the Collegium Budapest, Institute for Advanced Study, where he worked on a project entitled "The Rise and Influence of Think Tanks in Central and Eastern Europe" in 1997-1998. At present, Ivan Krastev is the Chairman of the Board and Research Director at the Centre for Liberal Strategies, Sofia, Bulgaria. |
| Maverick | Highly independent type of diplomat, opinionated, daring, and expressive character. Acts as a group catalyst when the agenda is prolonged, and is useful in situations requiring risk-taking, enterprising action to break the entrenched resistance and move on. |
| Mcluhan, Marshall | Herbert Marshall McLuhan, a communication theorist, was born on July 21, 1911 in Edmonton, Alberta, Canada. McLuhan got his MA degree from the University of Manitoba in 1935. In 1942 he earned a PhD at Cambridge University, and in 1954-80 he became a professor of English at the University of Toronto, where in 1963 he established the Centre for Culture and Technology-his intellectual base-camp. From that time McLuhan devoted himself to studies of the effect of electronic technology on the human community. His ideas had great popular success in the 1990s with the advent of the World Wide Web. *Wired* magazine has adopted him as their 'patron saint' and a number of new books have emerged using McLuhan's ideas: *The Mechanical Bride* (1951), *The Gutenberg Galaxy* (1962), *Understanding Media* (1964), and *The Medium is the Message* (1967). For more information see: *http://www.law.pitt.edu/hibbitts/mcl.htm; www.marshallmcluhan.com* |

*Contd. ...*

*...Contd. ...*

| Term | Definition |
| --- | --- |
| Mercantilism | A doctrine, developed in the West after the decline of feudalism, that the wealth of nations derives from possession and control of territories, people, and resources. The assumption that a nation's economy could be strengthened by governmental protection of home industries, by increased foreign exports, and by accumulating gold and silver, which in turn promoted a collection of policies of conquest and protectionism. |
| Nepad—The New Partnership for Africa's Development | A vision and a program of action for the socioeconomic development of Africa, which was formed on 23 October 2001 as a merger of the Millennium Partnership for the African Recovery Programme (MAP) and the OMEGA Plan, dealing with the building of infrastructures, including the new technologies of information and communication (ICT), education and human resource development, health and agriculture. NEPAD is a holistic comprehensive integrated development plan that addresses key social, economic, and political priorities in a coherent and balanced manner. It was conceived and developed by African leaders. Its primary objective is to eradicate widespread and severe poverty in African countries, both individually and collectively. Then to establish a path of sustainable growth and development to halt the marginalization of Africa in the globalization process. (*http://www.nepad.org/ http://www.dfa.gov.za/events/ nepad.htm*) |
| Network | An arrangement of interconnected people or operations, which can be either informal, such as among scientists or researchers, formal, with imposing structures and widely respected identities, comprising a core of officials serving both the institution and the network (such as OECD) or a blend of informality within a structured arrangement (World Bank consortia meetings). |
| OECD | The forerunner of The Organization for Economic Co-operation and Development (OECD) was the Organization for European Economic Co-operation (OEEC), founded in 1949, which was formed to administer American and Canadian aid under the Marshall Plan for reconstruction of Europe after World War II. Since it took over from OEEC in 1961, OECD provides a setting for its 30 Member countries to discuss, develop and perfect economic and social policy. Members compare experiences, seek answers to common problems and work to co-ordinate domestic and international policies that increasingly in today's globalized world must form a web of consistent practice across nations. Their exchanges may lead to agreements to act in a formal way—for example, |

*Contd. ...*

| Term | Definition |
|------|------------|
| | by establishing legally binding codes for free flow of capital and services, agreements to crack down on bribery or to end subsidies for shipbuilding. But more often, their discussion makes for better-informed work within their own governments on the spectrum of public policy and clarifies the impact of national policies on the international community. OECD is a group of industrial countries sharing a commitment to market economy, democracy, and respect for human rights. |
| OECD—The Online Library | The OECD online library, Source OECD, possesses a great number of books and 24 OECD periodicals, which serve as a precious source of information covering 20 subjects. This award-winning online library is now in its third full year of operation, and is loading new e-books every year. At the end of 2001, just under 2,000 institutions subscribed to it and about 12,000 e-books and 4,000 statistics tables a month from 160,000 user sessions were delivered via Internet. *(http://www.oecd.org/pdf/ M00029000/M00029254.pdf)* |
| OECD Member Countries | Australia, Austria, Belgium, Canada, Czech Republic, Denmark, Finland, France, Germany, Greece, Hungary, Iceland, Ireland, Italy, Japan, Korea, Luxembourg, Mexico, Netherlands, New Zealand, Norway, Poland, Portugal, Slovak Republic, Spain, Sweden, Switzerland, Turkey, United Kingdom, United States. |
| OECD Publications | OECD is the largest scientific publisher in Europe. It possesses great sources of diverse information, such as various publications (over 4,000 paperbacks including annual reports, 24 journals, magazines, studies and conference proceedings), research reports, conventions, working papers, country surveys and statistics (25 statistical databases on CD-ROM and 700 electronic publications on-line) on economics, social issues, trade, macroeconomics, education, development, science and innovation. OECD statistics are available to the public through electronic and paper publications and through the Statistical Portal. The OECD reports and statistical data on the economies of member countries represent harmonized, validated and comparatively formed up-to-date sources of information, which can be utilized by the governments, businesses, academics, NGOs, researchers, planners, journalists, ministries and policymakers. |
| Official Development Assistance (ODA) | Refers to funding offered by governments or aid agencies to disadvantaged countries or regions either free of charge or at rates below the market rate (also known as cheap or free funding). OECD defines it as grants or loans to countries and territories on Part I of the DAC List of Aid |

*Contd. ...*

| Term | Definition |
|------|------------|
| | Recipients (developing countries) which are: (a) undertaken by the official sector; (b) with promotion of economic development and welfare as the main objective; (c) at concessional financial terms (if a loan, having a Grant Element (q.v.) of at least 25%). In addition to financial flows, Technical Co-operation (q.v.) is included in aid. Grants, loans and credits for military purposes are excluded. Transfer payments to private individuals (e.g. pensions, reparations or insurance payouts) are in general not counted. |
| Ownership | Aid agencies have come to use this term in the sense of appropriating a concept, an idea, a technique or a particular form of know-how. It is often used in that sense as a measure of success, as ideas or activities that are not owned or appropriated by the recipient are likely to be abandoned once the donor ceases paying for it. |
| Paradigm | A model that forms the basis of something: an example that serves as a pattern or concept model, especially one that forms the basis of a methodology or theory. In the philosophy of science—a generally accepted model of how ideas relate to one another, forming a conceptual framework within which scientific research is carried out. Paradigms are the ground against which theories are formed, which in turn are influenced by the paradigms of the culture. Also used to reflect the way that the world is experienced or 'seen' by individuals or collectivities. |
| Passive Diplomat | Not very efficient type of diplomat: usually does not participate in debates, remains in the background, and satisfied with accomplishing the main tasks of the protocol and ensuring correct administration of the meeting. Because such behaviour does not stimulate group dynamic and enthusiasm, eventually would be replaced by more energetic member. |
| Peer Pressure | Effective tool used in the negotiation process, which helps to reach consensus; a kind of moral and political constraint that countries exercise on each other, but is quite different from that flowing from formal agreements. |
| Peer Review | Tool for cooperation and change, which can be described as the systematic examination and assessment of the performance of a State by other States, with the ultimate goal of helping the reviewed State improve its policy-making, adopt best practices, and comply with established standards and principles. Representatives of other member countries serve as a 'jury' to evaluate a sparticular country's performance. |
| Persistent Diplomat | Represents skilled, expert type of diplomat, who has |

*Contd. ...*

*...Contd. ...*

| Term | Definition |
|------|-----------|
| | extensive successful experience of chairing a number of committees, and ability to listen carefully and patiently to other delegates for a long period of time, aligning them along the main objectives of the meeting. |
| Policy | A decision, a course of action or a position to be preferred in the pursuit of one or more objectives of the government. Always implies a set of processes involving the participation of a great number of concerned actors such as other governments, international organizations and other government levels, representatives of the civil society including users, clients and stakeholders, scientists, legislators, and others, who will discuss the various alternatives and input into the choice to be made. |
| Policy Adaptation | The process of introducing and successfully launching new policies in the member country. The vital elements for successful policy implementation would be defined by openness, flexibility of the political and institutional systems, capacity to understand and to accept new foreign concepts, as well as the willingness to make necessary changes in the existing policy regime. |
| Policy Adoption | The act or condition of choosing and accepting a policy or recommendation for its further consideration. |
| Policy 'Regime' | Sets of implicit and explicit principles, norms, rules, and decision-making procedures around which states or government expectations converge in a given area of international relations, including subjects such as regional economic cooperation. |
| Policy Community | Refers to a group of people, usually consisting of different backgrounds (parliamentarians, experts, civilians, the media, researchers, NGOs) who share and promote a broad single interest and form various specialized committees to hear and discuss their viewpoints and arguments, thus exercising public involvement and citizen participation in policy debates and formulation. |
| Public Good, or Social Products, or Collective Products | Any good or service that cannot be provided other than on a group basis because the quantity supplied to any individual cannot be independently varied unlike private products. They are paid out by general taxation and not by individual consumers buying in the market place. These were traditionally few in numbers, involving for example, national defence, police protection, heavy communication infrastructure. Over the 20th Century, they have come to include education, health, housing, municipal services such as water and sewerage and public transport, etc. National accounts and national statistics are also considered public goods or institutions, such as the |

*Contd. ...*

*...Contd. ...*

| Term | Definition |
| --- | --- |
| | OECD, may be included in the definition. |
| Public Policy | A decision, a direction, or a position to be preferred in the pursuit of one or more objectives of the government, which implies a set of processes involving the participation of a great number of concerned actors (other governments, international organizations, representatives of the civil society—users, clients and stakeholders, scientists, legislators) who will discuss the various alternatives and input into the choice to be made. |
| Ritual | An established and prescribed procedure for a ceremony, where form of doing things becomes more important than the content. It is a pattern of behaviour repeated (often mindlessly) in a fixed form and order as though prescribed by custom or authority. It occasionally happens that a useful routine or an administrative procedure is transformed into a ritual, thus inducing mindless and error-prone behaviour. It has been deplored that a number of practices introduced by donors have been ritualized , and in this process have lost their usefulness. |
| Routine | A regular course of action, day-to-day copied precise way of doing things, a repetitive activity that never changes. Sahel Club was founded in 1975 by OECD as a friendly donor consortium intent on providing policy advice and support to the West African region. As an informal forum for exchanges of views, attuned to African thinking, the Sahel and West Africa Club facilitates links between North and South and between private and public sectors. It works toward improving development assistance and encourages the southern partners to control their own development and shape their own strategies. |
| Savvy President | Chair/representative who plays the key role in moving the agenda forward for the committee, keeps the group focused on the substance of the issues, helping the organization to foster 'cooperation' among its members at all the times. Elected from the country members of the committee, subcommittee, or workshop based on savvy, knowledge of the subject, leadership, interest, and in accordance with the rules, precedents, and habits of the organization. |
| Standards | Documented agreements containing technical specifications or other precise criteria to be used consistently as rules, guidelines, or characteristics, to ensure that materials, products, processes, and services are fit for their purpose (such as internationally accepted ISO 15000 quality standards). Here it refers to unification of the quality standards, their harmonization and the |

*Contd. ...*

*...Contd. ...*

| Term | Definition |
|---|---|
| | process of the 'common' standards formulation within member countries. Such standards allow effective communication and exchange: they breed connectivity and confidence between trading partners, support increased trade and economic growth of the member countries. (*www.iso.c00h.html*) |
| Story Line | A term derived from cinema used here to describe the series of sufficient arguments, developed by the delegate and acceptable in their own culture, which can be presented to various levels of decision-makers and influential parties for a new policy to be adopted in any OECD member country. |
| Summary Record | An analytical, descriptive document, usually prepared by a Secretariat, which recapitulates the process of the discussion and its main points, underscores agreements and consensus reached as well as goals achieved and lessons learned. At the same time it complements the role of the agenda and provides the delegation members with a succinct review of all key arguments, which serves as a useful tool to share values and experiences with their national policymakers back home, validate the amount of work done, while reporting to the headquarters and justifying the cost of the meeting. |
| Synergy (Synergetic Partnering) | Co-operation partnering among the countries, which creates a state-of-the-art synthesis of knowledge and offers a more effective, more efficient, and more resilient approach to enhancing the wealth of each country, and all countries through constant improvement of their economic efficiency. |
| Technical Assistance | Includes both grants to nationals of aid-recipient countries receiving education or training at home or abroad, and payments to consultants, advisers, and similar personnel as well as teachers and administrators serving in recipient countries (including the cost of associated equipment). Assistance of this kind provided specifically to facilitate the implementation of a capital project is included indistinguishably among bilateral project and program expenditures, and not separately identified as technical co-operation in statistics of aggregate flows. |
| Tied Aid | Type of aid where the giving (or donor) country also benefits economically. This happens because the receiving country must buy goods and services from the donor country with the money provided for that purpose. |
| Time Management | Time management is about controlling and use of time. Effective time management necessitates a sense of balance and high achievement. High achievement implies the |

*Contd. ...*

*...Contd. ...*

| Term | Definition |
| --- | --- |
| | optimal use of personal energy and time, purposefulness and effectiveness of the actions, as well as flexibility and readiness for new opportunities. Balance is about the time distribution in the key areas of your life, including family, work, money, health, social, and spiritual areas. Balance and high achievement form a foundation for the self-actualization, career, business, and financial success. Personal time management is about the skills, habits, and tools that bring you there. For references, please, see: *http://www.time-management-guide.com* |
| Transfer of Technology | Refers to "the sum of information, knowledge, methods and tools necessary to use and make useful things" (The Economic and Social Council of UN). It's a 'know-how' that is being transferred. Such transfer is a process that involves many different techniques and methods: *Public technology*—whatever knowledge is in the public domain and can be transferred free; *Privately owned technology*—falls under industrial property rights and must be purchased before it can be used; *Imbedded technology* or techniques that are imbedded with tools, which implies that one has to buy the tools along with the manual or training that comes with it to master technology or 'know-how' specific to that tool. It could be an entire industrial process with all management techniques that had been recognized as the essential components of the process. Thus, transfer of technology may refer to the distribution of various knowledge through training and/or through the provision of expertise in the form of reports. And lastly, it may be related to the provision of specialized equipment. |
| Transparency | Availability, share, and exchange of information, when all economic data and analyses, as well as government procedures, are made public and are available to international and domestic institutions, citizens, domestic critics, and opposing parties. It is measured by the degree of its accessibility and distribution within the country. |
| UNDP/GEF—United Nations Development Programme/Global Environment Facility | Established in 1991 as a result of the Rio Conference (1990), The Global Environment Facility (GEF) forges international cooperation and finances actions that address six critical threats to the global environment: biodiversity loss, climate change, degradation of international waters, ozone depletion, land degradation, and persistent organic pollutants (POPs). GEF brings together 175 member governments, working in partnership with the private sector, NGOs, and international institutions to address complex environmental issues, while supporting national sustainable development initiatives. GEF helps developing |

*Contd. ...*

*...Contd. ...*

| Term | Definition |
| --- | --- |
| | countries fund projects and programs that protect the global environment and foster international agreements. GEF has allocated US$ 4 billion in grants and leveraged an additional US$ 12 billion in co-financing from other sources to support more than 1,000 projects in over 140 developing countries with economies in transition. In August 2002, 32 donor nations pledged nearly US$ 3 billion to fund the work of GEF for the next four years. *(http://www.gefweb.org/)* |
| Weights | Specific values, biases, and characteristics of the society, which influence its policy decision-making process. |
| Win-Win Negotiations | Reaching agreement, sale, resolution or impasse favourable and mutually beneficial to both sides involved in the negotiations, and achieved as a result of thorough discussion, compromise, and willingness to tackle arising hazards and problems. Win-win negotiations preserve the ecosystem and, overall, are the most effective means of accomplishing goals as they provide the means for achieving better results and terms for both parties. "In business you don't get what you deserve—you get what you negotiate!" The Golden Rule is to adopt a winning-for-everyone strategy or getting everything you want by helping others get what they want. |
| Wise Director | Metaphor used to describe the unit directors in the OECD Secretariat. The team act as diplomatic mediator within OECD, to ensure successful collaboration between national representatives, help them influence each other in a constructive manner, find a 'common language' and unblock prolonged negotiations, which occur as a result of cultural misunderstanding and suspicion. They possess objectivity, moral integrity, impartiality, professionalism, intellectual and moral independence, balance, and conflict-avoidance talent. |

## OECD Resources and Other Useful Links

- *www.oecd.org*: The OECD main website
- *http://cs3hq.oecd.org/scripts/stats/ source/index.htm*: Worldwide Statistical Sources
- *http://www.oecd.org/EN/about/0,,EN-about-20-nodirectorate-no-no-no-20,00.html*: OECD Statistical Portal
- *http://www.oecd.org/EN/document/0,,EN-document-notheme-12-no-3-32570-0,00.html*: OECD Investment Policy Reviews: Ukraine—Progress in investment reform 2002
- *http://www.oecd.org/pdf/ M00009000/M00009570.pdf*: The Centre for Cooperation with Non-Members (CCNM), OECD

  2, rue Andre Pascal,
  75775 Paris cedex 16–France
  Tel.: (331) 45 24 82 00
  Fax: (331) 45 24 91 77
  E-mail: ccnmcont@oecd.org
  Consult *www.oecd.org* under the rubric
  "Emerging and Transition Economies"

- *http://www.oecdmoscow.org/*: OECD Moscow Office
  **c/o The Institute for the Economy in Transition**
  Building N3, Gazetny per. 5
  103918 Moscow-Russia
  Tel.: (7 095) 229 7089, (7 503) 956 4721, (7 095) 956 4721
  Fax: (7 503) 956 4722 or (7 095) 956 4722
  E-mail: *oecdmo@glas.apc.org*

- CCNM Activities: Tax Policy via OECD Multilateral Tax Training Centres, the Joint Vienna Institute courses on applied market economics and financial analysis

| *OECD and Western Europe Co-operation Outcomes:* | *USSR and Eastern Europe Isolation Outcomes:* |
| --- | --- |
| Promotion of cooperation among countries | Excluded from the synergy of international development |
| Financial and technical assistance | Economy degeneration |
| Rebuilding trust, hope and social peace | Failure of confidence |
| Stabilization of the political situation | Vertically structured network |
| Information sharing (transparency) | Poor connectivity (its absence) |
| Constant economic policy reviews | Antidevelopment syndrome |
| Reducing the barriers of trade | Ambiguous quality standards |
| Emerging of many great ideas within OECD | Creativity and innovation blocked |

# References

## Chapter 1

Koehane, Robert (1989). *After Hegemony*. Princeton University Press, p.57.

Peyrefitte, Alain (1995). *La société de confiance*. Paris: Odile Jacob.

Reysset, Pascal & François Pingaud (1995). *Awélé*. Paris: Chiron.

Ruggie, John (1982). *International Regimes, Transactions and Change: Embedded Liberalism in the Postwar Economic Order*. International Organization, Spring.

Stiglitz, Joseph E. (2001). "Information and the Change in the Paradigm in Economics", Nobel Prize lecture, December 8. Available at: *http://www-1.gsb.columbia.edu/faculty/jstiglitz/papers.cfm*

Wilson, R. (1977). "A Bidding Model of Perfect Competition", in *Review of Economic Studies*, Vol. 44, pp.511-518. (quoted in Stiglitz, 2001).

## Chapter 2

Beasley, W.G. (1992). *The Modern History of Japan*. Tokyo: C.E.Tuttle Company.

Bernard, Anne K. (1996). *IDRC Networks: An Ethnographic Perspective*. IDRC.

Carden, Fred and Stephanie Neilson (forthcoming). in Diane Stone and Simon Maxwell (eds.), *The Challenge of Transnational Knowledge Networks: Bridging Research and Policy in a Globalizing World*.

Collins, James and Jerry Porras (1994). *Build to Last*. New York: Harper Business.

Guilmette, J. and I. Iskra (2001). "IDRC's Experience in EMDU", in *Research Capacity in Developing and Transition Countries*. Berne : Swiss Commission for Research.

Hately, Lynne and Kamal Malhotra (1997). *Between Rhetoric and Reality: Essays on Partnership in Development*. Ottawa: The North-South Institute.

Hopper, W. David (1970). "Statement to the Inaugural Meeting of the Board of Governors of the International Development Research Centre", October 26. Ottawa: IDRC,.

Hulse, Joseph (1981). *A Decade of Learning*. Ottawa: IDRC.

Lattès, Robert (1988). *L'apprenti et le sorcier, les défis de l'innovation*. Paris: Plon.

Lusthaus, Charles *et al.* (2002). *Organizational Assessment, A Framework for Improving Performance*. Washington and Ottawa: IDB and IDRC.

Lyzogub, I. 2001. *Final Report: Environmental Management Development in Ukraine and its Influence on Public Policy*. The full text of report can be found at the following web address: *http://web.idrc.ca/en/ev-31684-201-1-DO_TOPIC.html*

USAID (1995). *New Partnership Initiative Report*, (Draft). Washington D.C: USAID. (quoted in Hately and Malhotra, 1997)

## Chapter 3

Berger, Peter L. (1973). "*Homeless Mind, Modernization and Consciousness*", New York, Random House.

Bonvin, Jean and Christian Morrisson (1998). *L'Organisation de Coopération et de Développement économiques (OCDE)*. Que sais-je, Presse Universitaires de France.

Chavranski, Henri (1997). *L'OCDE au cœur des grands débats économiques*. Paris: La Documentation française.

Griffith, Richard T. (1997). *Explorations in OEEC History.* Paris: OECD Historical Series.

Hill, Peter (1984). *Real Gross Product in OECD Countries and Associated Purchasing Power Parities*, OECD.

Maalouf, Amin (2002). *Les croisades vues par les Arabes.* France: J'ai lu.

McMillan, John (1992). *Games, Strategies & Managers.* Oxford: Oxford University Press.

OECD (2002). *Agricultural Policies, Markets and Trade: Monitoring and Outlook 2002.* Paris: OECD.

Thygesen, Niels (2002). *Peer Pressure as Part of Surveillance by International Institutions*, Discussion of the Economic Development Review Committee, OECD Internal Document.

Stiglitz, Joseph E. (2001). *Information and the Change in the Paradigm in Economics*, Nobel Prize lecture, December 8. Available at: http://www-1.gsb.columbia.edu/faculty/jstiglitz/papers.cfm. He quotes Wilson and this is the reference:

Wilson, R. (1977). "A Bidding Model of Perfect Competition", *Review of Economic Studies,* Vol. 44, pp. 511-518. (quoted in Stiglitz, 2001).

## Chapter 4

Chavranski, Henri (1997). *L'OCDE au cœur des grands débats économiques* », La Documentation française, Paris.

Bonthous, Jean-Marie (1994). "Understanding Intelligence Across Cultures", *International Journal of Intelligence and Counterintelligence*, Vol. 7(3), Fall.

Boyd, R. and P. Richerson (1987). "The Evolution of Ethnic Markers", *Cultural Anthropology*, Vol. 2(1).

D'Iribarne, P. (1993). *"L'enracinement culturel de la gestion des entreprises"*, in B. Ponson (eds.). *L'esprit d'entreprise*, Paris: John Libbey Eurotext.

Homer-Dixon, Thomas (2001). *The Ingenuity Gap.* Canada: Vintage.

McMillan, John (1992). *Games, Strategies & Managers.* Oxford: Oxford University Press.

## Chapter 5

Johnston, Donald J. (2001). "The Complete Healthcare System", *OECD Observer*, December 11.

Sacerdoti, Giorgio (2000). *To Bribe or Not to Bribe,* "No Longer Business as Usual, Bribery and Corruption", Chapter 2, Paris: OECD.

## Post Face

Guilmette, Jean-H (1995). "Proceedings", International Francophone Meeting *Conflict Prevention: African Perspective*, September 19-22. Ottawa, p.65.

# Additional reading
## that the reader may wish to consult

*Below a few titles related to:*

## Peer Review

Pagani, Fabrizio (2002). *Peer Review: a tool for co-operation and change*. An Analysis of an OECD Working Method SG/LEG(2002)1. *http://www.oecd.org/dataoecd/33/16/ 1955285.pdf*

## Policymaking

Neilson, Stephanie (2001). *IDRC-Supported Research and its Influence on Public Policy. Knowledge Utilization and Public Policy Processes: A Literature Review*. Ottawa: IDRC. *http://intra1.idrc.ca/evaluation/litreview_e.html*

Lindquist, Evert (2001). *Discerning Policy Influence: Framework for a Strategic Evaluation of IDRC-Supported Research*. Ottawa: IDRC. *http://intra1.idrc.ca/evaluation/documents/publicpolicy/discerning_policy.pdf*

## Cross Cultural Management

Hofstede, Geert (1993). "Cultural Constraints in Management Theories", *Academy of Management Executive*, Vol. 7(1), pp.81-94. Maastricht, the Netherlands: Academy University of Limburg.

> Hofstede is often quoted for his research in this field. His first body of data came from a survey conducted throughout the various subsidiaries of IBM worldwide. He has a site at *http://pages.stern.nyu.edu/~wstarbuc/mob/hofstede.html*. He has also published:

Hofstede, Geert (1990). "Motivation, Leadership and Organization: Do American Theories Apply Abroad?", in *Organizational Dynamics*, Summer, pp.42-63.

See as well:

*International Journal of Cross Cultural Management*, Vol. 1(1), 1 April 2001. *http://sagepub.co.uk/journals/details/issues/j0326v01i01.html*

Noorderhaven, Niels G. and Bassirou Tidjani *Cultural, Governance, and Economic Performance: An Explorative Study with Special Focus on Africa*, as well as those of G. Hofstede et de H.C. Triandis.

With respect to Europe see:

Adler, N. (1983). "Cross-cultural Management: Issues to be Faced", *International Studies of Management and Organisation*, Vol. 13(2), pp.7-45.

Holden, N.J. (2001). *Cross-cultural Management: A knowledge Management Perspective*, Harlow, UK: Financial Times/Prentice-Hall, especially Chapter 13, "Remapping the Domain of Cross-cultural Management".

Joynt, P. and M. Warmer (eds.) (1996). *Managing across cultures*. London: International Thompson Business Press.

Picq, Thierry (1994). *Vers un modèle de management européen multiculturel*. Gestion, Printemps, pp.15-21.

> In this article, Picq examines German, British, French and Italian idiosyncrasies, values, professional attitudes, and the usage of tools and management techniques.

Tagliabue, John (2001). "At a French Factory, Culture is a two-way street", *New York Times*, February 25. Section 3, p. 4. This article provides the case of adapting French and Japanese mentalities in a Toyota plant in France.

## History and the Economy

Braudel, Fernand (1976). *Afterthoughts on Material Civilization and Capitalism.*

Hobsbawm, E.J. (1994). *The Age of Extremes: The Short Twentieth Century.*

Jacobs, Jane (1984). *Cities and the Wealth of Nations.*

## Room Set-up

*Concerning room set-ups, a great number of articles and books have been written on this subject. Here is a selection of a few that can be consulted.*

Carlopio, J.R., and D. Gardner (1992). "Direct and Interactive Effects of the Physical Work Environment on Attitudes", *Environment and Behaviour*, Vol. 24(5), pp.579-601.

Howells, L.T. and S.W. Becker (1962). "Seating Arrangements and Leadership Emergence", *Journal of Abnormal and Social Psychology*, Vol. 64, pp.148-150.

Maslow, A.H. and N.L. Mintz (1956). "Effects of Aesthetic Surroundings, Initial Effects of Three Aesthetic Conditions upon Perceiving Energy and Well-being", *Journal of Psychology*, Vol. 41, pp.247-254.

Mehrabian, A. and S.G. Diamond (1971). "Effects of furniture arrangement, prop and personality on social interaction", *Journal of Personality and Social Psychology*, Vol. 20, pp.18-30.

*The following book contains a comprehensive bibliography:*

Kiesler, Sara and Jonathon N. Cummings (2002). "What Do We Know about Proximity and Distance in Work Group–A Legacy of Research" in P. Hinds and S. Kiesler (eds.), *Distributed Work*, Cambridge, MA: MIT Press.

*http://basic.fluid.cs.cmu.edu/articles/Kiesler02-ProxmityfDistanceWorkGroup.pdf*

*An America Department of Defence site provides useful information concerning nonverbal communications in the context of "technical negotiations".*

## Nonverbal Communication

5.3 Describing How the Physical Environment Affects Negotiations

*http://www.acq.osd.mil/dp/cpf/pgv1_0/pgv5/pgv5c5.html#5.3*

## Conclusions

Johnston, Donald J. (2001). "The "Complete" Healthcare System", *OECD Observer*, December 11.

OECD (2001). *Health at a Glance.* OECD.

Oxley, Howard and Stephane Jacobzone (2001). "Healthcare Expenditure: A Future in Question", *OECD Observer*, December 9.

## Statement of Preliminaries for the Creation of the OECD

CONSIDERING that economic strength and prosperity are essential for the attainment of the purposes of the United Nations, the preservation of individual liberty and the increase of general well-being.

BELIEVING that they can further these aims most effectively by strengthening the tradition of co-operation which has evolved among them;

RECOGNIZING that the economic recovery and progress of Europe to which their participation in the Organization for European Economic Co-operation has made a major contribution, have opened new perspectives for strengthening that tradition and applying it to new tasks and broader objectives;

CONVINCED that broader co-operation will make a vital contribution to peaceful and harmonious relations among the peoples of the world;

RECOGNIZING the increasing interdependence of their economies; DETERMINED by consultation and co-operation to use more effectively their capacities and potentialities so as to promote the highest sustainable growth of their economies and improve the economic and social well-being of their peoples;

BELIEVING that the economically more advanced nations should co-operate in assisting to the best of their ability the countries in process of economic development;

RECOGNIZING that the further expansion of world trade is one of the most important factors favoring the economic development of countries and the improvement of international economic relations; and

DETERMINED to pursue these purposes in a manner consistent with their obligations in other international organizations or institutions in which they participate or under agreements to which they are a party;

HAVE THEREFORE AGREED on the following provisions for the reconstitution of the Organization for European Economic Co-operation as the Organization for Economic Co-operation and Development:...PARIS 14th December 1960